STARSTRUCK

Cosmo Landesman writes regularly as a feature writer
and film critic of the *Sunday Times*.

Cosmo Landesman

STARSTRUCK

Fame, Failure, My Family and Me

PAN BOOKS

First published 2008 by Macmillan

First published in paperback 2009 by Pan Books
an imprint of Pan Macmillan Ltd
Pan Macmillan, 20 New Wharf Road, London N1 9RR
Basingstoke and Oxford
Associated companies throughout the world
www.panmacmillan.com

ISBN 978-0-330-44706-5

1 3 5 7 9 8 6 4 2

A CIP catalogue record for this book is available from
the British Library.

Typeset by SetSystems Ltd, Saffron Walden, Essex
Printed in the UK by CPI Mackays, Chatham ME5 8TD

Visit **www.panmacmillan.com** to read more about all our books
and to buy them. You will also find features, author interviews and
news of any author events, and you can sign up for e-newsletters
so that you're always first to hear about our new releases.

For the Jaybird,
who despite his best efforts
showed me how to put the fun back into success
and take the sting out of failure.

The author would like to thank the
following people for their help with this book:
Maxine Landesman, Toby Young, Helen Hawkins,
Adrienne Connors, Peter York, Robert Hewison,
Bryan Appleyard, Stephen Pile, Ed Barrett,
Bruno Vincent, Richard Milner and
my agent Eugenie Furniss.

'Every man, however hopeless his pretensions may appear, has some project by which he hopes to rise to reputation; some art by which he imagines that the attention of the world will be attracted; some quality, good or bad, which discriminates him from the common herd of mortals . . .'

Samuel Johnson, *The Rambler*, 1751

Contents

1

Meet The Family

Dad

Early one morning in June 2000 I got a telephone call from my American dad, Jay Landesman. This is how it went.

Jay: Have you got a minute?

I could tell by his tone of repressed excitement that he was in the grip of that thing I had come to fear the most: a new project.

Me: Well, actually I'm a bit . . .

Jay: Do you know a good scriptwriter?

Me [*alarm bells going off*]: Why?

Jay: Big news . . . I'm doing the movie of *Landesmania!*

(*Landesmania!* is the name of a book about my dad's life that he paid a friend of his to write. I later learned that he was paying another friend of his to write the screenplay of the book.)

Me: But you've already written two film scripts about your life and . . .

Jay: Them? Ahh . . . they were just . . . well, first drafts.

Me: And who's going to make this film?

Jay [*excitedly*]: Nic Roeg is directing! Sandy Liberson is producing!

(Nic Roeg is the British director of such films as *Performance*, *Walkabout* and *Don't Look Now*. Sandy Liberson is the producer of *Performance* and many other films.)

Me: Jay, take a deep breath and tell me exactly what's going on.

Jay: I'm having drinks with Roeg next week and . . .

Me: Does Roeg know you're having drinks?

Jay: Yes. Sandy Liberson is setting up a meet.

Me: Does Roeg know that he's directing the movie of your life?

Pause.

Jay: No, not exactly. But the *Landesmania!* script would be perfect for him.

Me: What script?

Jay: That's why I called. Do you know any good scriptwriters?

Me: No.

Click.

My father never got a script to Nic Roeg.

Yes, drinks had been arranged with Nic Roeg.

But only inside my father's mind.

My dad has had an interesting life. He's never had a job that bored him. He is an original man, a man who has opened minds and emptied a few rooms in his time.

In America during the late 1950s, he started a theatre/nightclub in the city of St Louis called the Crystal Palace where performers like Woody Allen,

Lenny Bruce and the young Barbra Streisand appeared. He's taken tea with Bette Davis, cocktails with Bessie Smith and LSD with Timothy Leary. His is a life that many would envy; I know I do. And yet my dad has never thought of himself as a success, for one simple reason: he isn't a big name. His life has always lacked the imprimatur of celebrity.

But Jay must be one of the most well-known unknowns in the world. He's had two volumes of autobiography published, both by respected firms, and has been the subject of numerous newspaper and magazine articles. He's appeared on radio and television and his name turns up in studies on the beat generation and in showbiz memoirs. He even acquired a whole new kind of local fame as 'that bloke with the painting' who appeared on the BBC's *Antiques Roadshow*.

So this is a man who is not unknown. He's not what you'd call a nobody.

Yet he's not a somebody.

And that makes him feel like a nobody.

Mum

My mother, Fran Landesman, started her career as a songwriter in the early fifties and has enjoyed considerable success. Two of her songs, 'Spring Can Hang You Up The Most' and 'The Ballad Of The Sad Young Men', are jazz standards. Everyone from Ella Fitzgerald to Chaka Khan has covered her work. She now performs her poems and sings to small but adoring audiences.

My mum is always begging me to come to her gigs. She's been doing this for twenty-five years and each time she insists that I will love it. In the past I would go and I never loved it. Actually, watching her perform I felt a mixture of horror and embarrassment. My brother Miles accompanies her on guitar and it's one of the worst acts in showbiz. But amazingly, people love it. She recites poems, which she does well. But Fran also sings, which she does badly. As a performer she moves like the bride of Frankenstein; as a singer she sounds like Shirley Temple being strangled.

Shortly after Jay's phone call I get a call from Mother.

Fran doesn't bother with the usual pleasantries: enquiries about her grandson / me / my wife / my work or anything like that. Fran gets right down to the point, which is always Fran.

Mother: I'm doing a gig really near you guys and I thought maybe you and Maxine would like to come along?

Me: Well the thing is . . .

Mother: Oh come on, it's not that far from you.

That sounds reasonable, doesn't it? But her tone suggests that what she's really saying is this: *You selfish, lazy, shit-of-a-son . . . why won't you come to my gig? I always support you in your work and it wouldn't cost you anything and it would mean a lot to me and I haven't got long to live and you never come to my gigs . . . so would it kill you to come, just this once, you selfish cunt?*

Me: Everything is about you, you, and you!

Mother: I just asked if you'd like to come to my gig!

Me: That's what you said, but your tone of voice was

trying to pressure me into going ... you're trying to make me feel guilty. And besides, did it ever occur to you that we might be tired, with the baby and all?

Mother: You're fucking crazy!

Me: You're fucking self-obsessed!

Click.

Of the two my mother has always been hungrier for success than my dad – or at least more open about it. She has been on television numerous times, had six books of poetry published and even appeared as Sue Lawley's guest on *Desert Island Discs*. So this is a woman who has enjoyed a great deal of success, attention and acclaim. For decades her public and her peers – including Stephen Sondheim – have praised her and told her she's wonderful. And yet it's not enough. She wants more attention, more praise.

My mother is seventy-eight years old and when she grows up she would like to be a star.

Miles

My brother Miles has played in over two dozen rock bands in the past thirty years. He's never had a hit record. He's never had a hit band. He's never even had a record contract.

Miles has made over two hundred demo tapes, written one rock musical and a book of poetry that my dad published. Miles is forty-seven and still lives at home with my parents and has no regular job other than looking after them.

This is a man the world would call a failure.

But Miles thinks of himself as a success.

Miles says, 'I'm doing what I want, I'm making music. I feel lucky. I've made it!'

The week of the Fran and Jay calls ended with a call from Miles. His band Fancy Dress was playing a gig and they had this big A&R guy coming down to check them out.

So could I come along? Could I bring my wife? Could I bring a friend? Could I bring all my friends, my baby and my boss too?

Miles: Come on, Cos, it will be brill!

Click.

That's the trouble with my family: to them everyone is just gig fodder.

Once I was the adored first-born son, then the older brother to look up to. Now I'm a face, a guest, a plus one; I am a bottom to place on a seat. I am human filler, to fill out the rooms that my family can't fill.

At first I thought it was funny that my seventy-eight-year-old mother was turning into Norma Desmond, the crazy silent-movie star from the film *Sunset Boulevard.* She would sit on her bed and tell me about last night's performance and, throwing her head back, declare, 'They *loved* me . . . They *loved* me!'

Then I started to notice that my dad was turning into Norma Desmond as well. Feet up on his desk, cigarette dangling from his mouth and with a Martini glass in his hand, he'd tell me, 'They're gonna go wild when they read this script! It's the best thing I've ever written. Here, take it home with you.'

And Miles made it three: 'Cos man, you gotta listen to this demo we've made. It's a number one!'

Me

I like to think that I'm not like my family, that I don't have their craving for attention and public affirmation. I think I'm content with my life. I have a wonderful wife (Maxine), two great sons (Jack and Dexter), and one of the better jobs you could have in journalism – I'm the film critic for the *Sunday Times* and a feature writer for various magazines.

I like to think I belong to that small group of people who look at the absurd frenzy of longing that surrounds the famous, who see the seductive allure of success and say: 'No thanks.' We small band of happy dissenters quietly get on with our lives and our work, oblivious to the cacophony of the celebrity carnival as it passes by.

Then there are times when I think: *You old phoney! You know that you want fame and you want to walk into a room and feel like a somebody just like everyone else. You are just like your family; you crave it, you need it, you dream it . . . but you don't have the balls to go out and grab it!*

The thing is I don't want to end up like my dad, feeling like a nobody just because I'm not a somebody. To base one's sense of self-worth on such shallow criteria is the dumbest thing a smart person can do.

And yet I do it. It sneaks up on me. Here's how it happens.

Step One: Envy. Someone I know has been given a column/someone I know has been asked to do a radio or television programme. Why didn't they ask me?

Step Two: Self-pity. The reason is you're crap/shit/useless/too old/too American/and most important of all YOU'RE NOT A BIG ENOUGH NAME!

Step Three: Self-loathing. Look at yourself . . . fifty-two years old and what have you accomplished? Then out comes the old mental baseball bat and the frenzied attack on myself begins – and all because my life lacks the validation of a form of celebrity I don't even believe in.

At times like these I fear I'm turning into my dad.

☆

Members of my family have always been a little self-centred. People in show business are; it goes with the territory. That's to be expected and tolerated, and Maxine and I used to joke about it. But somewhere along the line their self-centredness grew into an all-consuming self-absorption. They stopped pretending to be interested in other people and talked about themselves *all* the time. At this point Landesmania stopped being funny.

Going to visit my parents for dinner with Maxine became an ordeal. It was like going to the theatre and seeing a one-man show and a one-woman show . . . *simultaneously*. We would sit there at the dinner table as Fran and Jay talked about *their* careers, *their* plans, *their* future projects, and we would smile and make encouraging noises as they read from *their* works in progress – and often their *past* works – and discussed *their* reviews and *their* letters of rejection/success.

I would look at my wife and the look on her face said: *My God, what sort of family have I married into?*

And when he could get a word in Miles would mention the names of illustrious music-business people who were interested in hearing his latest demo.

'Do your parents ever talk about anything but themselves?' Maxine once asked in the early days of our marriage.

It did not take her long to discover the answer . . .

☆

Here are some of the other signs that got me wondering about my parents.

In 2003 my mother got hit by a motorcycle while crossing a road. I came to visit her and I was shocked by her appearance: she was covered in bruises. I wanted to talk to her about her accident and how she was feeling, but all she wanted to talk about was the gig she'd done before the accident.

Fran: You should have seen that audience, I had them eating out of my hand.

Me: And how are you feeling now?

Fran: Fine. That gig was one of the best I've done in ages. You should have been there!

Then there was Jay and his book *Landesmania!*.

When I first learned that Philip – a friend of my

9

father's – was writing a biography of Jay, I was pleased for the old man. Honest. I figured he could use a little attention. And then I discovered that Jay was paying Philip to write the book and I was shocked. It was like discovering that one of your parents pays for sex.

I wasn't too worried because I figured that the book would never find a publisher. But then I discovered that Jay was intending to publish the book himself. It was like learning that your dad pays for sex – with two people at the same time.

When he told me the title of the book I panicked.

Jay: We're calling it *Landesmania!*.

Me: You can't call it that. People will think you're delusional. There's no such thing as Landesmania.

His response was classic Jay: he let out that little sardonic chuckle of his, the one that says: I find what you are saying *très* amusant, but it is you, my friend, who is delusional!

The book appeared in 2004. Jay said it was the best thing that had ever been written about him. The opening line went: 'Who is Jay Landesman and why does the 20th century owe him a favor?'

So far it has sold two hundred copies.

After the *Landesmania!* project I thought there was nothing that could surprise me.

And then along came the Jay Landesman Museum project. The idea was simple: Jay was going to create a museum dedicated to the life of Jay Landesman. For a certain number of months, Jay would open the house so the public could come and visit and see what an interesting man Jay Landesman was.

Exhibits for the Jay Landesman Museum would include:

a) His entire collection of *Neurotica* – a literary underground magazine that Jay started in the 1940s.

b) His collection of sixties Destruction Art – including a large mattress that resembled a gaping octogenarian vagina.

c) Photos of Jay. (As young, handsome man.)

d) The complete correspondence/plays/biographies/press clippings of Jay Landesman.

e) Jay Landesman's collection of hats.

Miles and Fran thought it was a terrible idea because they feared having strangers roaming around the house. Jay loved the idea because he thought it would show people how to live a more interesting and fulfilled existence by studying his life. Jay arranged for a man from the Association of Independent Museums to look over his place and proposal. I don't know whether he thought it was a good idea or if he thought Jay was a lunatic, but he rejected the idea on the grounds of public safety: there were not enough fire exits from Jay's basement den where the bulk of the exhibits would have been.

When the museum project collapsed Jay was not downhearted because an old project raised itself from the dead. Somehow he had met a German film producer living in Hackney, who liked his screenplay for *Spring Can Hang You Up The Most*. It was a film based on

Jay's unpublished novel *The Nervous Set* that was a semi-autobiographical account of Jay and Fran's life as a young couple in New York amongst the beat generation.

Jay phoned to give me the news.

Jay: Got a minute?

Me: Actually . . .

Jay: I've found this terrific German director who wants to do the *Spring* screenplay! He says he can get Joe Pesci to play me and Drew Barrymore to play Fran.

Me: What films has he made before?

Jay: His last film was on German bunkers in World War II.

Me: Sounds perfect.

Jay: I think so too . . .

Click.

☆

Around 2001 I kept reading articles in newspapers and magazines about the way England was changing. It was said that we were becoming a nation of attention-seekers, exhibitionists, gossips and voyeurs. Reality television had come into our lives and the machinery of fame had gone into overdrive, churning out an endless stream of instant celebrities.

Something like a cultural revolution seemed to be taking place: the submerged mass of 'nobodies', the 'no-talents', the 'boring', the 'ugly' and the 'ordinary' were charging the media barricades, pushing their way into the media spotlight and into our lives. Everyone, it seemed, wanted to be a recognizable name, a somebody. Of course people have always dreamt of being famous;

now they were demanding it. It was no longer a reward but a human right.

It was said that we were becoming more materialistic and selfish and that the notion of public service had given way to personal self-aggrandizement. There was much talk about the digital narcissism of the young with their blogs and webcam exhibitionism.

My wife had once asked: do your parents ever talk about anyone but themselves? I was now asking myself: does *anyone* talk about anything but themselves?

One word summed up the rampant egotism and the mass craving for visibility, public adoration and the ubiquitous trivia of modern Britain: *celebrity*. An army of commentators lined up to deliver the news about what was happening to England. We were now living in the age of celebrity (A.A. Gill), celebrity was our new religion (Sam Taylor Wood) and it drove the British economy (John Grey). It was what we all wanted (Chris Rojek) and what we most valued (Bryan Appleyard). Will Self declared it an 'addiction' and Clive James said it was a 'disease'. The critic Ziauddin Sardar made the startling claim that 'Nothing moves in our universe without the imprint of celebrity.'

I wanted to know if this was really an accurate reflection of the condition of England. Had things changed so much or were these commentators just over-reacting? Or maybe they were feeling a kind of social and cultural anxiety because as a class they were losing cultural authority?

What worried me was the idea that the way we measure our worth as individuals – and the value of other individuals – had undergone such a major change. Could it be that the very thing that had made a successful man like my father feel like a failure was making others feel that way too?

In contemporary Britain celebrity – and not class or wealth – seemed to be the new measure of success.

So how I was to react to these changes? Should I take a stand and end up like some grumpy old guy complaining about the trivialization of our culture? Or should I give in to that inner voice that demands to be part of the thing I profess to loathe?

I also wanted to know about my parents. I should point out that since writing this book we have become very close again and their phase of crazed self-obsession has passed – well, almost. But for a time it seemed that they had disappeared up their own dream of making it. I nearly lost them.

I sometimes wondered if they had really become monsters of megalomania or whether the problem was with me. Maybe I was overreacting to their legitimate pursuit of success – a pursuit I was envious of?

So I thought I would write this book to find out two things:

a) What happened to my parents?

b) And what happened to my England?

2

When Jay Met Fran

It's New York 1949 and a party to mark the death of the crazy French playwright Antonin Artaud is under way in a girl's apartment in Greenwich Village. Darkened rooms are full of smoke and sad faces armed with sardonic smiles. In the background you can hear the squeals, shrieks and flatulent bleeps of serious jazz.

Here are the hip at play: bohemians, beatniks and would-be artists, aspiring writers, actors, musicians, street people, poor little rich girls from the Upper West Side and lunatic poets from the gutters.

The topics of conversation are typical of the day: problems with my analyst, the death of the theatre, sexual repression, French cinema, selling out and the New Criticism.

The names and terms to drop are: Kafka, Freud, Bird, Sartre, Beckett, Djuna Barnes, gestalt, existentialism and Kandinsky. The poses to strike are: supercynical, supercool, latently neurotic or full-blown crazy – take your pick, but for God's sake don't act normal with this crowd. And if you're happy, better keep it to yourself.

The women are dressed in various shades of black, tight sweaters, dark tights or peasant chic; the men are mostly in the standard beatnik uniform: beards, black shades and polo-neck sweaters.

But not Jay. Not tonight. He wants to make a statement, to stand out from the oh-so-hip-crowd, so he wears a suit. It's a daring act of social suicide, a put-on and a put-down to these oh-so-cool New Yorkers by a boy from the Midwest of America.

At any other New York party of the time you'd see Jay – a skinny, handsome man – in a black button-down shirt, yellow hand-painted tie, a crumpled seersucker suit and pair of Clarks desert boots. In the 1950s you'd find him in his *Nervous Set* suit – the one with six buttons, multiple vents and triple lapels. It looked like a suit for George Raft designed by Salvador Dali. But tonight he's wearing the real 9 to 5 suit of the suburban square. You can imagine the crowd's reaction – *who's the Martian in the straitjacket*?

In the corner of the room Jay sees a very pretty girl. Twenty-three-year-old Francis Deitsch is sitting with a group of her girlfriends, talking and laughing. She's having a good time and doesn't care who knows. Obviously, playing it cool is not her style.

He thinks: *a little square, but cute.*

A writer friend of Jay's – John Clellon Holmes – described what Fran was like in those days: '. . . her face luminous with the hip chick's soulfulness; a girl who bore an astonishing resemblance to Zelda Fitzgerald – only lovelier, softer, more remote, the kind of girl with a certain pang behind her intelligence and chic.'

She and Jay exchange a few words, and end up in a verbal collision.

Fran has made a crack about the large breasts of the hostess and Jay, rushing to her defence, says, 'That's not very nice.'

She retaliates with a verbal slap: 'Don't be so square!'

Fran turns her back on him and carries on talking to her friends. She dismisses him as a businessman; he thinks she's a bitch. But then Jay could resist anything but a pretty, bitchy girl who'd give him a hard time.

A week later Jay is in Central Park and sees a stunning blonde wearing a peasant blouse, a wide belt and a flared skirt: it's the cute chick from the party called Fran.

He picks her up and they have drinks at the San Remo bar. He discovers she has problems galore, dirty fingernails and more tales of rejection than he could ever hope to match.

She likes him because he's handsome and funny, and she's impressed that he's the editor of a new little magazine called *Neurotica*. She tells him, 'I told my girlfriend about you and she was jealous. Her boyfriend edits a magazine called *Blood*, which nobody has ever heard of.'

He likes her because she's a pretty Jewish princess in full rebellion against her rich parents, but then he's a nice Jewish boy in rebellion against being a nice Jewish boy.

There's a sadness to her story that he can't resist. She was a Jewish princess in the making who was sent away to a fashionable boarding school and came back fat. Her successful father never had any time for her or interest in her, and Fran's mother said she felt sick every time she looked at her obese daughter.

Fran attended art school but got her education hanging out in Greenwich Village. There she took a series of misfit lovers for solace. The lonely, love-hungry little fat girl was now gone; in her place was a fast-talking wisecracking beauty, who was studying textile designs by day and playing the rebel at night.

Soon after they met Jay wrote a letter to his mother, who was known as Cutie.

Dear Cutie,

Yesterday I saw New York's fabulous skyline from a penthouse on Central Park West. A pretty girl lives there who is as crazy as I am. I think I'm going to marry her. I miss you.

Love and kisses,

Jay

Jay was right. After a whirlwind romance they got married and were pronounced Fran and Jay.

3

Little Magazine, Big Dreams

Jay hadn't gone to New York looking for love but literary glory, which I guess is love by another name. He was a young man with his own little magazine and a big dream; he was going to knock New York on its ass and wake up the rest of America.

It was a bold mission for a young guy who till then had been working in his mother's antique shop in St Louis, Missouri. But it wasn't as crazy a plan as it might seem today, because back then little magazines had a special place in American cultural life. They were the shock troops of the avant-garde: small groups of guerrilla rebels making daring assaults on orthodox thinking and cultural values. Little magazines lobbed grenades of the experimental and fired rockets of the new: ideas, writers, poetry, left-wing politics and polemics. It was through the little magazines that modernism entered the bloodstream of American culture; in these publications T.S. Eliot, Ezra Pound and Joyce's *Ulysses* first appeared.

In 1948, Jay decided he'd had enough of working in his mother's shop and St Louis. It was a city that was once known as the Gateway to the West and some would say that was because no one would want to stick around a place as dull as St Louis.

Jay was twenty-nine, restless and eager for a different life – just like those other post-war rebels from the American Midwest who would take off for the bright lights of bigger cities. Anxious guys and magnificent misfits like Marlon Brando (Nebraska), Montgomery Clift (Nebraska), James Dean (Indiana) and William Burroughs (St Louis).

The idea of self-reinvention has become so central to popular culture that the idea itself has become trivialized. These days any third-rate female pop singer who changes her hair colour or gets breast implants is celebrated as a model of triumphant self-reinvention.

Of course a nation of immigrants like America was built on this idea. The newly arrived masses from Europe had to shed names, customs and even languages before they could dive into the melting pot and emerge as Americans. It was different for their children, coming of age in the 1950s. Their self-reinvention was not to fit in, but to break free.

Jay's personal journey began when as a teenager he read *The Great Gatsby* and decided to change his name from Irving to Jay after its hero, that master of self-reinvention Jay Gatsby. Then he decided to leave his mother's store and launch himself as a publisher, playboy, dandy and cultural crusader. So he created a magazine called *Neurotica*.

Having his own magazine was a good excuse to hang out with interesting people, throw parties and meet beautiful women. Yes, he was serious about exposing

the neurotic state of American culture, but he wanted
to have fun in the process. In retrospect he was the
hipster's Hugh Hefner – mixing Martinis, girls and
interesting minds into an intoxicating social cocktail.

He wanted to create a magazine written for and by
neurotics; one that took their side in a society that
considered them sick. The manifesto from the first issue
stated: '*Neurotica* is a literary explosion, defence and
correlation of the problems and personalities that in our
culture is defined as neurotic.'

Neurotica – it was to be a quarterly – offered a
psychoanalytic examination of American popular culture and life that would appeal to a hip, non-academic
readership. Jay drew up a list of proposed titles of
articles for the first issue that sum up what the magazine
was all about. 'The New Look Is The Anxious Look';
'American Sexual Imperialism'; 'The Theatre as Subli-
mated Suicide'; 'The Castration Complex in Animals'
and 'Can You Slap Your Mother? A Semantic Problem'.

It was a crazy, inspired and truly original idea that
was way ahead of its time. (Years later *Newsweek* called
Neurotica 'Brilliant and bizarre . . . an impishly arcane
magazine'.) In an America that was coming under the
influence of psychoanalysis, to suggest that neurosis was
something to be celebrated and not cured was a radical
proposition. Jay's magazine – long before the work of
R.D. Laing appeared – challenged the orthodox idea
of what it meant to be a well-adjusted human being.
A decade after *Neurotica* first appeared, even as mainstream a magazine as *Readers Digest* (circulation 12 million) could carry an article entitled 'The Danger of Being

Too Well Adjusted'. The article quoted a psychiatrist who claimed that 'We've made conformity into a religion.'

Neurotica spotted early on the way the neurotic would become a new kind of American anti-hero. In the first edition (May 1949), Jay published an essay called 'The New Look Is The Anxious Look'. Two years later the neurotic left the subterranean world of bohos and beatniks and entered the cultural mainstream with the publication of J.D. Salinger's *The Catcher in the Rye*. Its protagonist, the troubled teenager Holden Caulfield, is telling his story from a sanatorium after having a breakdown.

It wasn't long before Hollywood realized that the new look and new style of post-war youth was anxious. By the mid-1950s the three 'fascinating neurotics', Montgomery Clift, Marlon Brando and James Dean, had all become movie stars. They played psychologically troubled and emotionally tormented anti-heroes in films such as *From Here to Eternity* (1953), *The Wild One* (1953) and *Rebel Without a Cause* (1955). By the end of the 1950s popular culture had caught up with *Neurotica*'s mission to explore 'the problems and personalities that in our culture is defined as neurotic'.

It was when Jay teamed up with the eccentric polemicist, raging paranoid and sexual folklorist Gershon Legman – a man known to be unpublishable, uncompromising and unbearable – that he found a brilliant crazy man and a new crusade for *Neurotica*. It was Legman who encouraged Jay to drop all the 'look at me I'm neurotic' stuff and the experimental poetry. Together, they were going to fight censorship and expose a culture that welcomed murder and violence as entertainment and condemned sex as immoral. Jay and Legman believed that America was on the verge of a nervous breakdown – and they would do their bit to help it on its way.

When *Time* magazine mentioned *Neurotica* in an article on the new wave of little magazines that had appeared in 1949, Jay thought he was on his way to success. When a year later Henry Luce – the publisher of *Time* magazine – let it be known that he'd be interested in buying *Neurotica*, Jay was certain of it.

But it didn't happen, for reasons I will go into later. After eight issues Jay felt he had said everything he wanted to say. Besides, he was exhausted: the legal battles with the American Post Office (who wanted to prosecute the magazine for obscenity) plus long struggles with the abusive and confrontational Legman had taken their toll.

New York's bohemia – that small world centred in Greenwich Village – had lost its charm and fun. The constant cynicism, the pressure to put everything and everyone down; the proud boasts of sexual malfunction and creative impotence, once so daring and honest, had become so tedious – at least to Jay.

Then there was his troubled marriage. He and Fran were drifting apart. To fill the growing gap they crammed their apartment with people and covered the silence with parties. (A friend of theirs said at the time, 'Through those doors pass the most beautiful and neurotic people in the world.') Jay knew he had to do something quickly to save his marriage, so he decided to split and go back to St Louis and Mother.

Fran received Jay's plan for going back home like it was a prison sentence. She didn't want to leave her beloved New York and began to wonder: *what happened to the handsome, hip magazine editor I married? What kind of rebel heads back to the sticks and Mother?*

Jay asked Fran to try St Louis for a year and if she didn't like it she could always return to New York. So she decided to give it a go and packed her bags and checked her pillbox. 'I'm covered for any emergency,' she told Jay. 'Sugar substitute, aspirin, Contact, sleeping pill, painkiller, appetite depressant, Miltown – all the usual equipment for the modern girl.'

So in 1951 they climbed into Jay's battered Ford Dodge, headed down the West Side highway and drove off to St Louis. Jay had promised that the three-day drive would be the honeymoon they'd never had. He looked at his bride and saw the sad face of a kidnap victim who knows there's no chance of escape.

A few weeks into their new life, Jay realized that Fran's look of sad resignation had collapsed into a look of deep boredom. She was suffocating in St Louis. So Jay and his brother Fred decided to open a nightclub – part cabaret, part theatre – to keep her amused. They called it the Crystal Palace.

Jay became the club's producer and brought the plays of Samuel Beckett to middle America, along with Lenny Bruce, the unknown Woody Allen and Barbra Streisand. It was Bruce who said that the Palace, with its stained glass, looked like a church that decided to go in for a spot of bingo and ended up having strippers.

In St Louis Fran made a discovery that would change her life: she could write lyrics. Her first attempt was with the composer Tommy Wolfe and it was inspired by T.S. Eliot's line, 'April is the cruellest month'. She decided to translate that into hip speak and came up with 'Spring Can Hang You Up The Most'.

While she scribbled away at lyrics, Jay decided it was time to write his first novel. All his old buddies – John Holmes, Jack Kerouac, Chandler Brossard – were getting published. It was time to lose his literary virginity. He had an opening line that summed up his whole take on success: 'You can't stay married if you want to make it in New York.' He called his book *The Nervous Set* and it was essentially the story of Fran and Jay living the bohemian life in New York. It ends with Jan – the Fran character – committing suicide. The book went through a round of rejections and ended up in Jay's rejection trunk.

The Crystal Palace was a fabulous party that lasted about twelve years and then sometime in the early 1960s, Jay suddenly decided that he was bored with America and tired of his nightclub. The fun had gone. Now that he had to attract audiences with Habeba the Belly Dancer instead of daring acts like Lenny Bruce, he knew that the glory days of the club were behind him. And without the Palace – his own personal playground – there was no point in sticking around. It was time to make a move. The question was: where to?

Jay was forty-eight years old and dreaming about dropping out and living the life of a full-time idler. Maybe as a country gentleman in Connecticut or perhaps he'd move to a Greek island and spend his days watching the flowers grow.

The only thing that Fran wanted to watch grow was her career. By now she was a respected songwriter working with Alec Wilder. Her song 'Spring Can Hang You Up The Most' had been recorded by Ella Fitzgerald and Sarah Vaughan. She wanted the phone to ring with wonderful offers from producers and singers. Her dream was to write songs for big musicals.

There you have it. He wanted a Greek island and she wanted Broadway.

So they settled on London.

☆

Why London? If they had to leave America Fran wanted a big city where they spoke English. And Jay? I once asked him why he chose London, and he said, 'I thought it was a good place to be a failure in.'

Like many Americans of his generation, Jay admired the English because he believed they were indifferent to both the seduction of success and the stigma of failure. They knew that success was overrated and that failure was nothing to feel bad about. After all, it was the British poet Kipling who had said that when faced with triumph and disaster, we should treat these two 'impostors' just the same.

When my family moved to London fifty years ago the English still had a reputation for being fond of plucky underdogs and heroic failures. They were ready to take a loser to heart like no other nation. As George Orwell pointed out, 'The most stirring battle poem in English is about a brigade of cavalry which charged in the wrong direction.'

Such a country was perfect for Jay. The trouble with Americans – or so some Americans like Jay claimed – was that they were obsessed by success. In a letter written to H.G. Wells in 1906 William James complained of the 'moral flabbiness born of the exclusive worship of the bitch-goddess *Success*. That – with the squalid cash interpretation put on the word success – is our national disease.'

That 'disease' posed a problem that my father spent his whole life confronting: how does a thoughtful, sceptical and ironic person function in a society in thrall to celebrity and success?

Jay tried to solve this problem by cultivating what he called a 'lifelong romance with failure'. This romance can be seen as a desire to pursue the forbidden; and nothing was so forbidden to an American of Jay's generation as failure. He thought he could puncture the prestige and power of success with laughter; inoculate himself with large doses of irony, send the fucker up, mock its followers; turn his back on success and make a pass at its ugly sister failure.

Back in New York Jay and his hip little buddies used to meet around cocktail time at P.J. Clark's, a famous bar on the Upper East Side of Manhattan. One of their favourite activities was to sit and watch the successful people from Madison Avenue drown their sorrows.

Jay's crowd were success snobs who regarded everyone else as 'sell-outs'. Selling out was the big concern in the 1950s, the ultimate act of betrayal. The sell-outs were the ones who just did things for money, the writers who prostituted their talents to Hollywood (this was a big complaint of Holden Caulfield's), or sold their souls to the big advertising agencies.

Jay's romance with failure wasn't all pose and perversity, but rooted in the perceived poverty of success. The thinking goes like this: success has no poetry, no grandeur and no song. Success may produce money, but failure produces myth.

My parents used to argue about the value of success.

Jay would say, 'Success is overrated.'

And Fran would reply, 'Don't knock it till you've tried it.'

'That hurt,' Jay would reply.

I think I've inherited from my father his fascination with success and failure. It was something I became aware of at a very young age. Jay loved to tell Miles and me stories about his friends who, like him, had gone to make it in New York and found nothing but heartbreak and humiliation. There was the failed actor who summed up his time in New York as 'the forty-five-year *insult*'. There was the writer who was invited by a top American publisher to come by the office and collect his manuscript – from inside a toilet bowl. My dad always used to chuckle when he quoted the *New York Times* book critic who said of his best friend's book: 'If the American novel isn't dead, this book will kill it.'

Listening to these stories as an impressionable and

sensitive ten-year-old, I came to the conclusion that New York must be the cruellest city in the world. People there were always *dying, bombing, striking out, flopping, empty- ing the room* and *going down the toilet*. They couldn't get *arrested* or elected *dogcatcher*. This mythological world was made up of *somebodies, nobodies, winners* and *losers*. People in New York, my father insisted, had no time for what he called *the little people* – they only cared about the big shots.

Thank God we were moving to London.

4

The Oldest Swingers In Town

My parents arrived in London in March 1964, two loud, middle-aged American bohemians in the land of the stiff upper lip.

Or so they thought. Very few people knew that London had become the most 'swinging' city in the world. (That only happened a year or two later, when the public began reading magazine articles about Swinging London.) American tourists came to London for the treats of tradition: the changing of the guard and the taking of afternoon tea. They wanted a London wrapped in the comfort blanket of the past.

But what they, and my parents, found was a very different England in the making, a loud, brash, yeah-yeah-yeah youth-driven England. You could see it in the outlandish fashions of the young on the streets and you could hear it in the hysterical screams of Beatlemania. Some Americans were disappointed by what they found, but not my parents. They had arrived just in time for the great four-year party that was Swinging London and couldn't believe their luck.

Jay found a dilapidated Georgian house in Islington for a home, and a nearby school for Miles and me. We quickly made friends with the local kids, who introduced us to the joys of soccer, or 'football' as we learned to call it. Jay had his morning chores and work on the house to keep him busy. Meanwhile our melancholic mum lay in bed, homesick for America. It would take her a little time before she got in the party mood.

Those early London days were full of uncertainty. My parents liked London but weren't sure if London liked them. 'Three months in London and the phone has become remarkably silent,' Jay noted in his diary.

Slowly they began to make friends with people and the city itself. For a man like Jay with a 'romantic attachment to failure' London seemed like the perfect city: a Paris for underachievers. He was convinced that he'd managed to find a city where they didn't care if you were a somebody or not. 'We were amazed at how easily people accepted us without knowing or even caring about our economic or social background,' said Jay. 'It was such a relief not to be asked, "And what do you do for a living?"'

It was a question he found hard to answer, because he didn't know what he was doing for a living or how he wanted to live. When he had told Fran that he just wanted to sit on an island and watch the flowers grow, he was only half joking. Now he was playing with the idea of quitting show business and becoming a middle-aged dropout.

He'd produced, promoted and written numerous plays but had never had a big hit, at least not outside of St Louis. God knows my parents had given it their best shot back in 1959 when their musical *The Nervous Set* –

based on Jay's book, with lyrics by Fran – opened on Broadway. Everyone said that this was going to be the one that made them. They were set to be the golden couple of New York, the new Scott and Zelda.

The Nervous Set was a hip, funny satire on the beat generation, but the show only lasted 23 performances. It was too cynical, sophisticated and angsty for the times. What chance had a musical with that crazy title and one featuring a four-piece jazz combo on stage and a suicide for an ending? What chance had they against the hit musicals of the season like *The Sound Of Music* and *Gypsy*? So they bombed on Broadway and returned to a St Louis that was just starting to turn its back on them.

Now Jay was beginning a new life in London, so why go back to his old ways? He was tired of the game; tired of producing plays, tired of showbiz talk and showbiz bullshit. But most of all he was tired of the whole be-a-success game, a game he had never really wanted to play in the first place. It was time to lie back, dig London life and just watch the flowers grow. He wanted to devote himself to the art of what he called 'creative living'.

For Jay this meant being a good husband to his wife and a good father to his children, and having art and interesting people in his life – and of course as many lovers as he could. So Jay, who has been dabbling in journalism since the move to London, quits writing articles for his home-town paper, the *St Louis Post Dispatch*. He had this crazy project he'd been producing, a musical version of *Dracula*, and that goes on the back burner. No more meeting with theatre people or schmoozing with the great and the groovy and the people who can help your career.

On sunny days you'd find Jay lounging in a park soaking up the rays and reading *Variety*; there's lunch with Robert Rauschenberg, celebrity encounters at parties (Marlene Dietrich and Jay discuss the fine art of French polishing), exhibitions to catch, new plays to see and people to meet.

Jay's diary entry of 20 July 1964 describes a typical afternoon in these early London days, out drinking with the gay Labour MP Tom Driberg and his Filipino houseboy.

'We pub-crawled with Tom D. Ended up in a pub that could well be called "The Spare Nobody Bar". Lesbians, transvestites, young Danish sailors powdered from head to toe, whores, ageing pederasts and young couples all in good humour. Tom D said it helped him to keep in touch with his constituency.'

London was a loafer's paradise in those days. There were plenty of people around who just wanted to hang out. Work was something they did to finance the real business of life: drinking, parties, pubs, sex, falling in love and falling on your face drunk in some smoke-filled Soho dive.

Even those devoted to their careers felt obliged to keep up appearances and pretend they lived the life of an idler. You'd find the painter Francis Bacon and the novelist Keith Waterhouse drinking away the after-noons, looking like men who would never soil their souls with creative labour, when in fact they'd been working away since dawn.

Jay would spend the morning devouring the newspapers, writing letters, working on the house; but the afternoon was always playtime. Back in St Louis he used to meet with an American artist called Ernest Trova at 2.30 p.m. to just hang out, have coffee and watch all the anxious men in suits rush back to the office after lunch. Not Jay and Ernie. For them it was crucial that a man was free to do anything he wanted to at 2.30 p.m.; that was the measure of a successful life.

Now Jay was off looking for new playmates, and he found them in the pubs and afternoon drinking clubs of Soho and Chelsea – places like the Kismet, the Pickwick Club and the Colony Room. Jay (sometimes accompanied by Fran) mixed with what was left of British bohemia: cult novelists, jazz musicians, junkies, painters, fading beauties, publishers, poets, journalists and actors. The afternoon drinking clubs – pubs in those days closed at 3 p.m. – provided sanctuary from the routines of responsibility and the demands of middle-class respectability.

One of Jay's favourite places was the Kismet, a leprous cellar off Tottenham Court Road that was known as 'Death in the Afternoon' and the 'Iron Lung'. Legend has it that a newcomer once entered the club and asked the bartender: 'What's that terrible smell?'

'Failure,' said a drunk at the bar.

In this world a man could be anything, a vicious drunk or a drug addict, and no one would care. But even bohemia has its taboos, and a man who was openly ambitious or a conspicuous success was branded that most loathsome of all creatures known to bohemian kind: 'a bore'.

In that world to be a bore was the greatest of sins. British bohemia had clear ideas about who and what was boring. Money was boring. Success was boring. The famous were boring. People – i.e. the aspirational, suburban middle class – who wanted to 'get on' in life were boring.

It's an attitude that was articulated by the critic Alan Brien in an article for the *Spectator* (1963) entitled 'The Anatomy of a Bore'. Brien set out to list the great bores of contemporary Britain. Two groups in particular stood out: the successful and the famous. Brien condemned 'all stars of stage, screen and television' as bores.

But at least he was honest about why such people deserved to be dismissed as bores: 'We often tend to be bored by those who hold superior positions to our own.'

The trouble with such people, claimed Brien, 'is that they deny your individuality. They transform you into a one-man audience . . . you can have no function but applause.'

That's something I knew all about, growing up in my family. Life was a cabaret, old chum – and in my family you belonged to the exciting people on the stage or you sat in the audience and provided the applause. Nobody ever imagined that one day the audience would demand their right to be the exciting people on stage.

☆

My father might have been at home in the louche bars of bohemia, but his social confidence soon disappeared when he entered the rooms where the big names on the London scene congregated. The rules that governed this society were very different from those of bohemia. Here admission was based not on the charm of failure but the charisma of success. In those days, said actor Michael Caine, 'everybody was a success and you didn't know anybody who wasn't.'

Here are some snapshots of the London scene in the sixties:

Snapshot One

Host – *Daily Mail* gossip columnist Quentin Crewe.

Where – Elegant sitting room in his flat on Wilton Crescent, London.

Names – Peter Sellers, Dudley Moore, Princess Margaret, Keith Richards, Sandie Shaw and Bernard Levin.

High point – Jocelyn Stevens arguing with Bernard Levin about Karl Marx.

Low point – A naked George Melly entering the room first as a man, then as a woman and then backwards as a bulldog.

Snapshot Two

Hosts – Theatre critic Kenneth Tynan and wife Kathleen.

Where – Flat on Mount Street, London.

Names – Gore Vidal, Richard Harris, John Mortimer, Michelangelo Antonioni, Marlon Brando.

High point – Marlon Brando arriving drunk.

Low point – Marlon Brando kissing Kenneth Tynan in the bathroom.

Snapshot Three
Hosts – Peter and Wendy Cook.
Where – The Cook home in Church Row,
    Hampstead: dinner.
Names – John Lennon, Paul McCartney, John Cleese,
    Michael Foot, Michael Caine, Fran Landesman,
    Jay Landesman.
High point – A celebrity asking who that funny
    American guy Jay Landesman is.
Low point – A celebrity *not* asking who that funny
    guy Jay Landesman is.

I once asked Jay how the name-packed rooms of London compared with those with New York, and he said, 'London rooms were much kinder. They were friendly towards me. In New York rooms it was all about how much money you made and how many copies your last book sold or how successful your show was. In New York rooms they'd check out your status straight away and if it wasn't up to scratch, then it was see you later, loser.'

My parents arrived in London with only one phone number: that of the comedian Peter Cook. He and his wife Wendy moved back to London in 1964 after appearing in the satirical revue *Beyond The Fringe* on Broadway. He had left London a big star, the golden boy of the satire movement. Now he was coming back and everyone was telling him that satire was finished. Cook was worried that nobody would know his name. What's more he discovered, to his utter horror, that his fellow Cambridge undergraduate David Frost was now a big star.

But it wasn't long after teaming up with Dudley Moore that Cook found success and fame. He and Wendy were as glamorous as any couple in England. It was through the Cooks that my parents entered the world of Swinging London. Their dinner parties featured a glittering collection of names like Ken Tynan, Peter Ustinov, Malcolm Muggeridge, Paul McCartney, John Lennon, David Frost, Joan Collins, John Cleese, Barry Humphries and Joseph Heller.

So what were my parents doing there? The Cooks always had places at their table, and in their lives, for people who were not quite as illustrious as them. Cook's biographer Harry Thompson wrote: 'Most of the guests were purposely selected for their fame and interest value'. Clearly, my parents had got in on the grounds of 'interest value'.

Entering the Cooks' star-studded living room made my dad nervous. The gracious Peter and Wendy tried their best to make him feel at home, as did their starry guests. Simon Gough, a close member of the Cook family who became Wendy Cook's lover, says of Peter: 'He never, ever was rude; never pointed me out for what I was ... a nobody. It was always almost a shared joke between us that this was his world and I was welcome to it. I remember him saying to me once, "God, I envy you, Simon," and I said, "What for? What could I possibly have that you envy?" Peter replied, "You're anonymous. You can go into any porn shop in Soho and nobody will know you."'

But despite the graciousness of the Cooks, Jay found it impossible to relax in a room with wall-to-wall names.

He was acutely aware that he was the token non-celebrity. That old status anxiety of his New York days was rearing its ugly head even in a London that – in theory at least – didn't care about such things.

Many of the Cooks' crowd formed what was called 'the new aristocracy'. And like the old aristocracy, there was an etiquette to dealing with fame. You were expected to regard the whole business of celebrities and stars as an absurdity imported from America. To express an interest in the famous – especially of the Hollywood sort – was a social taboo. That didn't stop people from having that fascination. Ken Tynan was as star-struck as any teenage girl. The writer Colin Wilson complained of Tynan's hypocrisy, 'he spent his life chasing after the famous, worshipping success and preaching a rather muddled sort of Marxist collectivism.'

To be famous was not a suitable ambition for an intelligent or talented person. And the famous person was expected to regard their renown as something silly or tiresome. ('This celebrity business is quite chronic,' said Virginia Woolf.) Just as a member of the old aristocracy would never make someone from a different class aware of their social 'inferiority', no member of the new aristocracy would be so ungracious as to make a guest aware of their lack of fame.

I asked Jay why he felt it was so hard to function at the Cooks' and he told me, 'They were all big shots. I found it discouraging to be with heavyweights like Ken Tynan and Bernard Levin. What was I?'

The funny thing is that Jay wasn't alone in feeling this way. Alan Bennett – who had appeared in *Beyond*

The Fringe and was something of a star himself – felt a similar kind of status inadequacy at the Cooks'. Many years later he confessed to Wendy Cook, 'I remember coming to a party and the Beatles were there and I thought, "I am nothing really now."'

Even though this was London, Jay was painfully conscious that his was the smallest name in the room. His only hope of social survival was to try and be the funniest person in the room, but to be funnier than Peter Cook was Mission Impossible. There are many comics who aren't funny offstage. Unfortunately for Jay, Peter Cook wasn't one of them. And if you try to dominate a room with people used to dominating a room like Cook, then you had better be good. It's one thing to bomb in front of ordinary people; it's another to bomb in front of professional comedians who know all about bombing. That's a double dose of humiliation. Not that anybody expected Jay to perform or to be outstandingly funny; nobody expected this except Jay.

So he had to play his ace comic card: the one marked failure. He got laughs by playing the loser. It was a refreshing novelty to hear an American actually boasting of his flop plays and his disastrous attempts at stand-up comedy. Wendy Cook paid him the ultimate compliment when she said to Fran, 'You're so lucky to be married to such a funny man.'

☆

Jay's dream of creative living may have been a nice idea but it had its downside. Fran hated it when she didn't have a project to work on. She came to dread the times when people would ask that worst of all questions: 'And what do you do for a living?'

Jay once tried to give her some advice on how to deal with this. The conversation went like this:

Fran: I get so tired telling people that I'm not doing anything.

Jay: Tell 'em you're catching up on the art of living.

Fran: I can't.

Jay: Why not?

Fran: Because it's a lie. I'm miserable!

Jay: Why don't you tell them you're a part-time schizoid looking for full-time work?

For all Jay's talk of creative living, the old career longings keep coming back to tempt him. There's a play that Jay had written back in St Louis called *Nobody Knows The Trouble I've Been*, about an ageing, neurotic and washed-up female jazz singer called Stella trying to make a comeback. She's one of those walking-wounded women you find in the work of Tennessee Williams. Jay gets a copy to Anne Bancroft, who would go on to star in *The Graduate*. Word comes back that Anne is reading it on the plane back to New York. Jay gets a copy to Ava Gardner. No word. He waits. And waits. And then Ava passes. Message from Bancroft arrives: thanks, but no thanks.

OK, never mind. Who needs Ava? Who needs Anne? He has a wonderful wife and great kids and a rewarding life of creative living. Then one morning Jay is in the park, getting ready for a day of enlightened loafing, when he reads in the paper that a sick Judy Garland has been admitted to a London hospital.

Straight away Jay is back in full-on high-speed career-achieving mode, and creative living can go fuck itself. This is too good an opportunity to miss. He picks up the phone and calls his agent: 'We need to get a copy of my play to Judy straight away! I don't care if she's dying. This play could bring her career back to life – even if it does kill her!'

He offers to take it to the hospital himself. What does he care if the poor woman is dying/suicidal/drunk – she'd be perfect for the lead role of Stella! His agent advises him to wait for Judy to recover. Time for a new agent, thinks Jay.

Like an AA member who takes a drink, Jay returns to his old ways. He's pursuing his career in journalism, pitching article ideas to the *St Louis Post Dispatch*. He also has lunch with the editor of British *Vogue* about doing a column for them. He writes a sample column and she writes back: 'Too hip for us'. He's working on raising money for *Dearest Dracula*.

And despite his various efforts as producer, playwright and journalist, Jay is reluctant to admit that he's back in the game. He tells Fran, 'I can't take any of it seriously.'

When Jay says that, what he really means is: *I don't want to take it seriously.*

Fran, on the other hand, is serious. She starts searching for an agent. Bingo. One comes along, reputed to be the best in the business, and they discuss their future together.

Agent: I'm a lousy agent, but a terrific lover.

Fran: Too bad. I have a lousy lover, what I need is a terrific agent.

Projects find Fran. She stays up all night writing songs for a revue with jazz singer Annie Ross. She is so excited about what she's writing, she wakes up Jay in the middle of the night and asks him what he thinks of her newest song. It's called 'Piss Off, My Love'.

Fran gets a top agent who starts teaming her up with various collaborators. She writes a song with John Barry for the new Michael Caine film *The Ipcress File* – the lyric is rejected. She teams up with Dudley Moore, he sets some songs but nothing happens. And then Fran gets her first London break. The hot BBC satire programme *Not So Much a Programme, More a Way of Life* wants to do one of her songs. We huddle around our new black and white television set and watch Millicent Martin singing a Fran song.

'Baby, this could be the start of something very big,' says Jay.

A few weeks later the programme is taken off the air in preparation for the forthcoming General Election.

☆

In December 1964 the *Sunday Times* carries a profile of my family by Hunter Davies that begins: 'There's a very way-out Salinger family just arrived in London called the Landesmans.' The profile makes us out to be a crazy American family, with bizarre decor and a neurotic relationship between Mother and me.

OK, maybe we are a little crazy, but we're close. We all go to the local library together every fortnight. We shop together at the local open market. We help Jay fix up our new house by tearing down plaster, scraping off old wallpaper and removing rubbish. Fran makes curtains and sews pillowcases. We're all mucking in and building a new life together.

On Sunday mornings we go to Petticoat Lane so that Jay can scout around for house bargains, and in the evening we have the big family treat of the week: a meal at the local Wimpy bar.

It's hard to convey what a thing of wonder a Wimpy bar was in 1964. We tasted our American past in its burgers, fries and milkshakes and saw our British future in that eccentrically sliced frankfurter they served; it resembled a miniature pink accordion. For dessert we'd devour such creamy, architectural wonders as the Knickerbocker Glory, and then go home to bed.

My parents liked us. Miles and I weren't regarded as children to be raised and fussed over, but as a curious form of entertainment to sit back and enjoy. We were a double act, a mini-revue. Jay writes about us in his diary like a theatre critic at work. We were 'funny ... sophisticated ... charming'. In one entry he pays his children the ultimate critic's compliment: 'they're the best show in town.'

When the era of those Wimpy meals ended, I no longer really enjoyed going out to dinner with my parents. The self-consciousness of adolescence would change everything. Dining out was suddenly an ordeal to be endured, a banquet of family embarrassment.

Part of the problem was that Jay had this unconscious need to act out his troubled relationship with his mother. His desire for attention often became acute at the dinner table. At the age of fourteen he had a nervous breakdown that was triggered by a plate of prunes – Jay felt he wasn't getting his fair share. So the slightest sense that he was being ignored in a restaurant led to a primordial cry for attention and affirmation from some poor waitress he wanted as a mother substitute. He once said to a waitress in an Angus Steak House, 'Madame, do you realize your aggressive delay in bringing my Black Forest Gateau has undone thirty-two years of psychoanalysis? If I relapse into a pre-oedipal stage it will be your fault!'

Such outbursts invariably led to people looking at us. We were always the loudest family in any restaurant. Our American voices seemed to shatter the quiet background hum of English whispers. I started to see us as I imagined others saw us – a loud, crazy American family – and I would bury my face in my hands and squirm in my seat.

And that's how I was to spend the next forty-five years.

☆

Around 1965/66 things start to change in London. Doing a whole lot of nothing is going out of style. The Swinging London theme has hit the headlines. The capital, once the centre of an empire, is now the international centre of cool. It has become a celebrity city, famous for being famous.

There's a lot of new American money sloshing around the creative economy. Any hack can knock out a film idea about Swinging London and sell it. Publishers are going out for three-hour liquid lunches and handing out advances for dessert. Funny money, they call it, and even the loafers want to get in on the bandwagon.

Jay's been doing nothing on the career front for months and has discovered that inactivity is a drag. He's tired of hanging out. The thrill of that 2.30 p.m. freedom is gone. He finally admits to himself: 'I thought I found a way to beat the game. I lost.'

So he talks the situation over with Fran. He says he's still anxious about getting back into the arena, but he has to do something. London is no longer a place to hang out and just enjoy yourself. There's this big creative surge that's going on and everybody is on the make and still having fun.

Fran is sympathetic. 'Yeah, It's too bad we can't just enjoy ourselves without it, but let's give it one more try.' And so they give what they imagine to be the final push to fame.

Jay finds a top agent. He starts writing a one-act play that the *St Louis Post Dispatch* has commissioned and he spends more time getting *Dearest Dracula* off the ground. Vincent Price says he's interested. Jay's sending the script to just about everyone in British theatre; he even gets it to the legendary king of the West End theatre, Binky Beaumont. He starts to get a lot of negative feedback on the project: too much humour, not enough horror is the common complaint.

Meanwhile, Fran is trying to make the transition from writing jazz songs to pop songs. Her new collaborator is Tom Springfield, brother of Dusty, producer and writer for the Seekers who get a number one hit, 'I'll Never Find Another You'. She and Tom write various songs together and nothing happens.

Bursts of hustle and creativity are followed by silence and the long, agonizing wait for people to get back to you. It's like waiting for a jury to deliver their verdict as to whether your project will live or die. When Fran gets down about her career Jay rushes to her rescue with advice and strategies for dealing with their situation. Instead of taking it all 'so seriously', Jay tells Fran that they should treat their careers like they were playing a game. That way success would no longer be a matter of life and death. Ideally they would play the game with style and panache, and if it doesn't work out, so what? *It's just a game.*

I know Jay's game approach well and so does every freelance journalist or person with a project. You send out your pieces and/or your proposal and you tell yourself, *don't take any of it seriously! If it happens, it happens. If doesn't ... c'est la vie. Why worry? Why fret and fuss? Life goes on. Life is so much bigger and richer than our petty projects.*

And then you spend all your time waiting for the phone to ring. There's no piece of modern machinery that's as sadistic as a silent phone. And when it seems that your prayers have been answered and it does ring, it's your mother, or your best friend wanting to tell you that there's a frenzied bidding war for their new book!

You check the emails – twenty new ones. Wow! At least one of them has to be good news, right? Wrong. They're all offers for on-line Viagra and pills that will make your penis grow. And just when you've given up hope, the reply finally comes and it's 'no thanks, not one for us'. Then as the tears fall from your eyes and the grief snot pours from your nose you tell yourself: *it's only a game.*

☆

In the early sixties, Americans like my parents looked at England and saw a country that was less wealthy and money-driven than the United States, but a country that was more *civilized*. Jay couldn't believe how polite people were – they said 'thank you' all the time and called you 'love'.

Were they just naive? I don't think so. Other Americans in London had the same impression. At the same time as Jay was writing articles for the *St Louis Post-Dispatch* about the pleasures of life in England, so too was Anthony Lewis, the London correspondent of the *New York Times*. He too lived in Islington and wrote about going to shop at Chapel Market and visiting the antique shops of Camden Passage, just like Jay did. In an article for the *Atlantic* magazine, Lewis looked back on six years in London and concluded that by comparison with America, 'life is gentler, in many ways more congenial; a declining Britain proves that wealth and power in a nation have very little to do with happiness.'

But Americans were coming to England at the very moment when there was much excited talk of a 'New Britain' in the making. Harold Wilson, the leader of the Labour Party, was its most visible and vocal champion. The Big Idea of Labour's 1963 election campaign was a vision of this New Britain – dynamic, youthful, classless, meritocratic – forged in the 'white heat' of science and technology.

This New Britain, however, was to be forged in the white hype of media myth-making; and they called it Swinging London. In reality, London wasn't swinging. For most Londoners it was business as usual, or boredom as usual. A piece of Sixties graffiti appeared that summed up life for many: 'Tube-work-dinner-work-tube-armchair-TV-sleep-work. How much more can you take?'

But there were a small number of Londoners whose lives and faces provided the copy and the photographs upon which the whole myth of Swinging London would be founded. They were young creative people, maybe a couple of hundred at best, that included pop stars (the Beatles), photographers (David Bailey), fashion designers (Mary Quant), actors (Terence Stamp), models (Jean Shrimpton), interior decorators (David Hicks), hairdressers (Vidal Sassoon), artists (David Hockney) and the posh photographer (Antony Armstrong-Jones). They had their own network of fashionable restaurants, nightclubs, art galleries and hair stylists.

These stars of Swinging London were hard-working and hedonistic, young and sexy, and a handful of its leading figures – David Bailey, Terence Stamp, and Michael Caine – came from the working class. The media were fascinated by what they did, who they did it with, where they lived, what they wore and where they ate.

Swinging London marked a change in the aspirations and style of youth. If you were a hip young thing in the 1950s you adopted a style of alienation. To be cool you had to be out in the cold. You wanted to be a rebel, an Outsider, a beatnik or an Angry Young Man. But for the young ones of Swinging London all that alienation and rebel stuff was passé; youth didn't want to change the system, they wanted to own it.

Jonathan Aitken – then a twenty-four-year-old journalist with the *Evening Standard* – went out and interviewed 200 leading figures of Swinging London for his book *The Young Meteors*. Aitken offered this snapshot of their aspirations. 'If one had to name the qualities most admired by the younger generation in London today, a quick attempt might run: wealth, sex appeal, fame, youth, talent, novelty and quick success.'

Much has been written on how Sixties youth rebelled against orthodox morality, especially when it came to sex and drugs. The rebellion against orthodox thinking about success and celebrity, however, has not been recorded in much detail. The Swinging London set raised two contemptuous fingers to the taboos that surrounded money and 'making it'.

There was still a lingering contempt for success, found not only in bohemia but a small but influential section of English society: high-minded liberals, leftists, academics, public servants, the arts establishment, sections of the BBC and those who feared the Americanization of Britain. Success itself wasn't frowned upon, but to be too ambitious, to want it too much was considered bad form. You were expected to rise effortlessly and silently to the top.

The then seventeen-year-old singer Marianne Faithfull knew all about this. 'There's a whole group of English people, my father is one of them, for whom the idea of success, even wanting it is just not done,' said Faithfull. She had just had her first number one record – 'As Tears Go By' – and was worried about what her parents and boyfriend John Dunbar would say about her becoming a *soi-disant* pop celebrity.

But the Swinging London crowd had no sense of shame, or time for the English gentleman type, with his self-deprecation and embarrassment when it came to the pursuit of success. Where once the idea of the English gentleman epitomized all that was best about England, it was now seen by many as embodying all that was worst: the amateurism and lack of competitive drive that was so damaging to the British economy.

Around 1965/66 making money and making a name for yourself wasn't something to be embarrassed about, especially if you were a Swinging London star from the working class. 'To come from the Mile End Road and have a million quid by using your loaf must be a great sensation and that's what I'm aiming for,' said the photographer Terence Donovan. No photographer from the old school – Angus McBean, Cecil Beaton or Norman Parkinson – would have ever dared to be so blatant about their ambition.

Donovan and his fellow photographer David Bailey

were never shy about being photographed with their Rolls-Royces, or showing off about how much money they earned. Such ostentation used to be condemned as the height of vulgarity, now it was celebrated in glossy magazines as youthful 'vigour' and 'vitality'.

Another important change emerging at this time was the English attitude to publicity. The Swinging London crowd thrived on it. Journalist Anthony Haden-Guest, writing in *Queen* magazine, commented on the difference between old society and the 'New Class', as he called the movers and shakers of Swinging London. In the past, 'the important thing was to be in the limelight, but to find it all terribly distasteful.'

Haden-Guest goes on to point out the hypocrisy of old society, where a society hostess would secretly invite a gossip columnist to their party 'and spend the whole evening wondering how that dreadful man got invited.'

But for the new class, wrote Haden-Guest, publicity was 'essential . . . it's how the new class eminence is measured.' Youth, then as now, was frequently criticized for being hungry for fame. 'Publicity,' wrote the Sixties commentator Francis Wyndham, 'is something they all crave.' Being famous was the trump card held by the successful members of the Swinging London scene, in their contest with the figures of London society and the aristocracy.

That lot had always got by on the power of a name acquired at birth; now members of the 'new aristocracy' were names too – famous names who'd achieved theirs through work. This small handful of names, with the assistance of that distorting mirror that was the media, managed to create the impression that Britain had turned its back on the class system and was becoming a truly meritocratic society.

☆

Poor Jay. He was fated to arrive in England at a time when, thanks to Swinging London, success had never looked so glamorous, so sexy, and, here's the thing that must have hurt: *so much fun*. Swinging London success wasn't rooted in trade, industry, finance or even public service, but rather in the glamour industries of entertainment, the arts and mass media. And what's more you didn't have to shed blood, sweat and tears for decades before you achieved this success.

People like Jay couldn't stand on the sidelines and feel superior to the Swinging London lot. These weren't your stuffy pinstripe-suited Institute of Directors Jag-driving squares of old, but some of the most beautiful and talented people in the world. Success had never looked so photogenic.

Swinging London success was even more enjoyable because now it was down to your own efforts and talents, and not your family background or public school connections. You deserved it.

All this talk of money and making it may sound like the dress rehearsal for the 1980s and the rise of the 'selfish yuppies', but back then the idea of working-class boys like Terence Donovan and Terence Stamp achieving fame and fortune made success seem positively progressive, even a touch left wing, because they were breaking down the unjust barriers of class. This resulted in the forging of the very meritocratic society that progressive opinion saw as the post-class future for Britain.

Socially my parents were having lots of fun. There were dozens of parties they could go to every week. But on the career front it was hard to sit back and watch so many of the people they once knew become so successful. A young anxious comic who used to appear at the Crystal Palace called Woody Allen comes to London, and he's now a big name. A singer friend from St Louis, Will Hurt, turns up. 'He's now a star and we're broke,' Jay writes in his diary. Their old friend Mike Nichols (who directed *The Graduate*) and the comedian Elaine May are both stars, and so is the funny Jewish girl with a great voice but bad jokes that used to play the Palace, Barbra Streisand.

One afternoon Jay goes to the taping of his friend Peter Cook's new television show, with special guest John Lennon. He writes in his diary: 'Being at the show is disquieting. Always makes me wonder why we haven't gone further.'

Jay would spend the rest of his life asking himself the *why didn't we make it* question. And the answer is, what? Too hip for the times, not enough talent? The wrong kind of talent? All the above?

☆

Who or what constituted a successful man in the 1960s? Many people would have said David Bailey. In print and photographs his life looked perfect. It was a popular conception that Bailey was happy to encourage. As he said at the time, 'I think the photographer is one of the first completely modern people . . . He makes a fortune, he's always surrounded by beautiful girls, he travels a lot and he's always living off his nerves in a big-time world.'

The media portrayed Bailey as The Man Who Has It All. At twenty-four he was good-looking, wealthy, charming, cheeky, and the most famous and successful photographer of his time. Bailey had the beautiful model Jean Shrimpton for a girlfriend (and later French actress Catherine Deneuve for a wife), plus Mick Jagger for a best mate. To a certain sort of aspirational young Englishman in 1964 this was the dream life. And it's still the dominant dream of aspirational males today.

Confronted by David Bailey as an icon of success, my father would say, 'Ah yes, but is he happy?' When people say that what they really mean is: let's pray to God that this rich, good-looking, talented and successful guy is a miserable bastard!

So was Bailey happy? It's impossible to say for certain, but at the time he described himself as 'very selfish, anti-social, quite rich, lonely and *not particularly happy* [my italics]'.

If David Bailey personified Swinging London success, who was the symbol of Sixties failure? To anyone young at the time, one name that immediately comes to mind is Simon Dee. He was the good-looking former Radio Caroline disc jockey who hosted a 1967 BBC TV chat show called *Dee Time*. Dee was the Jonathan Ross/Chris Evans of his day, who had as his guests everyone from Jimi Hendrix to the historian A.J.P. Taylor. For the BBC it represented the spirit of Swinging London. It was an image the programme promoted in the closing credits of *Dee Time*. It featured Dee zooming off from Broadcasting House in a white open E-type Jag, with a sexy blonde by his side.

At its height *Dee Time* had an audience of 14 million viewers and Dee – who three years before was a door-to-door vacuum salesman – became a television star. Then after a three-year run, his television career crashed.

It was said that his ego got too big, along with his contractual demands on the BBC. In 1969 Dee was dropped by the BBC and then went on to do a new late-night chat show for LWT. But it bombed and his contract was terminated. The media plug was pulled and Dee disappeared from the nation's television screens. The golden boy of broadcasting next hit the headlines when in 1970 he signed on for unemployment benefit.

His fall was a very Sixties kind of failure: very fast and very visible. It was in the Sixties that *Schadenfreude* really came to the surface. Since then Dee has become a symbol of the 'vicissitudes of fame' and characterized as the 'Icarus of British television'. His story quickly became a modern morality tale about media, ego and celebrity. In the history of fame Dee occupies a unique place, for as his biographer Richard Wiseman points out: 'he has become significant for being the most famous man in the country for having *lost* his fame.'

☆

Throughout the days of Swinging London, Jay was haunted by the prospect of failure. His diary is littered with statements about impending flops and declarations that he and Fran simply can't make it.

Just as individuals can feel like a failure, so can a nation. But I suspect that only England could feel like a failure and still have so much fun. The Germans – after the defeat of WWI and the 'humiliation' of reparations during the 1930s – felt like a nation of failures and turned to fascism. The English watched the decline of their empire, the loss of international prestige, and decided to have the great party that was the early Sixties.

The Sixties have a reputation for being a time of optimism and hope. It's true that there was much excited talk about the creation of an energetic, entrepreneurial, classless and dynamic Britain. But alongside the English sense that things were getting better and life was brighter, there were also anxious concerns that Britain was a nation in decline, morally, culturally and economically.

This was something the British had been worrying about since the 1880s. What gave it new importance in the 1960s was that the nation's decline was now relative to countries other than the United States. Put simply, Britain was starting to slide down the national league tables that measured gross national product per head of the population.

So while people felt better off as they enjoyed the fruits of the consumer society, full employment and low inflation, the newspapers were constantly lamenting Britain's lost greatness. But that didn't stop the fun.

'It was tumble time for Brits,' says novelist Jilly

Cooper. 'We were all in an absolute panic about being the bottom country.' But despite Cooper's panic, she paints a picture of London society having a ball. 'There was so much sex around then. The first *Sunday Times* party I went to I danced on a table in a miniskirt. It was fantastic. Everybody got off with everybody.'

The early Sixties sense of failure was, I suspect, something found mostly amongst commentators and gloomy intellectuals. In his 1963 book *A State of England* Anthony Hartley argued that 'a loss of power means a loss of purpose.' For Hartley, the 'cheery chatter of the new Carnaby Street culture, while England got poorer under a Labour Prime Minister' left him feeling 'depressed'. Hartley was typical of those who believed that England's success was measured in terms of empire, military might and international influence. For the Hartleys of the world, if Britain wasn't a somebody on the international stage she must inevitably be a nobody.

Gloom-and-doom commentators might see nothing but a declining Britain, but that was not how the rest of the world viewed it. To young Americans it was the greatest place in the world. 'When fans fell in love with them [the Beatles], they were also falling in love with England,' wrote American authors Michael and Jane Stern. In their book on *Sixties People*, the Sterns note that after the Beatles, 'being English was the coolest . . . thing anyone could be. In 1966, just about anywhere in the Western world, the one and only thing to prove you were supremely hip was "I'm English!"'

Sometime in 1965 it became clear to my parents that all their projects and plans had crashed. His plays, her songs, had done the rounds and returned home like wayward children, who were promptly tucked up and put away in the darkness of my parents' filing cabinets.

The biggest rejection of all came from Jay's friend Peter Cook. That was perhaps the biggest hurt of all. He'd offered Jay a chance to fill in for him on a five-minute television spot that Cook had grown bored with. It could have made Jay a television star, so he decided to resurrect the Mystery Comic act he had pioneered at the Crystal Palace. He did ten minutes of stand-up comedy for Peter Cook and didn't get one laugh.

Jay, now drenched in flop sweat, pleaded with Cook. 'Peter, this is subliminal humour: I'm trying to take the laughter out of comedy!'

'Congratulations, Jay,' says Peter.

In his diary Jay poses the question: 'How much rejection can one take?'

The answer to that can be seen in the fact that by April 1965 my parents were actually contemplating leaving London. In his diary Jay wrote, 'It begins to dawn on us that we're not marketable at this time – we haven't what it takes to "make it". Aside from not being commercial, when we enter the commercial field we've failed. We can't even sell out!'

Then they got the Big Call.

The people at the Dublin Theatre Festival wanted to do *Dearest Dracula*. Suddenly all that talk about 'creative living' and not stepping back into the 'arena' and getting involved with the 'horseshit' of showbiz was over.

'It's the chance we've been waiting for!' declared Jay.

The play opened at the Olympia Theatre in Dublin in

1965 and received a standing ovation from the audience. The Irish critics raved about it. It looked like the Landesmans had a hit on their hands. Jay was dreaming big again: a transfer to the West End and then Broadway ... and then English theatre critics came, saw and destroyed. Harold Hobson of the *Sunday Times* said it was the most inept production he had ever seen. Even *The St Louis Post Dispatch* – the paper Jay had been writing for – published a round-up of the bad reviews under the heading 'Landesman Show A Flop'.

But that wasn't going to stop Jay. He had hit on a way of bringing Dracula back from the dead. He met with the great Hollywood choreographer Busby Berkeley in the hope of getting him to head a production of *Dearest Dracula* for Broadway, complete with a dancing chorus of vampires and a tango-mad Dracula. But then it all fell apart. Eventually Vincent Price passed on the lead role and the American producer who would take the show to Broadway got sick. Jay had to go back to Berkeley and tell him it was over. The show died.

The whole *Dracula* fiasco left Jay feeling pretty battered. Likewise, Fran was feeling down about the state of her career. In 1966 her father died, leaving them enough money to live without the necessity to work for a couple of years.

Fran continued to scribble away on her bed but was despondent – all those meetings and arranged collaborations had come to nothing. She would sum up their plight years later when I asked what she wanted written on her gravestone. And she told me:

'It was a good life, but it wasn't commercial.'

Jay admits he started to suffer from what Fran called 'lack of recognition blues'.

Yet they both realize that they may not have the success they so crave but they do have each other. It's not a complete compensation, but it's a kind of comfort. Despite their failures, Jay writes: 'we're closer than ever before. We could lead a lovely life without the career-driven problems.'

But love and closeness were not enough. London was another city they had bombed in. Jay thought that it was time to quit and head back to America. They were even thinking about Florida.

And then Hippy London came to the rescue . . .

5

Fifties Britain and
The Dawn Of Celebrity

Any thinking person over the age of forty is bound to look at contemporary Britain, with its expanding collection of celebrities, famous nobodies, exhibitionists, attention-seekers and celebrity-drenched media magazines, and wonder: *when did this whole crazy thing begin?*

You look back to your own youth and it wasn't there ... or at least it didn't *seem* to have been there. But look closer and you'll see it in the posters and pictures of your idols that adorned the bedroom wall of the teenage you. And wasn't it there in your head as you sat during drowsy afternoons in stuffy classrooms dreaming of being a movie star, or in those moments of imagined rock 'n' roll glory before your bedroom mirror?

Has anything really changed, or do the infatuations of the present always look garish compared to the infatuations of the past, which, after all, have had the facelift of time and glow with retrospective innocence.

So maybe you concede there was a little bit of this celebrity madness back when you were young. Then you quickly point out that we weren't *so* obsessed and there wasn't *so* much of it and it didn't loom *so* large in British life. Yes, we were interested in movie stars and entertainers. However, it was a private passion that remained in the background of life. Now it has become the tinnitus of modern times, the infuriating buzz that's always ringing in our lives.

It's when I start writing things like that I begin to wonder: *Am I being nostalgic for an age that never existed? Am I talking about the state of England or the state I'm in? Maybe it's just me getting old and becoming a grumpy old guy who thinks everything is getting worse.*

But if this were true you could never make any critical judgements about any aspect of contemporary life, because you'd always end up accusing yourself of being a grumpy old guy or woman when, in fact, you could be dead right about what is really going on.

So when exactly did Britain change? The danger of posing such a question is that it assumes there was a great change; that we once lived a celebrity-free existence, and then along came a certain century or a specific decade and *wham*: the fall from grace.

There's a school of thought that says there's nothing new about celebrity culture; people have always been interested in the doings of the monarchy, the aristocracy, the rich, and then later the entertainers and sports stars of the twentieth century.

That's true. However, human curiosity may not change, but the means by which celebrity is manufactured, distributed and consumed does. There comes a point in the culmination of celebrity where its volume and visibility is so much greater than anything seen before that it qualifies as a new phenomenon.

The eighteenth and nineteenth centuries had what we would call celebrities, and critics were already drawing a clear distinction between fame and celebrity. 'They had celebrity, Spinoza has fame,' wrote Matthew Arnold. But no one talked about a celebrity *culture*. To an educated man of the nineteenth century such an idea would have seemed like an obvious oxymoron. If you had said to a literary celebrity like Dickens or Byron that in the future everyone will be famous for fifteen minutes, they would have thought you were mad.

So, without getting all misty-eyed about the past, we can say that there has been a change, but amongst writers on the topic of celebrity there's no general agreement on when this happened. The biographer Katie Whitaker traces the origins of modern celebrity back to the seventeenth century and the fame of the Duchess of Newcastle. Her first book – *Poems and Fancies* – scandalized English society in 1653.

The English historian Stella Tillyard prefers the eighteenth century as her starting point, and in particular, 'London with its dozens of newspapers and print shops, its crowds and coffee-houses, theatres, exhibitions, spectacles, pleasure gardens and teeming pavements'.

Film historian Jeffrey Richards places the birth of celebrity in the nineteenth century. He points out that was when 'star' and 'celebrity' were first used in a modern way. Richards shows that long before hordes of crazed American movie fans in the 1920s hounded film stars, you had the famous of Victorian England being mobbed by a star-struck public. The Poet Laureate Alfred, Lord Tennyson was constantly besieged by autograph hunters, and often raged against those who would invade his privacy by climbing up trees to peer into his house.

As for the title of Britain's first celebrity, all sorts of unlikely people have been awarded this dubious accolade. Frederic Raphael claims that Lord Byron (1788–1824) was 'the first modern celebrity'. No, says Jane Smiley, Charles Dickens (1786–1851) was 'the first true celebrity in the modern sense'.

Forget Byron and Dickens and all the other monarchs, movie stars, housewives' heart-throbs and adolescent pin-ups whom scholars and commentators have proclaimed the first 'modern celebrity'. If you want to see the first face of modern British celebrity culture you have to go back to the evening of 15 February 1955 and comedian Arthur Askey's BBC television series *Before Your Very Eyes*.

That night millions of viewers saw something they'd never seen before: television's first sex symbol in action. She was a young, busty, peroxide blonde in a tight black dress making her television debut. Viewers watched in amazement as she slid off a sofa, walked towards the camera, and then slowly turned sideways to reveal the mountain range of her magnificent cleavage. One can only imagine the effect on the families watching: a collective gasp of wonder. Men would fidget on the settee; teenage boys would blush and women would go and put the kettle on.

This mysterious creature remained silent for the entire show. She didn't do a thing but stand there: a living, breathing pin-up. But no one was complaining.

The BBC had given the viewing nation a mute blonde with a cheesy smile, a 41½-inch bust towering over an 18½-inch waist ... and *shazam*! A star was born. Her name was Sabrina.

Actually, her real name was Norma Sykes and her mother ran a B&B in Blackpool. After her appearance on Askey's show Sabrina became a showbiz phenomenon, a national star who couldn't act, dance, sing, juggle or – so it seemed – even speak. She was labelled, displayed and dismissed as 'Britain's dumbest blonde'. And yet Sabrina had a huge following of fans. Even after she had left the BBC her popularity showed no signs of declining. She made money from public appearances and modelling, and hardly a day went by when newspapers didn't carry a Sabrina-related story.

Hers was a very British kind of Fifties fame: cheesy, cheap and cheerful. It was imitation Hollywood with a touch of saucy British seaside-postcard vulgarity: starlet meets harlot. Sabrina was paraded at glamorous film premieres and showbiz events, but her bread and butter came from doing the rounds of local openings and special events. She was hired glamour.

All over the backwaters of Britain you got these personal appearances of 'stars' – Rank school starlets, B-list actors, television personalities and even pop singers. Those were the days when you could see a young movie star like Dirk Bogarde judging a beauty contest to find Miss Hull.

Sabrina could certainly pull them in. She once went to Sheffield to open a new hardware store and a crowd of four thousand turned up to take a peek at her. It was widely reported that a 'riot' broke out when her dress strap broke.

In 1956 *Picture Post* announced that 'Sabrina worship has reached a new frenzy' and frenzied Sabrina fans broke through a police cordon to see her opening the Gondolier, Ipswich's first espresso coffee bar.

Sabrina is an important figure in the history of British celebrity because her fame so resembles the fame of our own time. Hers was an instant celebrity, one built on nothing but the thin air of glamour shots, gossip, newspaper headlines, magazine features and public appearances. And like so much fame today, Sabrina's fame in the 1950s had no connection to talent. She knew it and so did everyone else.

There were lots of famous people in Fifties Britain who didn't have much talent (the public loved Diana Dors, but it wasn't for her acting). But none of these no-talents were so ridiculed and savaged as Sabrina. God knows she tried to play along with it, cheerfully telling the press, 'I mustn't speak or I'll lose my reputation for being the dumbest blonde in Britain!'

Commentators were baffled. Sabrina seemed to defy the laws of show business, the first one being that you had to have some sort of talent – however modest – to be in the limelight. *Photoplay* magazine posed the great Sabrina question of the day when it pondered, 'Incredible, isn't it, that a girl who has done so little (one TV series, one film and a variety stint) should so soon have become a household word. How long can it go on? How far can she go on her dumb blonde gimmick?'

A year later in 1957 journalists were still asking how

long could she go on. *Picturegoer* magazine tells its readers: 'at this time last year the talk was like this: "She'll never last. She's not a real star. She's a freak who'll fade overnight." Bosomy Sabrina, who seemingly had nothing to commend her but a talented physique, was bitingly listed as The Girl Most Likely Not To Succeed in 1957. But has she faded? She has not. Talent she may not have – her embarrassingly amateurish theatrical appearances prove that – but the Treasure Chest revealed another attribute in 1957: PERSISTENCE.'

How a girl with such a conspicuous absence of talent could be so famous and successful was a question that haunted Sabrina herself. She wanted to become a proper part of show business, so she began to take singing and acting lessons. As she told one reporter, 'After all, a girl needs to have something more than a big bosom.'

But, as we shall see, there would eventually come a time in Britain when a big bosom would indeed be all a girl would need to find fame and build a successful career as a celebrity. Still, Sabrina – who now lives a quiet life in Hollywood – has had the last laugh. Where once she was dismissed as a dumb blonde, she has had a retrospective makeover and become the smart, media-savvy pioneer of the modern art of self-promotion. No longer a national joke, she is now seen and celebrated as the Jordan of her day.

☆

Sabrina's celebrity challenges some of the dearest assumptions we have about Britain in the 1950s. The self-indulgent, celebrity-obsessed 1960s are often contrasted with the good old sensible 1950s. Nick Clarke, in *The Shadow of a Nation*, portrays that decade as the golden era before the thick, unreal fog of celebrity settled across Britain. He points to the fact that we were then still a nation of radio listeners. Television, which he holds responsible for Britain's slide into celebrity culture, had not yet become the tyrant in the centre of our living rooms and our lives.

It's tempting to take a romantic view of the 1950s as a pre-*Hello!* Britain when people had *real* communities composed of family, neighbours, workmates and friends to gossip and relate to, and not the virtual communities of celebrities they have now. The psychologist Oliver James argues that it was a time when we were far happier because we were not so driven by material wants and the longing for celebrity. And instead of the opiate of *heat* and *Hello!*, ordinary people had socially aware magazines and newspapers like *Picture Post* and the *Daily Sketch*. Most important of all, in those days fame was hard to come by. 'The only route to fame and fortune was through achievements in some field of public endeavour,' writes Nick Clarke.

But, as the case of Sabrina shows, this wasn't quite true. All sorts of unlikely people, many utterly devoid of talent, found themselves inexplicably famous, thanks to a new cultural force in British life: television.

Although television broadcasting in Britain officially began in 1936, it only became popular in the late 1950s. At the start of that decade only 4 per cent of the adult population owned a television set; by its end this had risen to 80 per cent. Television had become a part of the daily fabric of ordinary lives. As Harry Hopkins noted in the *New Look*: 'Each morning at the bus stop, on the railway platform, in office and shop and factory there was a new conversation to replace "the weather" ... it was, "Did you see so-and-so on television last night?"'

What Henry Ford's assembly line did for the manufacturing of cars, television did for fame. It began the mass production of a whole new class of television-bred celebrities: presenters, announcers, entertainers, game-show hosts, soap-opera stars, weather girls and quiz-show contestants. They entered the homes and hearts of the British public, becoming, as Hopkins put it, 'invisible members of the family circle, and a part of the furniture of the home in a way that film stars had never been before.' That was because television created the illusion of intimacy between viewers and the viewed far better than the cinema.

Television could turn anyone – comedian, cook or serious commentator – into a celebrity for no other reason than that they appeared on television. Recognition became a form of renown. By simply being on 'the telly' you were a somebody.

Even such an august figure as Richard Dimbleby, who was then the BBC's most popular and prominent television presenter, found that he was subjected to the kind of fame once reserved for film stars. It was Dimbleby who provided the television commentary for grand occasions of state like the Coronation of Queen Elizabeth II in 1953 and the funeral of Sir Winston Churchill in 1965. For such work he became known as the 'voice of the nation'.

Due to his work on television – presenting *Panorama* and the BBC's Election night coverage – Dimbleby couldn't go out in the street or get on a bus without drawing attention. If he stood still in public, a crowd would gather around and just stare at him, or ask for autographs. A woman in the street once stopped him and said, 'Mr Dimbleby, do you mind, I just want to say that I have touched your coat.' There was nothing so trivial about Dimbleby's private life that it wasn't of public interest; if he caught a cold it ended up in one of the gossip columns. Dimbleby, unlike so many broadcasters and journalists from the pre-television era, actually enjoyed his fame.

Gilbert Harding hated his. He's often described as British television's first celebrity, and in the 1950s he was considered the most famous man in the UK. Bob Monkhouse once summed up Harding's fame thus: 'If you went into Madame Tussauds in 1955 you would see a statue of Gilbert Harding. And the plaque underneath didn't say Gilbert Harding, it simply said The Most Famous Man in Britain, and that's all it needed to say. Everyone knew Gilbert Harding.'

Harding was the original grumpy old man who found fame as one of the panellists of the BBC's quiz show *What's My Line?* With his bow tie, 'fruity saloon-bar voice' and old-curmudgeon crotchetiness he had the manner of an irascible schoolteacher. People used to love to watch Gilbert give some poor contestant a verbal going-over. He was the Simon Cowell of his day.

In private he was a tortured homosexual with a drink problem. In the fifties Harding was an ubiquitous media presence: his face appeared on the front pages of news-papers and in adverts; he wrote opinion pieces in magazines and newspapers, and books of memoirs.

The public felt that 'Gilbert' – as everyone called him – belonged to them. He couldn't go out in public without being spotted and confronted by a star-struck member of the public. Gilbert felt nothing but contempt for his celebrity status because he believed his fame was founded on no real talent or merit: he simply appeared on television. And for that he was cursed with fame.

In his book *Master of None* Harding complained that he was 'constantly pestered by cranks and plagued by crackpots' who want advice or friendship from him. He goes on: 'It is often impossible to shop . . . or impossible to walk along the pavement without having crumpled pieces of paper thrust under my nose for me to sign, or without show-offs attempting to pick a quarrel with me.'

Harding wasn't alone in hating his TV fame. Dan Farson, a reporter for Rediffusion who became a household name with a series of documentaries and interviews, gives a good insight into what it was like to be a famous television face in the 1950s in a letter he wrote to his parents in 1959. 'You'll find it hard to believe but this staggering thing of being recognized wherever one goes is torture and sheer unadulterated hell. One feels one is being hunted. In a pub, bus or on the street, to have constantly to smile back at people who make fatuous though well-meaning remarks gets one down.'

Though men like Harding and Farson hated their celebrity, there were plenty of people who longed for it. Harding complains that members of the public are forever writing to him for advice on how to become a celebrity, and in his book he suggests such people should be happy with their humdrum life. 'I hope you have a woman who loves you, a dog who adores you, a cat who tolerates you, and no more children than you want and can love,' writes Harding. 'There are very few things in life more worth having.'

☆

Television was slow to pick up on what newspapers and magazines had already realized: celebrity was a popular form of entertainment in itself. People liked watching celebrities being celebrities. An early example of celebrity TV was *This Is Your Life*, which first appeared in 1955 and gained an audience of between 12 and 14 million people. Although today we think of it as a rather anodyne and celebratory view of the famous it was a controversial programme in its time. Critics complained that it was 'torture by TV', and a 'voyeuristic feast of invasive exploitation', which makes it sound like the *Big Brother* of its day.

In 1957 ABC TV broadcast a game show called *Can Do*, featuring Jon Pertwee – later of *Doctor Who* fame – as the host. Celebrities were given various stunts to perform, and the contestants had to guess whether the celebrity could do it or not. One episode featured Sabrina in a bikini diving into a 20-foot glass cage full of water in order to find and open an oyster with a pearl inside.

Alongside television the other great driving force of modern celebrity was the rock 'n' roll boom that began in the fifties. It is often said that the Suez debacle of 1956 marks the end of Britain's pretence to being a great imperial power. But in the same year that she lost her imperial illusions, Britain produced something she had never created before: her first home-grown rock 'n' roll star.

He was an eighteen-year-old from Bermondsey called Tommy Hicks, who would become famous as Tommy Steele. In October of that year Steele got his first number one record with 'Rock With The Caveman'. It marked the birth of British pop and a new modern definition of what it meant to be British. For within a decade of Steele's success, Britain's standing in the world, thanks to the Beatles, would be dependent on her pop prowess.

The British film industry, from its earliest days, had never felt comfortable with the business of creating stars. While recognizing their importance in attracting audiences, there was a tendency to regard star-making as a rather crass practice best left to Hollywood. In the noisy world of rock 'n' roll things were different. There was a new breed of young, brash, fast-talking, streetwise managers like John Kennedy, Larry Parnes, Reg Calvert and Don Arden who had no such qualms. They knew there was a growing teenage market for rock 'n' roll stars. If some young singer didn't have the talent to become a star, they didn't care. In the early days of British rock 'n' roll most people in the music business thought it was just a fad that would be over in a year or two. So you had to move quickly to make a killing. Managers would take some kid off the street, groom him, give him a new name, hype him, get him a hit and then dump him and find a fresh face to launch.

Who cared if a singer couldn't sing or play guitar? It was all about the look, the image. 'British pop in the fifties was pure farce. Nobody could sing and nobody could write and, in any case, nobody gave a damn. The industry survived in a state of perpetual self-hyped hysteria,' is how Nik Cohn described the early days of rock 'n' roll.

Even those who worked at the coalface of modern celebrity – like show-business journalist Leslie Mallory – were surprised by the new power of hype. Mallory, a journalist with the *News Chronicle* in the early sixties, spoke for many in her profession when she wrote:

'I wish men who call themselves public relations counsellors and have three cornets on their note paper would stop ringing me up and saying in carried-away voices: "Decca have just signed Fannie Bloggs. She's receiving the press at the Savoy at 5.30." I wish that after I have told the men with the three cornets to drop dead, I could come back from lunch and not find a note from my secretary saying Decca have just signed Fannie Bloggs and by the time I get to the Savoy, Fannie Bloggs, whom nobody ever heard of before that morning, is already famous!'

☆

The British fame machine wasn't just turning out would-be starlets and instant rock 'n' roll stars. In 1956 it created its first existentialist superstar: twenty-four-year-old Colin Wilson. He was a bespectacled, geeky working-class writer from Leicester who wore white polo-neck jumpers and proclaimed himself a genius.

His first book *The Outsider* (a celebration of existential thinkers) became an overnight hit thanks to two rave reviews in the *Sunday Times* and the *Observer*, Wilson, like Byron before him, woke up to find himself famous. And he managed to stay in the headlines and gossip columns for the following year. It's interesting to note that Wilson was warned by friends and editors that all the publicity he was attracting would undermine his credibility as a serious writer, which is something that no one would suggest today.

The appeal of Wilson wasn't his work, but his life. The press were fascinated by the Wilson legend – a young working-class man, writes in the reading room of the British Library by day and sleeps in a sleeping bag on Hampstead Heath at night, and produces a book that all the eggheads love.

That a someone like Wilson could write an obtuse book of existential philosophy – one of dubious merit – and end up as famous as a pop singer shows just how powerful the fame machine had become. Even Wilson was surprised by his fame: 'Yesterday I bought a magazine on James Dean and meditated on this peculiarity of our age . . . the hysteria and success worship which has made me so successful, as it made Dean.' But Wilson's fame and success didn't last long. His follow-up book, *The Rebel*, was so badly received that he came crashing back to earth.

☆

Manufactured rock stars, television sex symbols, adored quiz panellists, Rank starlets, overnight sensations, synthetic legends, movie stars, television personalities, famous young writers – no wonder that by the end of the 1950s commentators were starting to say that fame wasn't what it used to be.

Writing in the *News Chronicle*, Tom Baistow complained that 'Today fame apparently awaits any youngster with a modicum of talent for the guitar, the microphone or the typewriter.'

Fame was becoming more accessible and moving at a speed never seen before. Harry Hopkins noted: 'Given luck, a good gimmick and a resourceful publicity man, a snack-bar girl or lorry-driver of small but particular talent could now attain, in weeks, a fame and income far eclipsing that of a Cabinet minister.'

In 1959 Anthony Sampson, a former gossip columnist for the *Observer*, wrote in *Encounter* of his worries about the growing power of 'the fame machine' to make instant names out of all sorts of nonentities. Sampson conceded that things hadn't got quite as bad as in America, where 'publicity organizations have taken over the whole business of creating reputations.'

Yet he went on to strike a note of alarm: 'But things are not what they were. The advent of television, the huge expansion of advertising and public relations, the "Americanization" of British life, have all immensely increased the powers of the fame machine.'

Sampson gives an example of how the fame machine in Britain in the fifties worked. He referred to the various press releases he would as a diarist get daily, the subject of each one hoping to receive a mention in his column. Most of them he rejected as no-hopers but then, writes Sampson: 'a few weeks later one notices the names creeping into print, the faces appearing on the television screen, and a reputation being established, with all the trappings of Fame.'

Other commentators went further and suggested that there was something pathological about the new interest in celebrity. Although they did not talk about our 'obsession' with the phenomenon, they were clearly concerned that something like this was already developing, at least among teenagers.

In 1956 a Rediffusion documentary called *Fan Fever* appeared, which set out to look at a new malady that was supposedly sweeping the nation's youth. The programme's premise was that screaming mobs of teenagers were going crazy over their pop idols. A typical teenager suffering from 'fan fever' was interviewed: a young girl who was so mad about singer Johnny Ray that she proudly wore a bit of carpet that Ray had stepped on as a top button of her coat, and had 'I Love Johnny' tattooed on her arm. The programme concluded that 'Fan fever may not be the most important problem in the world but it is symptomatic of the times we live in. When there are girls walking around with the names of their idols tattooed on their arms, isn't it time to get worried about it?'

The fifties had plenty of commentators worried about youth and their infatuations with the stars; today we are still worried. But the celebrity fixations of the present seem rather innocent compared to the violent teenage passions of the fifties. In 1956 the release of the film *Rock Around the Clock* provoked Teddy-boy riots in cinemas across Britain. Two years later, Tommy Steele's appearance at Dundee's Laird Hall led to a riot with fans invading the stage, pulling his hair and knocking him out.

In the fifties teenagers weren't the only ones susceptible to the excesses of fandom; even adults could get carried away. In 1951 the funeral of movie matinee idol Ivor Novello took place at Golders Green. Weeping elderly women fought with police to catch a glimpse of his funeral cortège. In 1956 the American entertainer Liberace was greeted by thousands of screaming middle-aged fans at Waterloo station. 'This appalling man hit the country as violently as Churchill receiving the cheers of VE Day,' complained the American musician Larry Adler.

There was, however, one key difference between now and then. In the early part of the 1950s the public's fascination with stars was carried out within a society that was still rooted in the world of family, neighbourhood, community, class and the workplace. It was here that most ordinary people derived a sense of belonging and self-worth.

However, things began to change in the late 1950s. Youth began to drift away from the sensible, secure – but dull – world of their parents and into a new and exciting Britain driven by affluence, consumerism, television celebrities, pop stars and fashion. Here was a seductive modernity in the making, one that offered new freedoms – of identity and consumption – but which at the same time destroyed the old comforts of family and belonging.

It was in the sixties that the social fabric would be torn and the bonds of tradition broken; but the modern self would be set free to make its own way in the world. As we will see, that self would try to reconnect with the world it left behind by the imagined goodies and glory offered by fame.

6

Hippy London Ate My Parents

Sometime around 1967 a great wave of weirdness started to slowly spread across the Western world.

People went hairy, music went psychedelic, everyday clothes turned into fancy dress. Minds were blown, taboos got busted and reality started to look less real.

Thing weren't 'fab' any more; they were 'far out'.

Even the Queen noticed this wave of weirdness, commenting that the once clean-cut Beatles were 'getting awfully strange these days'.

That aspirational dream of moving-on-up had been replaced by the dream of dropping-on-out. Swinging London had become Hippy London.

That wave of weirdness, which had begun in San Francisco around 1965, had by 1967 trickled down our street in London, seeped into our home and right into my parents' heads. It did strange things to their minds and scary things to their sense of dress.

If you want to see the difference between Swinging London and Hippy London, just look at the change in my parents.

Exhibit A: Swinging London Dad

Clothes – Smart grey double-breasted suits from the chic men's boutique Take Six. White polo-neck jumpers. Purple shirts, black knit ties. Shiny black 'Beatle boots' with high Cuban heels.

Appearance – He looked cool, like a Jewish Robert Vaughn in *The Man From U.N.C.L.E.*

Exhibit B: Hippy London Dad

Clothes – Tight-fitting fluorescent yellow hip-huggers with bright orange floral patterns. Leather sandals, love beads, plastic-leather trousers and purple-painted toenails. Shoulder-length hair. Dark shades.

Appearance – He looked like a Jewish Robert Vaughn on acid.

Exhibit C: Swinging London Mum

Clothes – Mary Quant dresses, big plastic earrings, miniskirts, mascara-soaked eyes, hair by Vidal Sassoon.

Appearance – Middle-aged dolly bird.

Exhibit D: Hippy London Mum

Clothes – Purple Afghan coat that resembled a dead sheep, tie-dye T-shirts, bare legs, sandals, badges, bangles, beads and no bra. (Please note: no-bra mums were a rarity in those days. I was the first kid on the block to have one.)

Appearance – Middle-aged hippy chick.

In 1967 only young people, aristocrats, flamboyant homosexuals and lunatics dressed like my parents.

Middle-aged people did not dress like young people; they dressed like middle-aged people. Their clothes said: we are grown-up, respectable and belong to a certain social class.

Young people dressed in a way that said: *we are not like our parents*.

My parents dressed in a way that said: *we aren't like your parents either*.

And so it was that during the Summer of Love I was a thirteen-year-old boy with two middle-aged hippy parents to raise on my own. (Miles wanted no part in my mission. He wanted to join the party.) It wasn't easy trying to get my parents to act like grown-ups. They were regressing back to adolescence at the very time I was advancing towards it; no wonder we crashed head on in the middle.

I was a hypercritical thirteen-year-old.

I criticized the way my parents dressed: 'You're not going out looking like *that*, are you?' I criticized their friends: 'They're disgusting weirdos . . . freaks . . . spongers!' I criticized their use of drugs: 'You're going to scramble your brains/you'll go blind/you're going to destroy your memory taking that stuff.' I complained, threatened and cajoled. But there comes a point when you have to let your parents grow up in their own time.

I'm fifty-two years old, and I'm still waiting.

☆

As they continued their descent into weirdness I reacted by retreating into straightness. My room was so tidy all the time that my father worried that I needed psychiatric help. Every evening I ironed and folded my school uniform with the care and precision of an army cadet. My hair was short, my tie was straight and my Dr Martens cherry-red skinhead boots were always shiny.

My parents in turn criticized me for being 'uptight', 'bourgeois', a 'fascist' and 'anally retentive'. I wasn't sure what 'anally retentive' was, but I didn't like the sound of it. What's more, I was guilty of the worst crime of all: taking myself *too* seriously.

Their criticisms of me left me feeling infuriated and baffled. Couldn't they see that I was the *normal* one and they were the *freaks*? No, because they considered *me* the freak, because I was normal.

Still, I wasn't the only one who couldn't get with this hippy thing. By the summer of 1967 the 'underground', as the hippy scene was called, had emerged into the bright lights of media attention and the public imagination. The hip people of Swinging London had to adapt to the hippy movement or die.

Some of them, like my parents, did it without missing a beat. The Beatles managed it; they went hairy and their music went strange. (They stopped wanting to hold your hand; now they wanted to blow your mind.) But the other stars of Swinging London couldn't get with the hippy thing. Mary Quant, Vidal Sassoon and Michael Caine were too ambitious and hard-working to be part of this new scene. Sassoon and Caine were from the working class and had spent their lives trying to get a foot in the door. Now they were in, the last thing they wanted to do was drop out and drop down the social ladder.

The most conspicuous hippy failure of them all was the king of Swinging London himself, David Bailey. Hippy London was mostly a collection of rebellious middle-class youth who hated Swinging London and everything it stood for. It thought Swinging London was shallow, materialistic, obsessed with success, celebrity, glamour and glitz. No wonder the hippies hated Bailey: to them he was the Leni Riefenstahl of Swinging London.

Bailey tried to give hippy life a go and grew his hair long and wore love beads, but he could never put his heart into it. He was too obsessed by his work and had no interest in drugs or expanding his consciousness. Bailey was an old-fashioned grafter, a working-class boy made good. But most of all he was too rich and success-ful for the hippies. Yet, as Bailey complained: 'They sat in the back of my Rolls-Royce, ate all my food, drank all my booze and called me a capitalist pig!'

Bailey's former girlfriend and protégée, model and icon of Swinging London Jean Shrimpton, experienced similar hippy abuse. In her case it came from Heathcote Williams, the old Etonian rebel who had dropped out to become a playwright and counter-culture hero. On their first meeting at dinner Williams verbally attacked Shrimpton for being a symbol of Swinging London. 'He accused me of being a capitalist,' wrote Jean many years later. 'He accused me of many things, all to do with fame, success, money and the triviality of the life I led.'

Williams's attack, it turned out, was just a form of seduction, a strange foreplay. Somehow he managed to overcome his disgust with Shrimpton's shallow fame, her materialism and her money, and became her lover.

☆

You might think that my parents would have felt embarrassed about leaping on the bandwagon at their age, but as far as Jay was concerned he wasn't joining the hippies – the hippies were joining him. After all, he'd been part of that first wave of rebels and dropouts from the late 1940s to the early 1950s who became known as the beat generation. He was smoking pot and rebelling against middle-class values before these kids were born. What was *Neurotica* if not a precursor of the underground press and magazines like *It* and *Oz*? Old beat figures like Allen Ginsberg and William Burroughs enjoyed a special status within the counter-culture; they were seen as the parents and inspiration for the new generation of would-be rebels.

Hippy London came into my father's life at the right time and offered what seemed to be the perfect solution to his eternal anxiety about success and celebrity. For at its heart the hippy movement was a rejection of the conventional middle-class idea of success. Success, said the hippies, wasn't about what you owned, the symbols of status, the size of your house or your income. Instead of playing the whole be-a-somebody game, you 'turned on, tuned in and dropped out'.

Of course Jay had been trying to do this ever since his days as a young bohemian back in Greenwich Village in the late forties/early fifties. He'd given it a go when he was first in London, without much success. So what gave him hope this time? He was not alone. When back in 1964 he wrote in his diary: 'it takes a lot of nerve to get outside the dying culture and develop one's own environment,' he was right. There was no movement, no underground that one could feel a part of. The counterculture was in its infancy, just a bunch of isolated individuals (writers, poets, musicians, beatniks, political activists and art-school students) who were often unaware of each other. But by 1967 they were a fully fledged movement with their own media, shops, leaders and lifestyles.

Their credo could have come straight from the Jay Landesman guide to the good life. For the hippies that life was about exploration, play, fun and creative fulfilment; not the blood, sweat and tears of constant consumption and competition. You should do your own thing, expand your consciousness by drugs, meditation, Eastern philosophy or whatever 'turned you on'. The dichotomy between art and life, work and leisure was declared to be over. Jay and his 'creative living project' were back in business.

That summer Jay was rededicating himself to the art of creative living. There was a whole new London scene to check out; underground clubs like UFO on Tottenham Court Road (home of the Pink Floyd), parties illuminated by swirling psychedelic light shows and featuring naked bodies; the Legalize Pot rallies and the first big event of the underground: The 24 Hour Technicolor Dream at Alexandra Palace.

When John Clellon Holmes (Jay's old beat buddy from the days of *Neurotica*) came to London, Jay did his best to show him the hippy sights. He introduced him to Christine Keeler and Yoko Ono; the spectacle of the Kings Road, the underground movies of the Arts Lab and the bands at the Roundhouse. Jay wasn't really showing Holmes London, he was showing off his new way of creative living.

Holmes wasn't impressed. He thought the London underground scene was full of desperate people trying to be hip and rebellious. To him it looked like a second-rate version of what had been happening in America. He made it clear to Jay that he'd seen it all before and these youthful attempts at rebellion bored him. Holmes told Jay, 'The whole hippy, flower-power thing is already dying in America.'

Jay felt depressed after Holmes left London. He confessed to Fran, 'He made me feel the life I was leading was a complete waste.' He saw that old friends were writing their memoirs and getting them published. Some were even finding success. *Newsweek* carried a full-page review of Holmes's book, *Nothing More To Declare*, that included an essay on Jay, which gave him a boost of confidence. Fran suggested maybe he should give the memoir-writing business a go. 'Why? It hasn't made them any happier,' said Jay. 'Frankly, I'd rather live my life than write it.' But Fran wasn't fooled. She spotted what was going on straight away. 'You're suffering from a lack of recognition blues.'

Jay must have felt frustrated living on the edge of the hippy scene. He wanted to do something, make his contribution to the cultural life of the city. In those days any third-rate hustler with a telephone could organize a festival, a conference or culture centre. Jay got his chance in 1966 when an American stockbroker with more money than sense decided that he wanted to open a nightclub in Covent Garden called the Electric Garden. He had no idea what kind of club it should be, so he hired Jay as his artistic director.

For Jay it was a chance to get back into show business, to repeat the glory days of the Crystal Palace here in London. But more importantly it was also a chance to establish himself as a player on the London underground scene. All these other Americans – Jim Haynes, Jack Moore, Joe Boyd – were key figures, so why not Jay Landesman? This was going to be his big comeback.

Jay knew exactly what kind of place he wanted the Electric Garden to be: part disco, part rock venue and part avant-garde art gallery. He sensed that the lines between Pop and Art, artist and performer were breaking down, and he wanted to be the guy who gave the barriers the final boot. He was certain that artists were eager to get out of their studios and perform in public; the Electric Garden would be their platform. As he told the owner: 'I can get you the kind of performers that know how to freak out an audience in the name of Art.'

Jay believed that the crucial factor in the club's success was the quality, not of the performers, but of the publicity. And if there was one art form that Jay had mastered it was the art of the attention-grabbing press release. His mission was to intrigue, infuriate and perplex people in the media. He did it by mixing psychoanalytical gibberish and avant-garde outrage with a hint of Dada absurdity.

He announced that the Electric Garden would host a series of 'environmental entertainments on Sunday nights' with such titles as:

Warp-In-Rites (a probing of contemporary tensions)

Drag-It-On-Home-Baby (a psychedelic drag show)

Coloured Tape (interlocking envy problems)

One evening's entertainment he called 'Fused'. It promised nine artists presenting a 'Neon Ballet' featuring 'visual dialogues based on recently discovered medieval texts, electronic confessions and heat waves based on audience paranoia'.

After a few days of such happenings Jay's avant-garde tastes proved too much for the indecisive management. They got cold feet and wanted to resort to the comforts of running a disco. The crunch came one evening with the appearance of Yoko Ono. She sat on a platform, bound in surgical gauze, and invited members of the audience to come up and cut off a piece as she began her banshee wailing. Some of the audience could dig it, but the majority wanted the dance music turned back on.

The management told Jay to cut Yoko's mike and turn on the music, but he refused. He stood on the side of the stage shouting out words of encouragement to Yoko: *'Keep screaming, baby! Keep screaming!'*

When the music came back on in the middle of Yoko's act her husband, Tony Cox, tried to intervene and turn it off again. He was grabbed by bouncers and dragged out of the club yelling, 'This club is run by gangsters. Somebody call the fuzz!'

Some of the audience, assuming it was part of the show, loved it. Here was a real happening! Jay felt the evening was triumphant. He'd managed to freak out everyone: artist and audience. He'd also managed to freak out the management, and got himself fired.

☆

By '67 even Fran had lost some of her ambition. And besides, writing for Broadway was considered terribly square. But she kept writing pop songs and still hoped for a hit. Her new collaborator was Georgie Fame, who recorded a song she wrote called 'Try My World'.

One Saturday evening we sat around the television and watched *Juke Box Jury*, a popular BBC pop programme. Each week the latest record releases would be played to a panel of celebrities and they would vote it a Hit or a Miss – and sometimes the performer, who'd be hiding behind a screen, would come out and have to go and shake hands with the panel after being given a critical mauling. That Saturday we saw the panel vote 'Try My World' a hit. (Only later did I discover that the pretty dolly bird on the panel who raved about it was Jay's girlfriend at the time.)

As soon it was over Fran turned to me and said, 'Hit or Miss?'

I assured her it was a hit. She looked relieved. By then I had become the family's own *Juke Box Jury* for everything: songs, plays, and projects. You name it and I usually knocked it.

My mother was very excited by the panel's verdict. She had another *This Is It!* moment, certain that at last they had finally got the hit they had been hoping for all these years.

Jay agreed. 'Baby, this is going to be the big one! You're on your way out of that old jazz and into the new rock-music thing!'

I was proud of Fran's record and had no doubt that it was going to be a hit. I told everyone at school about it. I was excited by the prospect of following the progress of 'Try My World' in the *Melody Maker* as it moved up the charts. On 13 September 1967 'Try My World' entered the pop charts at number 37.

The following week I rushed to purchase my *Melody Maker* to find out how far it had risen up the charts. 'Try My World' had already dropped out of the top 50.

☆

By turning into hippies my parents stopped being Mom and Dad and became Fran and Jay. In effect, I lost my parents and found two new middle-aged playmates. Don't get me wrong: they were the best middle-aged playmates a boy could have.

But I wanted a mom and dad.

In the sixties all that conventional Mom and Dad stuff was called into question. Philip Larkin said it in poetry – 'they fuck you up, your mum and dad' – and the radical psychiatrist R.D. Laing said it in books like *Sanity, Madness and the Family*. Laing was a well-known critic of the nuclear family, an institution that he saw as the cause of much mental illness. Mom and Dad were artificial roles that kept your children/the world from seeing the real you.

It was during the Summer of Love that Fran and Jay's drug intake increased. On weekends there would be parental acid trips which was like having your parents away for the weekend, and yet still at home. They never said anything or gave us a warning about their tripping. They didn't have to. I could see it in their eyes, the way they'd stare off into space and giggle about nothing in particular.

I think that a combination of LSD and R.D. Laing helped to free my parents from the conventional restraints and obligations of parenthood. I don't mean they didn't love or care for their children: they did. It meant that they were free to follow their own fancy, do their own thing as individuals, and if the end result embarrassed the shit out of their own children, well too bad.

Hippydom was an important turning point in the evolution of the Sixties: it marked the move away from social activism – the struggle for civil rights and the protests against the Vietnam War – towards a new project of self-fulfilment. To change society, said the hippies, you had to change yourself. The early Sixties concern for *us* increasingly became – as the decade wore on – a concern about *me*. In the name of personal liberation one had a duty to indulge in self-gratification, be it through drugs or sexual promiscuity. How else could you break free from the confining bonds of bourgeois society?

With hippydom my parents found freedom and self-expression, and I found something new, too: acute embarrassment. I know that every teenager feels embarrassment, but not all teenagers feel embarrassment *equally*. All teenagers get spots; but some teenagers get acne, the kind that leaves their face scarred for life. The same is true with embarrassment: you can get the spotty kind of embarrassment or the acne kind.

Those who get the acne kind belong to an embarrassment elite, a small core of sufferers who unlike their peers do not feel the occasional flush of embarrassment, but are condemned to endure it at all times. Even when their parents aren't being embarrassing, the embarrassment elite is suffering from previous episodes of embarrassment or anticipating future attacks.

I belonged to that elite. Everything my parents did, and everything about them, embarrassed me: especially the way they looked (like freaks) and the way they talked; they were so LOUD. Loud in those special ear-shattering American voices that cut through public spaces like an ambulance siren. I remember my father running after a man on a bicycle who sold fresh onions on a string like a Frenchman. Jay charged down the crowded high street, singing like a madman who had escaped from a musical, 'Mr Onion Man ... Oh Mr Onnnnion man ... I want some Oniooooons!'

Then there was my dad's swearing. When driving the family car and getting into an altercation with another driver, Jay would scream in a voice that it seemed to me could be heard across the entire United Kingdom: 'YOU FUCKING ASSHOLE!' You can't imagine how shocking it was to be called an asshole in Britain in the 1960s. It was the one bit of the human anatomy that the Brits had not incorporated into their lexicon of slang and swear words. You could call someone a 'cunt' or 'prick' – but arsehole was off limits. The loudness of the denunciation and the fact that it came from a Yank made it worse.

The public realm was a much quieter place then. The younger generation might be going wild, but grown-ups were still governed by a code of restraint. You didn't impose upon the public your phone conversations, your music or your voice. From my newfound mates I learned about one of the great taboos of English life: whatever else happens you must never *show yourself up*. This meant doing things that drew attention to yourself or made you seem foolish – like having hippy parents and a dad who yelled from his car: 'YOU FUCKING ASSHOLE!'

Another reason my parents embarrassed me so much was that they talked in public in exactly the same way as they talked at home. It was as if the world beyond their front door was just an extension of their living room. They talked about feelings, friends, intimate problems and private fantasies as if they were behind closed doors. Letting other people know their business didn't bother them. Their private life was open for all the public to enjoy.

There's a performance artist called Ursula Martinez who in 1998 did a show at the Edinburgh Festival entitled *Family Outing*. I first got interested in her when I saw the publicity photo for her show: it featured Ursula naked with her naked mother Mila and her naked father Arthur by her side. Looking at the naked Martinez family together for a publicity shot I felt an unfamiliar sensation: my family was normal.

Martinez describes her show as 'a piece of aversion therapy. As a kid I was embarrassed by my parents and I still am.' I guess the idea behind her show is that to escape the horror of parental embarrassment you have to bury yourself in it. I think she may be right, but I've always been too horrified to bury myself in the horror; the horror always buries me.

Family Outing features the Martinez family on stage talking about their relationships – some of it's scripted, some of it's improvised, and it's meant to be a postmodern deconstruction of our 'confessional age'.

That may be true, but you could tell the father and the mother were a couple of hams who loved being on stage. And Martinez claim that she's embarrassed by her parents is a little suspect too – I could tell that she thought they were a pair of lovable characters. But watching the Martinez family at work made me think of my own family and how they would give anything for us to be on that stage together, talking about our relationships. They'd even go nude.

In retrospect, I admire my parents' utter indifference to what other people, for example the neighbours, would say about their behaviour. (When it came to their careers, what people thought obviously did matter.) I was totally the opposite in that I was obsessed by what other people (the neighbours, my friends at school, strangers in the street) would think of me.

I think my embarrassment stemmed from my longing to gain acceptance in my new country. I wanted to fit in, to be one of the lads. I feared that my parents' strange appearance would rebound on me; that I would pay the price of their pursuit of freedom and self-expression.

I had reached that age when you start to glimpse your parents as the people they were before they became your mom and dad. In my case it wasn't a pretty sight. I began to see them differently when during that summer I found strange bodies in their separate beds. Bodies soon became boyfriends and lovers with names, who started to leave the beds and could be found at the dinner table.

I knew kids who were happy to have hippy parents, who claimed they were never embarrassed by their freaky looks and lifestyle. I envied them. How did they manage to stay so cool, to be so indifferent to what other people thought, especially the other kids at school?

The answer was simple: they went to progressive schools full of nice, tolerant middle-class children who embraced difference, who did not persecute those with unconventional names like Cosmo. I, on the other hand, went to a rough, working-class comprehensive called Holloway School in North London. Holloway boasted an illustrious collection of skinheads, thugs, nutters and football hooligans. If there was one thing this lot hated more than 'Jews', ''omos' (homosexuals), 'Pakis' and 'wogs' it was ''ippies', or to give them their correct title: ''orrible-stinking-junkie-filthy-fucking-'ippy-cunts.'

So it should come as no surprise that my greatest fear at the time was that my classmates would discover my secret: I had hippy parents.

☆

School Open Day, 1967. My classroom.

It's hot. The mood of the classroom is pensive. Silence is punctured by outbursts of nervous laughter. We are waiting for our mums and dads to arrive, like defendants waiting for the jury to return with their verdict.

Boys are sitting at their desks, boys are sitting on their desks, boys are loitering around by the big French windows that look out onto the front of the school and the school gates. That's where parents will be picked up on the radar of their anxious children. It's the only time of year when all your classmates, and not just your mates, get to check out your parents and take the piss.

At around 2 p.m. mums and dads start to trickle in. They stand in the courtyard, awaiting collection by their children. I go over to the windows to watch. I see men in smart suits, polished shoes, hair immaculately parted, and women nicely dresed – they could be going to a wedding or a funeral.

The thing is about these parents from the white working class, they don't want to *show themselves up*, or their children. Now the descendants of these very same people line up to expose themselves on reality TV shows all the time. They don't care or even think about showing themselves *up*; they're too busy showing themselves *off*.

So you waited until you spotted your parents coming through the gates and then you went down and collected them, took them through the main entrance and into the large assembly hall where your teachers were waiting to talk about your progress.

Having seen a sample of the parents, I'm back at my desk. I sigh, I sweat. I have that big anxious smile of a nervous chimp on my face. I bury my head in the small pool of darkness inside my desk and inhale the smell of the ancient remains of pencil rubber.

I wonder: will they come?

That morning I had pleaded with them not to come. 'But,' I said for good measure, 'if you do come, please try and look normal.'

Jay laughed and gave me a quizzical look that said: how did I ever get such a freak of a son?

Back at my desk I console myself with the thought that it is unlikely they will come, and I'm getting all worked up over nothing.

I consider the facts.

Fact One. They've never bothered to show up to school events in the past. They don't fancy the tedium of all that PTA crap. School is just one of those draggy things you have to endure as a child. Whether I come bottom or top of the class, it's all the same to them. So why would they trudge to school like anxious pushy parents obsessed with their little darling's grades?

Fact Two. Jay is ideologically opposed to the very idea of the school system. For him it's an institution for brainwashing the young. To attend would be a kind of collaboration, an act of gross hypocrisy. He is one of those men who believe that you learn the really important stuff – how to mix a perfect Martini, how to seduce beautiful women and make a room laugh – by going out and making an interesting life for yourself.

Fact Three. This is a man who likes to boast to his friends, 'We sent our children to the worst schools that money could buy.'

I emerge from my hiding place. But within minutes I dive back into the darkness.

I'm having scary my-parents-are-coming thoughts . . .

Fran likes to do the conventional 'good mum' bit, and this time she might feel that they really should see how the kids are doing at school. Also, there's the possibility that Jay would want to go because he thinks it might be good for me to undergo a kind of shock therapy. One big-neutron Bruce Banner/Hulk-like blast of embarrassment might change me into a cool kid.

In the dark of my desk my worst nightmare comes to mind. It goes like this: my parents in full hippy gear, stoned out of their minds, come skipping through the school gates. A group of the school's most vicious skins are loitering nearby, smoking. They spot the colourful intruders. The herd of skins spread out and head for the hippies. In seconds my parents are surrounded. The skins stop and stare.

'Hey guys, what's happening?' asks Jay.

'Shut it, fucking 'ippy!' says the leader, Trev, a large youth in jeans, Ben Sherman shirt and cherry red Doc Martens.

'What's with the negative vibes?' asks Fran.

'I'll give you fucking negative vibes, you 'ippy slag!'

I'm there on the periphery, wondering what to do. I see the skins move in. I hear the crack of bone, the pulping of flesh. The frenzy of fists, boots and curses lasts for a few seconds.

The gang move off and I approach my parents' dead, mutilated bodies. I stand over them, shake my head and say, 'I told you to dress normal . . . but you just wouldn't listen, would you?'

I know it sounds like a ridiculous scenario that only a fearful boy with a feverish imagination could conjure up, but in 1967 these kinds of attacks really happened. This was the age of the infamous North London skinhead gangs like Somers Town – who were featured in *Rolling Stone* magazine – and the Camden Tongs. They were the avenging devils in that Summer of Love. Their victims were anyone with long hair, and everyone with long hair knew somebody who had been given a beating by the skins.

So I sat and waited. With the passing of every minute it seemed that they weren't coming. By 2.30 p.m. I was breathing a sigh of relief. That's when I heard the cry of, 'Fuck me, the Martians have landed!' I knew that meant only one thing: my parents had arrived in full hippy regalia. Bra-less Mum and purple-toed Dad were strolling through the gates.

I was a dead man.

Yet here's the strange thing that happened that day: *nothing*. I wasn't mocked or beaten, and my parents weren't attacked either. In retrospect I wonder if that's what I really subconsciously wanted to happen – for them to be punished for being so embarrassing. They strolled into the schoolyard, a riot of colour and cool vibes. I greeted them with a silent nod of recognition and led them to the assembly hall, walking way in front of them as if to signal to onlookers that the freaks behind me had nothing to do with me.

Later that afternoon I returned home full of indignation and anger at their refusal to compromise. I rehearsed my case against them on the number 43 bus throughout the journey.

Couldn't you have made the effort *just this once* to put on some normal clothes, look normal and act normal? Would it have hurt? All you had to do was play it straight for one afternoon at my school. I wanted you to do this one simple thing for me and you wouldn't do it. I've grown to accept your way of life, why can't you learn to accept mine? But my reasoned case with its modest demands fell on deaf ears.

'Oh for Christ's sake don't be so square!' was my dad's reply.

'You need to learn to relax,' said my mother.

'Yeah, Cos, you need to learn to relax!' said Miles.

It was then that I realized things had changed in the family: my brother had become one of *them*. I stormed out of the room, slammed the door and went to my room to seethe.

Some of the boys actually told me that I was 'lucky' to have parents like mine. But they were the ones with emotional problems, who were bullied and existed as tormented outcasts. To them Fran and Jay were exotic creatures, in whose crazy clothes these victims saw the promise of personal freedom and parental understanding. They looked like parents you could talk to. You could . . . but that was no guarantee they'd listen.

I, on the other hand, thought they were lucky to have parents like theirs. By which I meant 'ordinary' parents.

Such parents existed back then. Maybe you think I'm being nostalgic? I saw them with my own eyes coming through the school gates. I saw them in their own homes, where I was served sumptuous teas of thick white slices of bread with jam by tidy mums who wore bras and kept themselves nice and never ever showed anyone up.

In such modest homes I met reticent dads who came home from work, grunted a greeting and that was it for the evening. They did not dominate the room with twenty minutes of dynamite comic shtick as soon as they walked in, like my dad.

I wanted one of these invisible dads because I wanted the attention from my friends. I wanted to be the star in the room.

Away from school I was hanging out with a group of teenage girls and guys, and I longed to be the funny one, the one who would shine and seduce. Humour was my only hope because I was short, chubby and uncool. I figured that if I was funny enough there was a chance that one of the girls would sleep with me. But I could never be the star as long as Jay was in the room, because he always had to be the centre of attention. And he used my only weapon – humour – to achieve this.

I wonder: do they make ordinary mums and dads any more? You know, the kind of dull but decent figures who hover quietly in the background of their children's lives? Those invisible men and women who were really appreciated and loved, usually after they were dead.

That weird wave I mentioned? Well, it got me too and in 1967 I became a hippy.

Believe me, I tried to resist. I sat in my small cell-like bedroom in the basement of the house reading Dostoevsky or Nietzsche, and fuming at the 'decadent freaks' – i.e. my parents and their friends – upstairs. Their crazy music and the sound of their stoned laughter wafted into my monkish room like the musky scent of their incense. But resistance was ultimately useless. There were just too many pretty girls and too much fun to be had.

My transformation began one night after I ate some of Mother's hash cookies by mistake. I lay in my bed as the room started to go wobbly. First the walls began breathing, then came the hallucinations and swirling colours. At first I was afraid, but I learned to relax and enjoy the ride. In the morning I awoke and was ready to become a freak. Out went Dostoevsky and in came Hermann Hesse and all the other classic hippy texts. I grew my hair long, took drugs and developed my own mini-hippy scene with my would-be hippy friends: Nicky (a teenage runaway), Chris (heavily into Transcendental Meditation) and Sylvia (the token bird). We had our own crash pad at the top of the house. Of course my parents felt vindicated by my defection from the world of the normals. I was now one of them.

After school and on weekends we spent our time crashed out on mats, smoking dope, listening to music. Drugs became the centre of our lives. We smoked pot every chance we got and took acid on the weekends. We talked about drugs and we read drug-related books.

Our heroes (Tim Leary, Ken Kesey) were all famous druggies.

We didn't think of ourselves as silly teenagers getting high. *We* were expanding our consciousness and learning profound truths about the nature of reality.

Just being a hippy made you feel like a success because you were a superior person. Unlike the straights you were mentally free, rather than a victim of 'false consciousness' or brainwashing.

To belong to Hippy London meant you were connected to the whole youth movement of America and Europe. The streets of rioting Paris, the demos in Chicago, the party that was Woodstock – we were all part of this great wave of change; we were the VIPs of history.

Alongside the idealism and utopianism of the counter-culture there was a strand of old-fashioned snobbery. We had a condescending contempt for 'straight' people. Everything about our lives was better than theirs: we had better music, better food, better movies, better relationships and (most importantly of all) better sex. As we all knew, straight people didn't have good sex. They were ashamed of their bodies and never had orgasms because religion/morality/parents/Western civilization had made them too uptight for that.

Yet the counter-culture believed in the equality of mankind. They protested against the great divisions of wealth, power, gender and race that divided contemporary society. They liked to believe that we were all 'brothers and sisters', 'children of the universe' and 'fellow travellers on spaceship Earth'. But the one group hippies had no interest in were ordinary people. By that I don't mean just the 'straights' or the 'bourgeoisie', but ordinary working-class people. In this the hippies weren't alone. People in the media, opinion formers, the liberal-left intelligentsia, only had an interest in working-class people when they were part of a social problem, the kind Britain saw in the landmark BBC television play, *Cathy Come Home*.

By 1967 the vogue for things working class had passed. The new wave in British cinema that had appeared in the late fifties was exhausted. The hippies had little interest in British film-makers and the kind of ordinary working-class people you saw in films like *This Sporting Life*, *Saturday Night and Sunday Morning* and *The Loneliness of the Long Distance Runner*.

But then the young characters in these films didn't have much good to say about ordinary people, either. Arthur Seaton, the hero of the film *Saturday Night and Sunday Morning*, regards his dad as a poor, brainwashed drone who spends all his time in front of the television – which was the same way hippies saw people like him.

Apart from the new wave of soaps (*Coronation Street*, *Z Cars*), you didn't see ordinary people on the television that much in the sixties. They turned up as participants in quiz programmes and as the audience in variety shows. They were support fodder, never the star.

No one in the sixties would have imagined that one day the kind of people we see lounging on *Big Brother* and other reality TV programmes would actually appear on television and become a source of national interest.

Who could possibly have cared what these people did or thought about anything? They were just *ordinary*, and being ordinary was the last thing anyone wanted to be.

☆

For the counter-culture it was the crazies and the freaks who were considered interesting. 'Autumn of 1969,' wrote *Oz* editor Richard Neville, was the time of 'the fabulous freak'. What or who exactly was a fabulous freak?

Freak was the pejorative name that society had used to label hippies, and one that hippies were happy to embrace. To be a fabulous freak wasn't easy. You had to get in touch with your inner lunatic. In the sixties there emerged the cult of craziness, the idea that the mad, the fucked-up were on a higher wavelength than the 'normal'. Crazy was cool. 'R.D. Laing's *The Divided Self* was one of the most influential books of the Sixties,' wrote Angela Carter, 'it made madness, hating your parents – it made it all glamorous.'

The fabulous freaks were the 'mad' people, the damaged people: psychedelic tramps, junkies, those who walked on the wild side and went right over the edge. Freak heroes included: the Fabulous Freak Brothers, Neal Cassidy (from Kerouac's *On the Road*), Carl Solomon (in a madhouse when Ginsberg dedicated *Howl* to him), William Burroughs (famous junkie), Holden Caulfield (the neurotic hero of *The Catcher in the Rye*), and James Dean (tormented soul). The book loved by hippies – at least the ones who bothered to read – was Ken

Kesey's *One Flew Over the Cuckoo's Nest*, with the inmates of a mental asylum the heroes and the doctors and nurses the villains.

Actress Julie Christie once said that the one thing she resented about the Sixties was the cult of the fabulous freak. She wrote of: 'the peer pressure – the whole business of being as freaky as possible and if you weren't you were labelled "straight" or "square."'

In the age of the freak what girl wanted a nice guy like me when they could get a colourful and captivating neurotic?

I discovered in my early teens that if you wanted to get girls to be interested in you, you had to be fucked up. But fucked up in the right kind of way, in a way that made you seem interesting. Being a drug addict was a good option because it had the aura of romantic self-destructiveness.

My problem was that I didn't have the right kind of problems. The worst thing I could boast of was the acute embarrassment I suffered at the hands of my parents, and that wasn't exactly a sexy malady to compete with drug addiction, schizophrenia or some grand, colourful form of self-destruction that women would swoon over and offer salvation for between the sheets. I was convinced that if I could pass for a lunatic I could get laid more. But no matter how long my hair got or how many trips I took, I was just serious and sensible old me.

By the end of the sixties I was sixteen and had absorbed many of the decade's ideas. I was also at the age when you first begin to think about your future and what you want to do, how you're going to earn a living. I was confused. Should I carry on at school or drop out and just see what turned up?

One afternoon I went to Jay for some fatherly advice. He had taken up residence in the basement. I found him there with his latest girlfriend, a young Jewish woman who called herself an artist; Jay called her the Surrealist Yenta. She was pale and wore purple lipstick and smelt of opium.

Jay: Ah, just the man I wanted to see. Come in kid, join us. Martini? Reefer?

Me: Maybe I should come back later.

Jay: Nah. Sit. I wanted to ask *you* something.

Me: I wanted to ask *you* something.

Jay: Shoot.

I never got a word in. The Surrealist Yenta, realizing that she wasn't going to be the centre of attention, got up and announced she was going. I could hear them kissing and exchanging whispers just outside the door. Jay came back, poured tea and started talking about his life.

Jay: The thing is I need a new project. I guess you could say that I don't really know what I should be when I grow up – got any suggestions?

Me: I was going to ask you the same thing!

We both laughed and father and son spent the rest of the afternoon getting high and figuring out what to do when we grew up.

I needn't have worried. In the same way that Hippy London saved my parents, it provided me with what seemed like compelling reasons for not thinking about my future. The idea of competing, revising and struggling with exams so you could get into a university seemed crazy. What mattered was the university of life. I was a Child of the Universe, and no way was I going to be some cog in the corporate machine. In effect Hippy London said to me, and lots of other middle-class kids: *why worry about doing well at school? Schooling is a means of brainwashing people. Fuck that shit, go sit in the garden and smoke a joint.*

My parents never once asked me what I was going to be when I grew up. This could be because a) they hoped I would never grow up, or b) they assumed that I would just do my own thing.

For me in that Summer of Love, sitting in the garden stoned on hash cakes, laughing so hard I thought I would choke, it seemed there was nothing in the world to worry about. Tomorrow would take care of itself. In the meantime, there were plenty of wonderful distractions. Our home had become an international crash pad for friends and friends of friends who happened to be passing through London.

There was a constant flow of new faces: writers, comedians, crazy poets, singers, beautiful women, handsome young men with Thai sticks of grass and guitars; art hustlers, people on their way up and people on their way down. These were people who were always flying off to a party in Milan or a pop festival in the States. They never worried about money, mortgages, paying bills or tomorrow.

With all these people to act as distractions the important things – homework, exams and my future – lost their sense of urgency. I wanted to hang out and enjoy the party. So instead of doing homework I decided to go with the flow. And for a time it was fun – until I realized that the flow wasn't going anywhere.

We kids of the counter-culture had the greatest luxury of any post-war generation: we did not have to worry about making a living and what we were going to do in the future. So much of the freedom and the optimism of those days was based on the belief that someone else would pick up the bill or provide the largesse: a record company, a rich couple who wanted hip people around, an eccentric millionaire or the welfare state. We didn't have to face the realities of life – i.e. the need to make a living – because we were in the process of remaking reality.

You saw the consequences of this thinking later in the mid-1970s – bright middle-class kids in a state of downward mobility. Instead of going to university they went to India or Morocco. They drifted from job to job, squat to squat. They worked for charities or were 'getting a band together' or 'writing a novel'. Creativity was their way of concealing from the world their own drift. They had been set free by the Sixties and now they were drowning. They tried to adapt by cutting their hair and putting on suits. Some lived with their parents and some couldn't live with themselves. They floundered and felt like failures. The ones I knew either turned to God or became junkies.

I decided to go for journalism.

7

Stars In Our Eyes

I keep looking back to my youth and wondering: were *we* obsessed by celebrity in the 1960s? This depends on who you mean by 'we', and which bit of the Sixties you're talking about. For it was a decade that came in a variety of contradictory shapes and conflicting flavours. How can you generalize about a decade that produced both *Sergeant Pepper* and *The Sound of Music*; a decade that loved *The Avengers* and *Dad's Army*? Whose Sixties was it anyway: Hippy, Housewife or Head? Are we talking about Swinging London Sixties, Swinging Manchester Sixties, Acid Sixties or Street Fighting Man Sixties? The Sixties have a guilty secret and it's this: everything changed and, for most people, everything remained the same.

Commentators today look back on the Sixties and say: yep, that's when it all began! '. . . the contemporary cult of celebrity was born in the sixties' writes Andrew Marr in his *History of Modern Britain*. But is he right?

Many of the young and with-it commentators at the time would have agreed with Marr. They stared with Sixties insouciance at the machinery of fame, pumping out all these shiny, disposable celebrities, and it seemed so ... *cool* ... so very *modern* ... so very ... *Sixties*. (That's how journalists back then wrote.) These glitzy gods were the inevitable by-product of our media-driven world. And thanks to pop artists like Peter Blake and Ian Hamilton, we learned to appreciate their brash beauty.

As we have seen, there was no shortage of celebrity fodder and tinned glamour in the late 1950s. But to the great and the groovy of the Sixties, television stars like Gilbert Harding, Katie Boyle and the TV chef Philip Harben were for mums and dads. In the Sixties youth got their own magazines, their own clubs, their own clothes and their own celebrities. Typical of the new breed was the high queen of mod Cathy McGowan, who hosted the pop programme of the time, *Ready, Steady, Go!* There was a whole army of young celebrity disc jockeys, celebrity photographers, celebrity models, celebrity hairdressers and even celebrity criminals (the Krays) to excite the young. Thanks to the likes of *Time* magazine, the young even got their own celebrity city – London.

So yeah, we were fascinated by the famous. To the hip people of London – all twelve of them – there was a hierarchy of fame, with pop stars at the top of the pyramid and the beautiful people next in line. At the bottom were the old crooners, game-show hosts, the 'stars' of variety and society figures. But to kids like me and, I suspect, most people, there wasn't such a clear divide between major star and minor celebrity.

In 1965, when I was eleven years old, a photograph of my best mate Bernard and me appeared on the front page of our local newspaper, the *Islington Gazette*. It showed us – two grubby street urchins posing as fans – asking pop singer Frank Ifield for his autograph. In the early sixties Ifield had had three number ones, including his best-known hit *I Remember You*. However, by the time Bernard and I had our Frank moment his big-hit days were over. But we didn't care because we didn't really know much about Frank. (The great rock critic Nik Cohn called him 'a large hunk of Australian baritone with an alarming line in yodelling'.) All we knew was that he was a famous pop star and that was good enough for us. Autograph-collecting was something young boys and girls just did, even if you weren't a real fan of the person. There was a kind of fame etiquette that required you to ask for an autograph of the famous one. It was almost bad manners not to.

But here is a curious fact about the English in the early sixties – they would charge at, claw, scream at and demand autographs from anyone who was a) semi-famous and b) had a pulse. There was a whole generation of Sixties television stars and minor celebrities who found that they were subjected to the kind of hysterical mob outbursts that had been the preserve of crooners and rock 'n' roll idols of the late fifties.

Looking back on those days, the comedian Bob Monkhouse once said of anyone who appeared on television: 'If you hadn't got a false eye and a hump on your back they'd mob you.' He remembers being stuck in a car that was being rocked by a screaming mob of five hundred girls, anxious to get their sweaty little mitts on the terrified and trembling Monkhouse inside.

The girls managed to turn the car over onto its side. 'I remember thinking,' says Monkhouse, 'we're going to die!'

Cheesy comedian or candidate for Prime Minister, no one was spared the pop-star treatment. On a visit to Liverpool in 1963 the leader of the Labour Party, Harold Wilson, was mobbed by hundreds of children asking for his autograph and chanting 'yeah, yeah, yeah!' as if he were the fifth Beatle. The bruising encounter left the future Prime Minister with a damaged arm.

You would see vast queues outside supermarkets as housewives lined up to catch a glimpse of some television celebrity or minor starlet, hired to give their opening a touch of glamour. Simon Dee remembers opening a supermarket in deepest, darkest Wales, and thousands of people having to be held back by the police. 'I thought to myself, my God, the power of television,' Dee later reminisced.

One reason for this was that in the sixties we finally became a television nation. (By 1967 nine in ten households had a television set.) That little box in the corner of the room moved into the centre of people's lives and their leisure time. But celebrities did not dominate the medium the way they do now. When families sat in front of the television there weren't programmes featuring celebrities dancing, celebrities cooking, celebrities losing weight, celebrities doing social work, celebrities being stranded in jungles, celebrities showing off their homes or celebrities flying off to Thailand for enemas.

But they were there, however small in number, and they were popular with viewers. When you turned on your television in the sixties you'd find celebrities on *This Is Your Life* and *Juke Box Jury*. In 1964 there was even an ITV programme called *The Celebrity Game* involving contestants having to guess a celebrity's view on a topical subject. That was the same year that Britain got its first television talk show, featuring chats with the famous: *In London Tonight* with Eamonn Andrews. And you had the greatest star spectacle of them all: *Sunday Night at the London Palladium*, featuring all the big-name acts from the Beatles to Bob Hope. Stars were now in our living rooms on a weekly basis and destined to become part of our mental furniture. We had glamour on tap.

☆

OK, so there are now plenty of celebrities around, making public appearances and providing the press with photos, features and gossip. Bruce Forsyth – the star presenter of *Sunday Night at the London Palladium* – has become a love machine and Bob Monkhouse is going to orgies at Diana Dors's flat. Housewives throw their knickers at Tom Jones and husbands fantasize about the leather-clad Diana Rigg as Miss Emma Peel in *The Avengers*.

But here's the important thing to remember: for all the emotional heat and media hype generated by television celebrities, the early part of the sixties was a time when great stars and even heroes still walked the earth. I could go into a long and dull analysis about the difference between a star and a celebrity, but let me just put it this way: Elizabeth Taylor was a star and Elizabeth Hurley is a celebrity.

It's hard to convey the power over the popular imagination that these great stars of the early sixties had. They were seen as an exceptional breed of men and women, whose trivial doings or dramatic actions dominated headlines throughout the Western world. It wasn't our multichannel, multimedia world with instant gossip available 24/7. Stars on the box were still an event.

There is no contemporary celebrity couple, be it Brad and Angelina or Tom Cruise and Katie Holmes, who commands the kind of global attention that Elizabeth Taylor and Richard Burton did in the early sixties. News of their affair – they were both married at the time – landed on the front pages around the world.

That was the same time that we first met Muhammad Ali, then known as Cassius Clay, and we were stunned. His personality hit us like a right hook. And though we've had the rise of global sporting stars like Michael Jordan and David Beckham, Ali commanded the world's attention by sheer force of talent and personality alone, and not by the seduction of multimillion-dollar advertising campaigns. He was a human being, not a human brand.

The great stars of the age weren't all connected to show business. There were old-fashioned heroes who found themselves scooped up into the machinery of fame and pushed out the other end as weird centaur-like creatures: half hero, half celebrity. Men like Yuri Gagarin (the first man in space), Francis Chichester (the first man to sail around the globe on his own, and the fastest) and Neil Armstrong (the first man to step on the moon) – they started out making history and ended up stranded in the headlines.

So the public realm was fast filling up with celebrities, but in the early part of the sixties we were still a star-struck country, arguably the most star-struck country in the world. America had all sorts of movie and pop stars – remember, Elvis was still in the building – but only Britain had produced four gods by the name of John, Paul, George and Ringo.

Beatlemania began in 1963 and lasted till 1966. It was a collective convulsion, a three-year binge of hormonal riot and tearful hysteria as great mobs of charging Beatle fans laid siege to theatres, airports and concert halls. Beatlemania was louder and more hysterical than anything this island had seen before. From all over Britain they came to see the Fab Four and they wept and wailed, sobbed and fainted.

What had started as teenage passion became, in the words of Beatle biographer Philip Norman, a 'national obsession'. The Beatles charmed the adult world with their down-to-earth ways and wit, and in 1965 they were given MBEs by the Queen. They provided Britain with something more than just entertainment: they gave the nation a sense of pride.

It's hard to convey what Beatle fame was like in those days. There was no fame bigger or brighter. When John Lennon made his infamous remark about the Beatles being bigger than Jesus Christ, he was stating what seemed an obvious fact. Everyone wanted to meet a Beatle: the Queen, Princess Margaret, Prime Minister

Harold Wilson, Field Marshal Montgomery, Elvis, Brigitte Bardot, Ken Tynan, Joe Orton, academics, intellectuals, your mother and your sister and your nan.

So you can imagine how I felt when my parents had dinner with John Lennon at the home of Peter and Wendy Cook. I insisted on hearing the story of the Beatle dinner over and over and over again. It was like a fairy tale, my perfect bedtime story: two unfamous, middle-aged Americans called Fran and Jay get invited to the ultimate ball: dinner with a Beatle. Then they got invited to dinner with *another* Beatle (Paul McCartney). This was the first time I had ever been impressed by my parents.

There's a famous Frank Sinatra joke that goes like this: a guy is sitting with his girlfriend at a table in a restaurant. He sees Sinatra at the bar, gets up and goes over to him. He asks Sinatra if he will come to his table and say hello to him so that he can impress his girl. Sinatra declines. The guy pleads with him. 'Frank, please just walk by and say hello Danny.' No, says Sinatra. The guy gets down on his knees and starts to beg. An embarrassed Sinatra says, 'OK, I'll do it.' So later in the evening Sinatra goes over to the guy's table and says, 'Hello Danny.' Danny looks up from his food and says, 'Fuck off Frank, can't you see I'm busy!'

There's a true family story about Jay that goes like this: one night Jay was at the Playboy club in London. He was in a lift with two glamorous women on his arms. The lift door opens and there's John Lennon. Jay sees Lennon, recognizing him from the Cook dinner, and says, 'Hi, Jay.'

'Sorry John,' says Jay, 'I can't talk to you now, 'I'm all tied up,' and he charges out of the lift with the two foxy chicks, leaving Lennon behind.

Jay actually had the moment that every nobody dreams about, a moment that forms the basis of the Sinatra joke: you turn the tables on *them* and they get to know what it's like to be *you*. For Jay there was only one thing better than meeting a Beatle and that was the chance to snub a Beatle. In retrospect it seems an innocent form of revenge.

Fifteen years later snubbing a Beatle wasn't enough for the nobody.

You had to shoot one instead.

☆

The late 1950s to the mid-1960s was the last great age of the big stars, the heroes and larger-than-life men and women. Television was cutting them all down to a uniform size so that everyone – great stage actor, distinguished historian, pop sensation and pools winner – looked the same. Stars were stripped of their aura and mystique, and served up to the public on talk and interview shows as mere celebrities.

Stardom as a style and statement went out of fashion. In the sixties Diana Dors, the very epitome of fifties British star glamour, said: 'The luxury and the glamour that was once part and parcel of being a film star is now passé. In 1966 one has to play it cool to be fashionable. The Julie Christie kooky-doll look is all the rage now.'

Dors was right. Britain was producing a new, young breed of actors – Richard Burton, Oliver Reed, Tom

Courtenay, Albert Finney – who were the very opposite to the matinee-idol types like John Mills and Kenneth More. Central to their appeal was that they were ordinary blokes, impatient with the studio system and the whole phoney rigmarole of stardom. 'I don't give a damn whether I'm a star or not,' Albert Finney told *Sight & Sound*.

There was a new emphasis on being 'ordinary', working class and 'genuine'. It was the age of the New Wave cinema and kitchen-sink drama. Even politicians tried to pass as ordinary. Harold Wilson let it be known that he was fond of HP Sauce. The Beatles managed the difficult trick of being like gods and yet the boys next door. Their talent made them exceptional; their personalities and accents made them seem like everyone else.

A sign that conventional stardom was losing its appeal was the fact that show business, which had once been the major provider of stars and glamour, was now facing stiff competition from a new force: youth and pop culture. Until the sixties show business was the only game in town, and if you wanted to get on you played by its rules. That's why Brian Epstein took the Beatles out of leather jackets and into suits, and even those bad boys the Rolling Stones appeared on *Sunday Night at the London Palladium*.

But around 1965 pop music started to strike out on its own and become an independent cultural and commercial force with its own media, slang, styles and tribes. By 1967, the pop world and not show business was providing the idols and the glamour that so intoxicated the decade. When, in 1966, Truman Capote threw his legendary masked 'black and white ball' at New York's City Plaza Hotel it marked the end of an era, the shift from High Society to the Beautiful People. Suddenly the kings and queens of Hollywood – Taylor and Burton, Sinatra and his Rat Pack – all started to look a little square.

They also began to look much more vulnerable. The old discretion and deference shown to stars by the media started to come to an end. Stars of the early sixties remember those days as a golden era, when the media did not invade their private lives. 'There were tabloids like the *Daily Sketch* and the *Daily Mirror* but they didn't look into your private life the way they do today,' says Bob Monkhouse.

A key turning point was 18 September 1960, when Gilbert Harding appeared on the BBC interview programme *Face to Face*. Viewers witnessed the invisible interviewer John Freeman give Harding a grilling the like of which no one had ever before seen on television. Freeman's secret intention was to get Harding to admit that he was a homosexual, but he failed. However, he did get Harding to admit that he was a lonely and profoundly unhappy man. The dawn of celebrity confession had begun. It was when Freeman got Harding to discuss the death of his mother that the gruff old Gilbert was on the verge of tears. Suddenly, we were up close and very personal with a television 'star'.

The public in 1960 claimed they were shocked by this display of celebrity cruelty, but the appetite for the private lives and secrets of the stars started to grow. When, in 1964, British photographer Ray Bellisario took a photograph of Princess Margaret in a swimsuit it was published in the *Sunday Express* and marked the arrival of the paparazzi into British life. The public no longer wanted formal portraiture and airbrushed photographs of smiling stars looking their best – they wanted the off-camera moments of the stars as they were really were: more like ordinary people.

The number of actual stars in the world couldn't keep pace with demands, so God (and press agents) created celebrities. They didn't have to shine; they were simply small morsels of instant human entertainment. But to create them on an industrial scale required a new type of fame that was fast and less fastidious than the old version.

In 1964 the pop artist Andy Warhol made what has become the most famous comment on fame ever made. But what most people don't realize is that Warhol got it totally wrong. For what he actually said was 'In the future everyone will be *world-* [my italics] famous for fifteen minutes.' Well, that future has arrived and world fame is still the preserve of the very few. It was only when the word 'world' was omitted by subsequent journalistic usage that everyone thought Warhol was such a prophetic genius.

Anyway, Warhol's prophecy reflected the arrival of a new type of fame that we saw in its infancy in the late fifties. Now in the sixties it had entered into its adolescence. This was an instant, disposable, democratic and market-driven kind of fame. Let's call it Pop fame. It didn't demand blood, sweat, tears and talent – it could work its magic on a big bust or a boy's pretty face. It relied on the alchemy of hype, the intoxication of the right image. Pop fame was the fuel that would drive the age of entertainment for a nation that expected excitement and spectacle served at breakfast.

Pop fame wasn't interested in the old crowd: the statesmen, the generals, the men of science and the arts, the aristocracy – all those crusty old faces that stared at you from the walls of the National Portrait Gallery and whose boring biogs filled books like *Who's Who* and *Debrett's*.

The promise of Pop fame was constantly sold to youth in the sixties. Newspapers and magazines ran countless stories about the ordinary nobody, the boy or girl from next door, who overnight became rich and famous. Look at Marianne Faithfull: she was discovered by Andrew Loog Oldham one night at a party and hey presto, she's top of the charts! Look at Leslie Hornby, a sixteen-year-old girl from Neasden who worked in a Queensway hair salon on Saturdays and woke up one morning to find, thanks to pictures of her in the *Daily Express*, she was famous as Twiggy. Or what about nineteen-year-old Shelagh Delaney, the theatre usherette who became famous with the success of her first play *A Taste of Honey*? Fame was a kind of national lottery and you had as much chance to win as the next person.

Did the young buy the dream? You bet. Just as now the young were criticized for preferring 'recognition' to 'the substance of achievement', or so Swinging London chronicler Jonathan Aitken claimed. He went even further and declared that 'publicity has become the modern *vice anglais'* and fame itself was now 'the ultimate dream of the masses'.

But as Swinging London slowed down and slipped into Hippy London, fame found itself facing a most determined foe: the counter-culture. Members of this movement saw the whole cult of celebrity as a by-product of narcissistic and image-obsessed Swinging London. They wanted to create an alternative society where all men and women were to be equal. No more classes, no rich and poor, no leaders and the led, and no more stars.

By 1967 an interest in Hollywood movie stars and pop stars, man, that was so uncool; it was what house-wives and dopey little teenyboppers talked about. Frankfurt School theorists like Theodore Adorno and the French philosopher Guy Debord had showed us that the star system as a means of social control, a way of keeping the masses docile by the distraction of entertain-ment. Stars were the leading figures in what Debord called the Society of the Spectacle.

Besides, to be a star meant you had prostituted your talent and integrity for money and fame. Look at Marc Bolan. He began life as a groovy troubadour in an underground acoustic folk group called Tyrannosaurus Rex, and then became a rich and famous teen idol in T.Rex in the 1970s. What a sell-out!

The hippy critique of fame went deeper. Life for hippies wasn't about seeking attention, becoming famous and having your ego stroked and pampered. No, the whole point of life was to *transcend* your ego, lose it and then, and only then, could you alter your consciousness and find spiritual enlightenment. Fortunately, the hippies had found a fast and effective solution to the problem of too much ego: lysergic acid diethylamide (LSD) or 'acid', as it would be called. This new miracle drug acted as a kind of solvent on the self; used correctly it could dissolve your ego in a jiffy.

Rock stars were keen to try acid, because by 1967 they didn't want to be rock stars any more. They wanted to be artists. You can see this in the transition from singles to albums, and from shaving to facial hair. Teen idol Jim Morrison of the Doors grew a big beard, got fat and moved to Paris to write poetry. In the hope of being a member of a group and not a star, Jimi Hendrix broke up the Jimi Hendrix Experience and created the anonymous-sounding Band of Gypsies.

The most dramatic example of this change was John Lennon. By 1966 the Beatles were fed up with the gruelling tours, the screaming hordes, the whole mad life of the rock star – so they quit touring, retired to the studio and grew moustaches. Lennon came under the influence of two powerful forces: LSD and Yoko Ono, a terrifying combination that was bound to make a man either an artist or a lunatic. In 1968 Lennon came out as a fully fledged artist with the release of the avant-garde *Two Virgins* album, featuring a naked Lennon and Ono on the cover.

☆

When it came to rock stars, the hippies practised the most blatant double standards. They looked down on those teenage female fans who would scream at pop groups – often the very ones that the hippies adored like the Doors and the Beatles – and dismissed them as 'teenyboppers'. Boppers, as they were called, were considered to be the lowest form of rock-fan life. They were innocent hysterics, manipulated by record companies and the media: they had no taste or real appreciation for music. The spectacle of teenyboppers besieging airports and weeping and fainting at concerts of their idols struck the hippies as pitiful. And yet women who opened their legs when faced with the same idols, were known as groupies and held in high regard.

Today the term groupie has certain sleazy associations, but in the sixties groupies were considered kind of cool and sexually liberated. Even a smart counter-culture star like Germaine Greer was a defender of the groupie way of life. In 1969 she appeared on the cover of the underground magazine *Oz*, standing behind the bemused figure of Vivian Stanshall (lead singer of the Bonzo Dog Doo Dah Band) unzipping his fly. The *Oz* cover bore the strapline: 'OZ talks to Dr G – the only groupie with a PhD'.

In the *Oz* article – entitled 'The Universal Tongue-bath: A Groupie Vision', in which Greer interviews herself under the pseudonym of 'Dr G' – she writes without any embarrassment: 'I guess I'm a starfucker really. You know it's a name I dig, because all the men who get inside me are stars. Even if they're plumbers, they're star plumbers. Another thing I dig is balling the great before the rest of the world know about them . . .'

Greer was later to claim that this was a work of

satire. Her unofficial biographer Christine Wallace doubts it. 'Germaine had relayed these precise views and anecdotes in all seriousness to Richard Neville before she wrote the piece some years earlier.'

Two years later, in a 1971 interview with the *New York Times*, Greer candidly admits to having been a 'supergroupie'. 'Supergroupies don't have to hang around hotel corridors,' she said. 'When you are one, as I have been, you get invited backstage. I think groupies are important because they demystify sex; they accept it as physical, and they aren't possessive about their conquests.'

There have always been women willing to have sex with a man who was famous, but until the sixties most women who did so kept it quiet. It was the sort of thing that could get a girl labelled what the Americans called a 'tramp' and the British a 'tart'. It shows just how star-struck the hippies – for all their anti-fame rhetoric – really were, because with them 'star-fucking' lost its stigma. What was considered vice had become a vocation.

Groupies were ahead of their time, pioneering a relationship with stars that would eventually be taken up by the rest of society. Like the paparazzi, they refused to stay out of the private lives of the famous. Theirs was the right of the non-famous to access all areas of the star life, both backstage and in the bedroom. The masses had the *News of the World* for tales of rock life behind closed doors; the counter-culture had Jenny Fabian and her novel *Groupie*.

But the great counter-culture battle against fame

ended in defeat: they simply got rid of the old stars and created a new bunch. Hippy London was as stratified and star-struck as Swinging London. As Andrew Bailey, the editor of British *Rolling Stone*, put it: 'I was slightly in awe of the underground heavies like Richard Neville and Germaine Greer. You'd meet them, you'd be in the same room at parties, but they were stars. The underground had a star system exactly as did pop music and films and everything else.'

I was as much a phoney as all the rest. I was a groupie, a teenybopper and a bored housewife all rolled into one when it came to rock stars. I know because my first Dad-as-hero moment involved a rock star. I was sitting having breakfast when my father came into the room in his bathrobe. 'I've got something for ya,' he said, slapped down a small piece of paper and headed off for the kitchen to make his morning tea.

I turned the paper over and read the following message, scribbled in blue biro.

> *To Cosmo and Miles,*
> *Stay cool, be groovy,*
> *Love, Jimi Hendrix*

And with that my dad became my hero, my very own Atticus Finch (Gregory Peck) in *To Kill a Mockingbird*. To me Hendrix's autograph wasn't just pop-star scribble, it was a handwritten message from a god. My dad was Moses, down from the mountaintop with the two commandments: Stay cool. Be groovy.

8

Macro-Whacko

Decades have a nasty habit of turning up late and never ending on time. The Sixties were like a drunken party guest that wants to keep going long after everyone else has gone home. But there was a sign that something was changing, at least in my family. By the start of the early 1970s a miracle had occurred: my parents were no longer star-struck.

It happened like this. By the end of the 1960s Jay felt he was suffering from too many parties, too many friends, too many good times and too little to show for it all. All that freedom can make a man's life go flabby. So as he faced the new decade Jay felt he needed some rules and restraints to give his life shape and structure. As he later wrote in his memoirs: 'The swinging Sixties had come to an end and what did I have to show for it? All my abortive projects had left me feeling I had to find God or a good substitute.'

Jay found his substitute for God, projects, fame and his mother's love in the most unlikely of places: his stomach. He became a born-again brown-rice-munching macrobiotic. Macrobiotics was a way of eating and a philosophy of life developed by the Japanese writer George

Ohsawa. Its core idea was that all food contained elements of yin and yang and that you should try to strike a healthy balance between the two. This was best achieved by eating brown rice, grains, organic vegetables and bread. Macrobiotics was the Talmud of the tummy: an elaborate set of rules about what you should eat and why. It even had rules about *how* you should eat. 'Chew each mouthful of food fifty times,' commanded Ohsawa. 'Chew each mouthful of food fifty times,' Jay told us every night at the dinner table.

Jay's conversion happened overnight. One day I left for school and when I returned home he was in the kitchen engaged in an act of dietary purification. He rushed around, black bin liner in hand, exorcizing the forces of evil: white sugar, white flour, white bread, processed foods, all dairy products, bottled sauces, meats and soft drinks. In their place came the foodstuffs of righteousness and the objects of the sacred: the wok, chopsticks, the organic brown bread, the bags of lentils, the soy sauce, the tofu and, the holy of holies, big sacks of organic brown rice. Our house took on the musty smell of tamari sauce and the wet-twig odour of Mu tea.

Once the kitchen was transformed Jay went to work on himself. He began to cook food, and talk food and think food. Gone was the self-indulgent hippy; in his place stood the puritanical health-food nut. Everything we ate was analysed by Jay in terms of yin or yang. 'Be careful, you're about to swallow a helluva a lot of yang,' he'd warn. And everything we did was audited for its yin and yang propensities. He once told me that I was whistling too much because I was suffering from a 'surfeit of yin'.

For Jay, macrobiotics became something more than a diet. It became an all-embracing explanation for the world and its problems. The war in Vietnam? 'Look at all that meat Americans put in their mouths,' he'd say, 'they're so yanged-up, so aggressive – no wonder they're at war.'

There was nothing that couldn't be explained by food. One day Miles got arrested for stealing money from a hot-dog vendor outside a Lou Reed concert, and Jay had to go and pick him up from the police station. Jay walked into the police holding cell, took one look at Miles and knew what had gone wrong. 'Miles,' he said, 'you've been eating those sausages again!'

'Yes, Jay,' confessed a contrite Miles. 'It was the sausages . . . they made me do it!'

☆

The soft lovey-dovey Sixties started to come to an end in 1968 with mass demos in Paris and London; revolutionary politics became all the rage. Going to Grosvenor Square to protest about the war in Vietnam was a must-do event, like going to see the free Rolling Stones concert in Hyde Park. Alongside the Hendrix and Dylan posters on my wall hung the faces of my new heroes: Che and the Black Panthers. Jay had his rice and I had my revolution. He quoted Ohsawa, I responded with Chairman Mao.

Now it was the turn of the hippies to be out of fashion. The bus of radical politics was heading off to that better world just around the corner and Jay was determined to get on it. He began preaching the doctrine of revolution through brown rice. In 1971 he wrote an article called 'Splendours in the Rice' for *Oz* magazine, with a message for all the yippies, protesting students, Black Panthers, New Leftists, Marxists and anarchists: 'The real revolution begins right under your nose – open your mouth and chew.'

☆

Jay had always believed that if a thing is worth doing it's worth overdoing, and his involvement with macrobiotics was no exception. It was around a year after the Miles arrest, when we were taking a trip through the South of France, that I realized Jay had crossed over from being macrobiotic to being macro*psychotic*.

It was a hot summer's day and Fran had purchased an ice cream. When Jay saw his wife (and fellow traveller on the great macro crusade) holding an ice cream in her hand he blew up and accused her of betrayal, threatening divorce.

If Jay had found his wife in bed with another man he wouldn't have minded. But catching her red-handed with an ice cream was, for him, the ultimate act of infidelity. A contrite Fran chucked her ice cream away and promised never to have anything to do with a dairy product again. The marriage was saved.

The macropsychotic Jay was a different man. He no longer had the need to be the centre of attention. He stopped trying to impress people with his conversation and tried to convert them with his cooking. Now the only names he dropped were varieties of organic beans or brands of tofu. For the first time in his life my father had become a bore.

He bored and alienated many of his old showbiz friends with his constant talk of organic this and that, yin and yang and how many times they should chew their food. The funny thing was that he didn't care; he simply went out and got new friends who were macrobiotic.

Jay and Fran began to move in the unglamorous world of the London macrobiotic scene. John Lennon and Yoko Ono might be spotted at the macro restaurant called Seed on Westbourne Grove, but macro people had none of the fixation with glamour and the famous that you found in Hippy London. They got excited by recipes for vegetable tempura and new developments in organic farming. They were mostly skinny, serious people who spoke softly and chewed loudly.

Since his conversion to macrobiotics Jay had dropped out of showbiz and was now in the organic-food biz. Instead of lurking in his lair waiting for a miracle at the other end of the phone line, he went out and got a job. Every morning he would deliver a tray of tea and toast to Fran in bed and take off for a day at the office. He was working for a company set up by Craig and Gregory Sams, two American businessmen in London who'd opened a macrobiotic restaurant, a health-food store and a wholesale distribution operation called Harmony Foods. Jay did all sorts of jobs – he worked in the restaurant as a singing waiter, he was a salesman for

Harmony Foods products and was in charge of public relations.

I can honestly say that during this period my parents were happy, healthy and fantastically boring. It was when Jay became a full-time publicist for Harmony Foods that some showbiz gene in his DNA kicked in. He was back in business with a new act. The man who had once reinvented himself as a daring playboy publisher in the 1940s had undergone another reinvention: he now called himself Stan Stunning, and wore a specially designed macrobiotic jacket made out of old brown rice sacks, displaying yin and yang symbols on it. His mission? To spread the macro message: you are what you eat.

It wasn't an easy task. In the early seventies the health-food movement was just beginning in the UK. It was rare to find shops selling organic foods. The typical supermarket manager regarded brown rice as nothing but bird food. Macrobiotics was just another offbeat, crazy cause that my father couldn't resist.

It was hard to tell what Jay was really selling: brown rice, or himself? But he was very successful at Landesman/rice promotions. He got John Pilger to write a feature about a macrobiotic baking competition for the *Daily Mirror*. He got the *Sunday Times* to do a feature about the 'ideal macrobiotic family'. The article included a picture of the Landesman family sitting around the dinner table, chopsticks in hand, enjoying the wonders of brown rice and umoboshi plums. My feelings about being dragged into the limelight to be part of the happy-chewy macrobiotic family can be seen in the *Sunday Times* photograph: I'm trying to hide my face behind my shoulder-length hair.

This article was the first of many attempts by my parents to parade their style of life as something special, something the reader should envy. In the article Fran is quoted as saying that the macrobiotic diet has done wonders for their marriage. 'No more of Jay's twenty-four-hour lunch conferences . . . we spend peaceful evenings at home reading gems from macrobiotic literature . . . life has become simple and loving.'

Soon Fran and Jay were famous figures on the natural-food scene. He was Stan Stunning and she became known as 'Ma Landesman' of apple-strudel fame. Jay discovered that food could be a fast route to a kind of celebrity. They even had a song written about them and recorded by Paul Jones – former lead singer of Manfred Mann – called 'Stan Stunning and the Noodle Queen'.

The irony of their success in the world of wholefoods wasn't lost on Jay. No sooner had he given up on trying to make it than he achieved a kind of celebrity. He later wrote, 'After a lifetime of struggling for recognition, in various fields of endeavour, how easy it was to become stars in the natural food world.'

Looking back it strikes me as rather sad that Jay could find satisfaction in that. Going from dreams of Broadway to dreams of brown rice – what a comedown! Fortunately, it didn't last that long. Slowly, Jay's macro crusade began to crumble. The austerity of my parents' macro regime eventually proved too much and they began to loosen up, indulging in once forbidden things.

One evening an old friend caught Jay tucking into a steak and remarked, 'My, they're doing strange things with brown rice these days.'

I knew that the days of macro were over when Fran took Miles and me to a new American-style hamburger place called The Great American Disaster. A friend of my parents, Phyllis Raphael, wrote of that night with Fran and her kids in her memoir of London in the seventies: 'She hadn't eaten meat since the macrobiotic diet entered her life. She lifted the bun off the hamburger and looked as if it were the face of God.'

It would be only a matter of time before I longed to have my boring macrobiotic parents back.

☆

It is nineteen seventy something. Miles is playing rhythm guitar in a progressive rock band called Renoir. One evening they're playing a gig at the Red Lion pub in Islington, north London. The place is packed, the band is on fine form and the crowd love them.

Watching them play it occurs to me that Miles is actually in a band that *might just make it*. Lead singer Phil Daniels is a charismatic frontman who writes catchy pop songs with his collaborator, keyboard player Peter Hugo Daley. The band mostly do their own songs, but their set usually includes a couple of Fran's songs as well. They finish one of hers and the crowd goes wild.

'Thanks. Cheers,' says Daniels. He turns and grabs a pint.

There's this quiet murmur you get in between numbers, when the band and the audience take a breather, and suddenly everyone hears this loud voice of a woman yelling: 'THAT'S MY SONG ... MY SONG ... I WROTE THAT! *ME! ME! ME!*'

It is Mother.

Everyone turns to stare at the crazy American woman in the middle of the room. Fran stands there and giggles. I look at the band to assess the damage.

Daniels looks like his face has frozen between a grin and groan.

Miles laughs nervously, and then rushes behind a stack of amps to hide.

The remaining members of the band look at each other as if to say: *what was that*?

Me? I'm on the verge of embarrassment meltdown.

So I leave the gig blushing and furious *How could she? Why would she? No, this time she's gone too far ... even Miles will have to admit that! ...*

As I walked home Fran's shriek of 'ME! ME! ME!' rang in my head. I had never heard anything like it before. It was as if her private longing for recognition could no longer be silently contained; it burst out in public like a flow of obscenities from someone with Tourette's Syndrome. Once my anger and embarrassment had subsided I felt a kind of pity and concern for my mother. In that cry I heard the Mayday call of a woman lost at sea and frantically waving; afraid that she was going to drown in the black waters of anonymity.

☆

It never happened for Miles. The times were against him. A band with a name like Renoir had no place in a

world where bands were now called the Clash, the Sex
Pistols and the Stranglers. They carried on for a bit till
Phil Daniels got the offer to appear in the lead role of
the Who's film *Quadrophenia*. After that came their inevitable bust-up. A bit later Miles heard that Daniels was
putting together a new band – with two of the Renoir
guys – and had a record deal. He waited for the call but
it never came. That must have hurt. But Miles remained
cheerful and wished Phil and the boys luck. Then his
hair started to fall out.

And it looked like it would never happen for me
either. I read Truman Capote's *In Cold Blood* and Hunter
Thompson's *Fear and Loathing in Las Vegas*. I read Tom
Wolfe, Norman Mailer, William Burroughs, Ken Kesey
and Kurt Vonnegut, and decided I wanted to be a writer
or a journalist. But I never wrote.

At nineteen I took a year off and travelled around
America collecting material for a book I would write on
my return to London. I tried to write about my journey
in America and produced nothing. Instead I hung out.
I went to pubs in Soho and parties in Hampstead.

I made solemn vows to write. I made writing sched-
ules. I read books on How to Write. I read books in
which successful authors talked about the art of writing.
I bought an expensive leather-bound notebook, the kind
writers take to cafes, where they sip espressos and jot
down their impressions of the world. I went to cafes and
sipped enough coffee to produce three novels. But I just
sat there thinking: what the fuck shall I write?

I did everything a writer should do, except write.
Instead, I smoked dope in the daytime. I watched tele-

vision. I binged on distraction and felt disgusted with myself. In 1971 the *Oz* School Kids' issue was prosecuted for obscenity. It became the trial of the decade. But I wasn't interested in the injustice of persecuting the *Oz* editors for obscenity. What got me angry was the injustice of not having been one of the school kids who got to work on that issue. Why couldn't I have been one of them? And here's the thing that really hurt: my parents even knew the editor of *Oz*, Richard Neville.

By now I was having full-blown regrets about the Sixties. That decade had whispered in my ear: *Relax . . . live for the moment . . . go with the flow . . . do your own thing . . . don't worry, something will turn up.* And that's exactly what I did: I relaxed. I flowed. I did my own thing. I gave tomorrow the finger, and tomorrow came and something did turn up: my first proper job – scrubbing toilets for nice Jewish women in Golders Green.

Fran had also found a new career as a performing poet. It all began when she was invited to read some of her verse at a charity event at the Crypt of St Martin in the Fields. She was a hit. In the audience that night was Michael Horowitz – poet and poetry promoter extraordinaire – who invited her to come and read at one of his poetry events in Hampstead. Fran went and was adored by the audience. More performances followed and more success, until she became a familiar face on the London poetry circuit.

Reading her poems in public gave Fran something she had never had before: instant injections of praise.

People would come up to her and say how much they loved her show and ask about buying her book.

Jay was spending more of his time getting her gigs at art centres, universities and poetry festivals, and she was even asked to do a platform performance at the Lyttelton theatre on the South Bank. Despite her new-found success she wasn't happy. Jay would come back from his office to find a depressed Fran in bed. A typical exchange between them went like this:

Jay: I spend my whole day trying to promote you, and I come home to a depressed angst-ridden wife.

Fran: What do you expect? I'm a poet.

☆

In 1976 Fran planned to take her poetry act to New York, for a one-off reading at a well-known jazz club called Bradley's in Manhattan. (The owner was a friend.) On hearing the news I panicked. Who in New York was going to be interested in Fran sitting on a stool and reading light verse, for Christ's sakes! I pleaded with Jay to rethink this whole trip.

Me: Fran can do her little poetry routine in funky London, but not the Big Apple!

She's gonna bomb. No one will pay her any attention. You're sending your wife out there to die! Remember what you told me when I was a kid – they have no time for little people.

Jay: What? Are you crazy? They're gonna love her. Trust me. I know a terrific act when I see one and that woman has a terrific act.

I went off thinking: my poor lunatic parents. Imagine going all that way to New York for something that's going to end in tears, heartbreak and humiliation. But it actually ended in a glowing full-page story in the *New Yorker*'s Talk of the Town page about the wonderful Landesmans coming to New York and Fran's entertaining performance.

Jay didn't say anything when he showed me the story in the *New Yorker*, but the look on his face said, *who's crazy now?*

Fran's next big challenge came two years later when she made her debut at the Edinburgh Festival. Jay had got her a week at Better Books, a place off the beaten track. Advance ticket sales were zero. So Jay went into action and took over Fran's publicity. On the day she was to make her first appearance he was pounding the streets of Edinburgh, handing out leaflets in the rain. He was like a crazed circus barker, the kind who would entice the crowds to come in and see some freakish spectacle: in Jay's case, his wife. 'Come on folks, step right up and see the hip little lady born in the smoky bars of Greenwich Village in the fifties perform her poems,' he'd shout, thrusting flyers into people's hands.

Jay got a few bums on seats, and a review in the *Scotsman* said her lyrics were funnier and truer than Stephen Sondheim's. More good reviews followed, and Fran was soon playing to packed houses. After every show people of all ages and from all sorts of backgrounds came up and told her how wonderful she was.

All this attention and praise had a profound effect on

her; Jay said it was just like the scene in an old Hollywood melodrama when the crippled girl suddenly
disovers she can walk. Only in the Fran movie, it was a
little fat girl whose mother had made her feel like a
freak discovering that people could love her.

A star was born . . . and so was a monster.

You can get a sense of this Fran in an interview with
a journalist from the *International Herald Tribune*. She
said: 'I just love going out there and giving of myself
and receiving all that love and energy. I want to go on
tour. I want to make an album. I want to be a star!'

Fran's newfound bid for stardom was given total
support by everyone in the family, except me. I was the
traitor to the cause, the scab who broke ranks.

'Baby, you're going to be a star,' said Jay.

'My mum is going to be a star!' said Miles.

'Look, lunatics,' I said, 'Fran isn't going to be a star.'

'Cool it with the negativity,' said Jay.

'Yeah, Cos, don't be so negative!' said Miles.

'You just wait and see,' said Fran. 'I'm going to be a
big *fucking* star!'

Fresh from her triumph in Edinburgh, Jay decided
that he was going to make that woman a star if it was
the last thing he did.

He would tell her at breakfast, 'Sweetheart, I'm going
to make you a star.'

They'd meet for lunch and he would discuss his plans
and strategies for her stardom. 'Wogan – you'd be
perfect for the Wogan show!' Jay would declare. 'I'll fix
that up right away.'

For dinner there would be talk of a new book of

verse, a new UK tour and a record of *Fran Landesman Live!*

Me [*sarcastically*]: How about a Fran Landesman television special?

Jay: Hey, that's a *great* idea! I'll get right on it.'

Me: Hello, crazy man? Time for your medication! For Christ's sakes, Jay, do you really think you can make a star out of that woman with that act?

Jay: Definitely.

Me: But why?

Jay: OK, Mr Negativity – what about Pam Ayers?

This was to be Jay's trump card, played whenever I expressed any doubts about the sanity of the whole Make Fran a Star project. I would always be put in my place with 'Pam Ayers'.

Pam Ayers was then a popular writer and performer of comic light verse. In 1975 she had shot to national fame with her appearance on the ITV talent show *Opportunity Knocks*. Since then she had had her own television series, released an album and, in 1977, she had appeared at the Royal Variety Performance at the London Palladium. Ayers had made the improbable seem possible: fame from light verse. I bet every woman and man throughout the United Kingdom who fancied themselves as a bit of poet believed that they could be the next Pam Ayers.

My scepticism didn't seem to matter, as I discovered a week later when I got a call from Jay. I had been working at my dad's new publishing company, Jay Landesman Ltd, reading manuscripts and trying to come up with ideas. So far I'd come up with nothing and was expecting to get fired at any minute. But it wasn't to be.

Jay: Got a minute?

Me: What's up?

Jay: Good news. I'm giving you a promotion. You're going to handle the PR for two of my biggest clients.

Me: Who's that?

Jay: Fran and Miles!

Me: *What?*

Jay: That's right. They've both got new books of poetry . . .

Me: You're going to publish a book of Miles's poetry?

Jay: Actually, they're a collection of his lyrics and they're sensational, have you read them?

Me: No.

Jay: I'm going to do a special limited edition. I want you to write the blurb for the back and get to work on Fran's press release. See you bright and early on Monday morning.

So instead of writing for something cool like the *NME* or doing my first novel, I was sweating over my masterpieces: the Fran Landesman press release and the Miles Landesman blurb. 'Miles Davis Landesman came to London in 1964, when his showbiz parents were forced into exile by indifferent notices . . . Miles has over three hundred unreleased demo tapes to his credit and is the author of the play *The Final Circumcision: A Jewish Rock Horror.*'

For Fran I'd come up with things like: 'From the

boozy nights and bright neon lights of the beat generation, Fran Landesman's verse is a funny and sardonic
look at love and a life lived on the wild side. She is the
hipster's Pam Ayers . . .'

And each day I would get a suggestion from Jay on
how to play up the Ayers angle. 'What about Pam Ayers
on acid?' or 'Fran Landesman, the Jewish Pam Ayers?'

Eventually I got one Pam Ayers phone call too many
and I cracked and said, 'Why not just cover all bases
and bill her as the beat generation's very own Jewish
Pam Ayers on acid for the thinking people who like
Dorothy Parker?'

Jay: Hey, that's not a bad idea!
Click.

☆

In 1976 I finally lose my writer virginity and get into
print. It's a spoof diary of a struggling health-food
convert and it appears in a macrobiotic magazine called
Seed. I am thrilled. Someone writes to me and says they
thought it was funny. I get my first compliment. What
a buzz. I suddenly understand what Fran wants. But
nothing else happens on the journalistic front.

I complain to Jay about my lack of success. He tells
me, 'You need to get out there and sell yourself. You
can't sit around waiting for the phone to ring. You got
to make those calls. You've got terrific ideas but no
hustle.' He's right. But I feel uncomfortable trying to sell
myself and my ideas. Instead of get-up-and-go I have a
sit-down-and-sulk attitude to life. But then I don't want

to be another self-promoting Landesman with a million projects for sale.

I quit writing and teach myself guitar, becoming another deluded rock 'n' roll dreamer. I end up playing in a band with Miles called Miles Over Matter. He will end up playing guitar for my mother, who will provide a space on her show for my father to read his memoirs.

By the way, as I write this the following happened two days ago. My father made a guest appearance at one of Fran's performances and read two chapters about himself from this very book. (He never asked me if he could read from my book, he just did it.) And here's the thing that really hurts: he bombed reading from *my* book! He totally lost the audience because he hadn't studied the text (or so I tell myself), and they told him to wind it up after a very long and lacklustre performance.

The fact that I was playing in Miles's band gave Jay a new idea: wouldn't it be great if we went on the road as a family, performing our poetry and songs? 'I could get us gigs at art centres up and down the UK!' he said.

I laughed nervously. He was only trying to torment me. I told myself it was just a crazy fantasy . . . and then he went and bought a big old school bus that could sleep six. Now I was afraid. I had nightmarish visions of us as the Partridge Family of bohemia – with Fran (poetry and lead vocals), Miles (lead guitar), Jay (memoirs) and me sulking in the background, banging a bloody tambourine.

It wasn't long before I hung up my guitar; but I could

never quite retire from show business. From Jay I learned that all the world is a stage and you had better have a damn good act to impress people with. Rooms – and the people in them – were to be 'dominated', 'worked' and 'won over'. You never went into a room like a normal person; you went into a room like a stand-up comic ready to do battle. Rooms did not contain people, they contained audiences. You didn't make conversation; you did shtick, you did your routine. You did not want to meet people or make friends: you wanted to *kill 'em, slay 'em, wipe 'em out* or *slaughter 'em* with laughter.

My father couldn't enter an empty broom closet without going into a routine. Dinnertime in our house was always showtime. At the dinner table it was permissible to pass out in the soup from drink or make a pass at one – or all – members of the Landesman family. The one thing my father could not tolerate was what he called 'dead air'. Dead air is what normal people call silence. (It's a term that dates back to the heyday of radio, when any silence during a broadcast was considered a major disaster.) To Jay people who did not talk, who didn't make an effort to be entertaining, weren't shy or simply incapable, they were guilty of 'negativity' and 'latent aggression'. Silent people were 'downers'. Jay called them 'vacuums' because they 'sucked up the energy in the room'.

Jay's performance attitude to life had clearly made an impact on me. Whenever I went out I was always anxious to be a social wow. I would come home from a dinner party and I would write a review of myself like I was a performer. But never once did I come back and say I was brilliant. I said I was awful/too loud/people thought me crazy/overbearing. Here is a typical entry from my diary at the time: 'I try so hard to shine and I always end up looking like a fool.'

As a consequence of eating with their parents as children, some people go on to suffer from eating disorders. Me, I have no problem with food. I have eating-food-*with*-people disorders. To this very day I can't sit down to dinner with people without being struck by a kind of stage fright. No matter how relaxed and informal the occasion, I am always worried about my performance.

For God's sake relax, I tell myself. *Nobody is judging you. Nobody is expecting you to perform. It's OK to be just you . . . It's just dinner. It's not the bloody Perrier Comedy Awards. You're not having dinner with your parents . . . you will not be dismissed because you aren't entertaining . . .*

So I relax and then a guest starts being funny. Not, mind you, incredibly funny; just funny enough to get me nervous.

Then he moves up a gear . . .

It's then that I realize that I'm dining with one of those very funny men who won't be content until he's shown everyone in the room that he's not just a funny guy, but that he's *funnier than you are*. When I meet one of these really funny people at a dinner party it comes back, the old fear that I'm not that funny . . . I am not brilliant tonight . . . I'm not as funny as he is . . . I am that most accursed of things . . .

I am dead air.

☆

On 4 July 1979 I went with my parents to a party of Victor Lownes's at his country estate. (Lownes was the head of the Playboy club in London.) Although I have seen celebrities in our front room, I've never seen so many en masse. I wrote in my diary: 'All of the beautiful people of London were there; Rod Stewart, John Cleese and Susan George.' At the time, Susan is the star of a film called *Straw Dogs*. Like all men then, I'm in love with her. If I were my dad's son I would have the balls to go up and introduce myself, be charming, make her laugh, arrange lunch.

But I don't. I just stand on the sidelines. I feel inadequate. Nobody knows my name. And I suddenly realize: nobody wants to know it, either. It's the first time I have the feeling that I'm a nobody. Jay comes up to me and says: 'Stop moping and start mingling. Look, there's that Susan George broad that you like so much.' I hear him yell, 'Hey Susan! I've got someone here I want you to meet!'

I blush and make a run for it.

☆

For me the seventies ended with a new form of embarrassment: my parents going public with their open marriage. What exactly is an open marriage? It is when a married couple reject a commitment to having an exclusive sexual relationship with each other, preferring instead the freedom to pursue as many sexual partners as desired without any concealment. An alternative definition is: two cohabiting sluts.

The term 'open marriage' was popularized by the

publication in 1972 of a book called *Open Marriage: A New Lifestyle for Couples* by Nene and George O'Neill, which sold over 1.5 million copies. But for the O'Neills the open marriage was more about revitalizing your marriage and finding friendship outside marriage, and not just about sexual licence. What they saw as the perversion of their concept was due to people like my parents, who never read that book – Jay would rather have been castrated than do something so square.

No child likes to think of their parents having sex, and no child likes to think of their parents having sex with other people. It is worst of all for the child who is aware of a) parental sex, b) parental sex with other partners, and c) everybody in the world knowing that your parents are having all this sex.

I knew other families where the parents had what was called an open marriage. But at least for the sake of their children they had the decency to be hypocrites and keep up the appearance of having a monogamous relationship. Not my parents. They just had to be so bloody open about their open marriage.

They first went public about this in January 1979. A full-page feature in the Living section of the *Observer* had the headline that said it all: 'The Semi-Detached Way to Swing'. In the piece journalist Sally Vincent referred to the 'sexual adventuring that has rounded the edges of the Landesman marriage. All this chat about Having Fun, as though it was nothing to be ashamed of.'

Jay was reported as knocking the shallowness of 'suburban swingers' and the article ended with him heading off to 'spend the rest of the day with a new lady friend in Balham' while Fran says, 'Have fun, sweet-heart.'

That was it. Suddenly they became the couple with the open marriage, and every journalist who subsequently came to see them made reference to their 'unconventional marriage', as they called it.

They were open not just in print but also in public. Their current lover would become part of our family life. There was no sneaking in and out of rooms; they sat at the dinner table at night and they were there in the morning for breakfast. And when other people were around, like my friends, neither parent ever bothered to hide whatever relationship was in progress. Displays of affection were there for everyone to see. Hands would be held, arms wrapped around shoulders. I would pretend not to notice and so would my friends.

I realized that I would never get my parents to grow up and give up their libertine lifestyle. So I offered them a deal. I said that I would accept their way of life only if they would live it with more discretion. I used to plead with them, 'Do you have to be so open about your open marriage? Could you please not talk about it to the media, it's so embarrassing.' I thought I was being reasonable; they thought I was being ridiculous.

I think their marriage was something that suited their emotional and sexual needs, but it became a marketing device that would generate publicity. Whenever Fran or Jay had something to promote, they knew their lifestyle would be a hook for journalists. I did try to confront them about using their marriage in this way. They were the only kiss-and-sell couple in the world who were actually married. But Jay always denied that they were after publicity. He thought it was just a part of their natural way of life, and so why should they cover it up?

Their marriage chimed with the mood of the times. There was much talk about the sexual revolution, when the battle of the barricades moved to the bedroom. According to the feminist historian Sheila Rowbotham, 'Sex by the early 1970s had become a cause.'

Monogamy was seen as a means of sexual control. It was believed by otherwise sane people that sex could offer a form of liberation that drugs and politics had failed to provide. Fucking and freedom became synonymous.

This was music to my father's ears. For Jay in particular, I think it was also a means of career compensation. Drawing attention to their marriage was a way of making themselves feel that they were still a daring and original couple.

So there I was coming of age during the sexual revolution – and my bloody parents were getting all the sex. They were the Marx and Lady Lenin of the sexual revolution, and boy did they have plenty of followers.

Amongst the bohemian set my parents moved in you often found men who had mistresses, usually a mature sensible woman with kids of her own. Not Jay. He seemed to have a stream of sexy dolly birds on tap. So while I sat in my room dreaming of Brigitte Bardot, he was in bed with her double.

The *Guardian* once referred to my parents as having

'a legendary open marriage'. Over the years people have asked me what it was like to have parents who were famous for their sex lives. What the hell did they expect me to say? 'Oh, I'm terribly proud to have a mummy and daddy who shagged their way through London'?

9

Back To The Future

It's said that contemporary Britain has become engulfed in a wave of narcissism and self-preoccupation. But the idea of a narcissistic decade, devoted to the selfish interests of the individual, is not new. It was said of the 1980s. And long before the 1970s got rebranded as the fun-loving era of Abba and bad taste, it was known as the Me Decade.

This tag came from a 1976 article by Tom Wolfe in *New York* magazine entitled 'The "Me" Decade and the Third Great Awakening'. Wolfe was writing about the boom in personal-growth movements and therapeutic fads that were spreading through America. He claimed that for the first time in history ordinary people had discovered the joys of thinking and talking about themselves. Beneath everything from feminism to gestalt therapy there lurked only one topic: Me.

The 1970s preoccupation with the self was the unintended legacy of the 1960s. The counter-culture believed that the old self was repressed by duty, deference and morality. It offered a new 'liberated' self, one based on self-expression ('be creative, man!'), self-awareness ('tune in, turn on') and self-gratification ('if it feels good, do it!'). But it wasn't all about the selfish pleasures of the individual, for it was assumed that if you created a better and freer self, you would create a better and freer society. In short, the personal was the best way to realize the political aspirations of the 1960s.

But the new liberated self that emerged from the rubble of sixties radicalism was a very different beast from what the counter-culture had envisioned. This being swaggered into the seventies with his hair still long; it was his social conscience that got cut. No longer interested in protest, politics and changing the world, the liberated self of the seventies was free to consume, be creative, self-expressive and talk about itself, incessantly.

People in the seventies, especially the young, wanted the hedonism and self-expressive individualism of the sixties, but not all that 'revolutionary crap' as Mott the Hoople put it their teen anthem, 'All The Young Dudes'. And rock music was happy to give them these things. It quickly changed its tune to fit the times and broke with its radical past and any pretence to be the voice of opposition. Nothing summed up the modest, self-satisfied aspirations of post-sixties rock music than the title of the Rolling Stones' 1974 album, *It's Only Rock 'n' Roll*. This was the same rock 'n' roll that had been set to change the world.

A great stimulant to the self-preoccupation of seventies youth was that strand of narcissistic pop – Bryan Ferry, Marc Bolan, David Bowie – where the peacock display of persona and style was even more important than the music. They showed ordinary working-class teenagers how to be fabulous individuals by dressing up in the Weimarian costumes of decadence, bisexuality and gender-bending.

The whole exhibitionistic carnival of the self that was going on in the world of pop, punk, fashion and the arts was played out against a social backdrop of national decline. A combination of the rise in the price of oil (following the Yom Kippur war in 1973), the rise of inflation (20% by January 1975) and the surge of industrial conflicts that culminated in the Winter of Discontent (1978/9) created a sense of a Britain on the verge of collapse.

Britain didn't collapse, but our sense of togetherness did. Despite the divisions of class and wealth, there'd always been a feeling that we shared a sense of belonging to the same society. But increasingly as the decade wore on it looked as if there was no such thing as society, only self-interest.

The sixties idea that we're all interesting, naturally creative and should express ourselves really took off in the seventies. (It even began to infiltrate the thinking of progressive-minded educationalists.) Little did the counter-culture know that the egalitarianism of the sixties would fuel the egotism of the seventies.

The sixties prepared the way forward by helping to break down the boundaries between high and low culture, art and life. If anything could be art – as the radical artists of the sixties claimed – then couldn't anyone be an artist? How could you tell who was a *real* artist or not? Was Charlotte Morman (the woman who played a cello made of ice in the nude in my parents' living room) an artist or an exhibitionist? Was Ralph Ortiz (the man who took an axe to my dad's piano in the name of 'destruction art') an artist or just another attention-hustler? Andy Warhol offered this as a way out of the confusion: 'art is anything you can get away with.' He made creativity sound like a clever con job or a bank heist. And there were plenty of people prepared to make a smash-and-grab bid for artistic fame.

The art critic Edward Lucie-Smith commented on this creative boom when he wrote that in the 1970s, 'The right to enjoy art became to some extent confused with a right to make it ... far more people aspired to be full-time artists, musicians and writers than even the most developed economies could support.'

Among sections of the cultured, affluent middle class, people were no longer content to have their status based on wealth and material consumption in the form of beautiful houses and beautiful things. In the seventies, these people wanted to be thought of as *interesting* individuals. You could no longer do this by coming on like some crazy freak, as they did in the sixties. Being a creative person was the best alternative, and everyone seemed to think they could be creative.

I saw these people at first hand in my parents' living room, which went from crash pad to open audition space. I watched performing poets bare their souls, women with guitars display their emotional scars, young men proferring unreadable novels and a whole gaggle of actors, comedians and film-makers. Even acid-heads, who couldn't remember yesterday, were writing their memoirs. (Jay began writing a surrealistic novel about the futility of freedom, called *Bad Nipple*.) Everyone seemed to think that they had a special talent and they were determined to share it with you. Not long ago these very same people had wanted to change the world; now they wanted to entertain it.

In 1974 Jay set up a talent agency for people with the kind of talent that conventional agents and managers would never touch, i.e. the kind that never made money. He called his agency Creative Artist Liberated (CAL) and it was to be the world's first 'anti-talent agency'. Jay got himself an office in a squat in Kentish Town, some new stationery, a secretary and a motto: *We Take the Sting Out of Success and Put the Fun Back into Failure.*

Jay's clients included a series of distinguished losers and lost causes. The first of his relaunched rejects was a black, middle-aged, ex-male-prostitute, ex-junkie and flamboyant homosexual from New York called Jason Holiday. Holiday was the subject of a celebrated underground film by Shirley Clark in 1967, *Portrait of Jason.* Jay got Jason an evening at the King's Head theatre in Islington, where he regaled the audience with his life and louche times.

Then there was Eddie Linden, a Glaswegian, ex-communist, homosexual and lapsed Catholic with a drinking problem and a passion for poetry. Jay published his autobiography entitled *Who Is Eddie Linden?* Judging by the sales nobody wanted to find out. But Jay didn't really worry about sales, until he was on the point of going broke. He believed that these marginal men like

Jason and Eddie, whom the world had labelled 'losers', had interesting stories that should be heard.

The most talentless of all CAL's clients was a young American kung fu stripper called Doshin, who recited poetry and sang while she took off her clothes. She had no talent, no beauty and no poetry, only a prehensile need for attention. Doshin could have been Madonna's ugly kid sister – one with a freakish lack of talent. But she was an early example of the wannabe who has to be noticed.

Doshin made her London debut at the launch party of CAL, where Jay, in the manner of Ed Sullivan, introduced her as a 'future star'. She then sang in a croaky, whiny, out-of-tune voice one of her songs, 'Better Blatant Than Latent', and gyrated around like a go-go dancer before a finale of kung fu kicks.

It was like one of those pitiful acts we see all the time these days on 'talent' shows like *The X Factor*. Her act finished to an embarrassed silence, followed by a fast, muted round of mercy applause. I didn't know whom I felt more sorry for: her or Jay. I never understood why he did it. Either he was motivated by some sadistic desire to watch this girl bomb in public or, even more horrible to contemplate, he really believed that she had talent.

☆

It wasn't just the dreamers, no-hopers and misfits that Jay managed who wanted to express themselves creatively, but those that society labelled as losers, delinquents, dole-queue scroungers, fuck-ups and failures – in short the punk generation. 'We are all extremely ugly people. We were the outcasts, the unwanted,' said the lead singer of the Sex Pistols, John Lydon, at the time.

That English cult of the loser found a new lease of life in punk rock. The very name punk – an American term for a worthless person, a criminal, a thug – reflected an embrace of loserdom. For punks loserdom was a mark of integrity and authenticity. Punk designer Vivienne Westwood – then married to the Pistols' manager Malcolm McLaren – said, 'Punks admitted they were victims or brain-damaged in a sense, and that was heroic in itself and clever.'

Being a working-class kid on the dole, with no educational qualifications, no job and no future, had something that money and class couldn't buy: *street cred.* Now there's a concept that has totally disappeared in our age of celebrity. Back then it meant that you were working class and 'real' and in touch with what was happening on 'the street' and with 'the kids'. Street cred was an unbeatable mix of class authenticity and pop-culture cool. It made you a noble savage who could survive the urban jungle; and it was something we nice, well-educated middle-class kids could never acquire.

In the same way that Hippy London had pushed the leading figures of Swinging London out into the cultural cold, so punk told anyone associated with Hippy London to piss off. They hated hippies, the sixties and all that middle-class-social-worker-compassionate-consensus-liberalism with the kind of visceral loathing that Norman Tebbit and the Thatcherites would exhibit in the eighties.

One reason for their hatred was that hippy was

considered so horribly middle class. The Sixties promise of a pop culture as an alternative to the divisions of class died with punk. Things got so bad that middle-class Joe Strummer, after he joined the Clash, refused to speak to his old hippyish friends from his squat days.

We middle-class boys who had grown up on rock culture assumed that there would be a place somewhere within punk for us. (And a lucky few like Malcolm McLaren and film maker Julian Temple did find acceptance.) We would never pass as proper punks, but hoped that at least we could be fellow travellers. OK, we had inflicted terrible things upon the world like Jethro Tull and Emerson, Lake and Palmer – for which we were truly sorry. We might be too old and too middle class to be actual punks, but we were punks at heart. Honest. Had we not been rebels too? Had we not done drugs? Had we not fought the law at Grosvenor Square in '68, and the law won? Weren't we all part of a great rebellious tradition that went from beats to Teds to mods to hippies?

To which the punks answered: *no, fuck off, you middle-class wankers.* What we didn't grasp was that punk was a tribe. As for drugs, we discovered we had been taking the *wrong* sort of drugs, i.e. too much acid, not enough speed. We soon realized that we weren't wanted in the great punk party of 1976. We weren't even allowed to write about it! Punks used to go up to Jon Savage, author of *England's Dreaming*, the definitive history of punk, and say, 'You can't write about punk because you went to Cambridge.'

☆

One night I was in bed with an American girl having sex when I heard my mother charging up the stairs screaming, 'Cosmo! Cosmo!' She began to bang furiously on the door. 'You've got to come down here immediately!'

What could it be? Was there a fire? Was Jay having a heart attack?

Before I could say anything she stuck her head in, ignored the girl and said, 'Johnny Rotten is here!' and with that she shut the door and rushed downstairs.

I leapt out of bed.

'Where are you going?' said the American girl.

'I'm going downstairs to see Johnny Rotten!'

I told her we had to get dressed, hurry down and see Rotten.

She said nothing and rolled over. I could tell she was hurt that I was abandoning her for the star below. At the time I thought she was just this square American girl. Americans didn't understand punk; she probably didn't even know who Johnny Rotten was. Poor girl. Now I think: what a cool girl she was. She stayed in bed and I ran off into the night to peep at the pop star like some dumb star-struck fan.

Rotten and a group of his mates had gatecrashed my parents' New Year's Day party (they had heard of it through friends of Miles's, a band of girls known as the Slits). When I got down they were getting stuck into the booze and food, and sneering at the guests.

Jay was overcome with excitement. He hadn't had a name as big as this in the front room since Barbra Streisand had arrived a year or two earlier. Jay tried hard to engage Rotten in lively discussion about Jay. What was said isn't clear, but you can bet Jay did his act with Rotten, who wasn't having any of it. Eventually he told Miles, 'Keep your dad away from me, he's getting on my nerves.'

Poor Rotten. No sooner had he escaped the routines of Jay than he got an earful of Fran. He was up in her room hanging out when she decided to read him her poem entitled 'The Ballad of Johnny Rotten'. It was all about how he would end up just another fat rock-and-roll star like Elvis. She had some chutzpah, reading that to the intimidating Rotten, who was surrounded by his adoring crowd of hangers-on. I expected him to spit out some nasty reply about the opinions of old fucking hippies but he simply said, 'Madame, I will have great satisfaction in proving you wrong.'

Punk always had an ambiguous relationship with stardom. Like the hippies they despised, there was an egalitarian anti-star strain in punk. They raged against the old rock stars for being old, fat and out of touch with the kids. 'They're bullshit people. They live in their rich mansions, fucking completely out of touch with reality,' said Johnny Rotten.

Some would say that Rotten was merely being hypocritical. 'Johnny loved being famous, probably even more than I did,' noted Bob Geldof. While Boy George claimed, 'The new punk stars were as every bit as pretentious and puffed-up as the seventies rock dinosaurs they despised.'

That night at my parents', when the booze ran out so

did Rotten and his crew. Off they went into the night for another party. I went back to the girl, full of apologies and anecdotes, but she was gone. On the pillow was a note that read: No Future.

Punk's enduring legacy was something more than music; it created the idea that anyone could form a band, get on stage and express themselves. A lack of talent, beauty, or craftsmanship was no longer a barrier to performing. One of the great beliefs that kept the old rock-star structure intact was the idea of musicianship. Rock music had grown up since its primitive beginnings in the 1950s and become a musically accomplished form. Rock musicians paid their dues, learnt their craft and developed their talent over years of touring and recording. Before punk it was assumed that you had to be an accomplished player to be part of a band. This was the time when progressive rock bands (Yes, ELP, King Crimson) were proudly displaying musical pyrotechnics. But punk said fuck all that, and advocated a rock primitivism that put music within the reach of anyone. A punk fanzine called *Sideburns* carried a page containing a diagram of the guitar chords A, E and G, and the command: 'Now go and form a band.' Could it really be that easy? Yes, said Sid Vicious: 'You just pick a chord, go twang and you've got music.'

In place of talent and musical aptitude, Punk believed in *attitude* and the willingness to give it a go. And this didn't apply just to music. Punk's DIY ethic meant you could start your own fanzine, open your own club or create your own fashion line. This have-a-go ethos influenced an entire generation of young people who would become pop stars in the 1980s. One of these was a young boy from South Wales called Steve Harrington, who became Steve Strange, co-founder of the Blitz club and lead singer of Visage.

Strange would later write of the Pistols' impact on his life, 'The Sex Pistols had the biggest effect on me. I saw those four lads and thought that anyone could get on stage and be in a band. They were saying "we can't play" and neither could I, but now it didn't matter.'

This must be one of the great turning points in pop music and youth culture. It's hard to think of any other cultural form in which you could be so lacking in ability. You can't play football if you don't know how to play football. You can't be a writer who can't write, at least in the technical sense. There had been plenty of pop stars who had made it despite the fact they hadn't actually played on their own hit records, but they never said it didn't matter.

As a movement, Punk quickly burned out. Many of the original members became disillusioned and disgusted when the vulgar pogoing masses started to move in on the scene. As a musical movement it was dead by 1978, but as a state of mind it's never gone away for its can-do philosophy has inspired hundreds of talentless individuals to demand their fifteen minutes of fame.

The creative democracy championed by punk was also taken up by disco. Like punk, disco believed that you had to get off your arse ... but only to boogie on down. It pushed forward the idea that even the common man and woman – who didn't have a discernible talent – could be a star, at least on the dance floor.

It's a sentiment found in Sly and the Family Stone's single 'Everybody is a Star' and Sylvester's 1979 disco hit 'Stars (everybody is one)' which proclaimed, 'There's a party feeling that outshines them all / if you're here you've earned it / And can't you hear that call / Everybody is a star.'

Unlike rock gigs, where a few distant stars strut around the stage, the real centre stage in a disco was the dance floor. It was here that the ordinary man or woman could shine and become a disco star, which was the idea at the heart of the film *Saturday Night Fever*. 'It made regular club-goers feel very important; they didn't have to look to a stage or a star to be entertained,' said Candi Staton ('Young Hearts Run Free'), 'everybody was a star.'

Music journalist Albert Goldman spotted the democratic promise of disco when he wrote: 'Thousands of young men and women have the looks, the clothes, the hair styling, the drugs, the personal magnetism, the self-confidence and the history of conquest that proclaim a star. The one thing they lack – talent – is precisely what is most lacking in those other, nearly identical, young people whom the world has acclaimed as stars. Never in the history of showbiz has the gap between amateur and professional been so small. Never in the history of the world has there been such a rage for exhibitionism. The question therefore is, what are we going to do with all these beautiful show-offs? Disco provides the best answer to date.'

☆

In 1978, Britain's most 'beautiful show-offs' could be seen at a club called Billy's on Meard Street in London's Soho district. Set up by Steve Strange and Rusty Egan, the club had a special Bowie Night on Tuesdays. The flyer advertising the club summed up the sort of people they were looking for: 'Fame, Fame, Jump Aboard the Night Train/Fame, Fame, Fame. What's your name?'

Billy's was essentially the Me decade on parade, a darkened basement underworld of wall-to-wall poseurs, self-obsessed exhibitionists and nocturnal narcissists. Here, the extravagance of fancy dress met the exoticism of the freak show. There were kids in tuxedos and wing collars, diamanté brooches, taffeta gowns, pillbox hats, Cossack outfits with harlequin lips. You would have found famous faces on the club scene like Boy George (in a kimono looking like a geisha), Claire the Hair (dressed like Bo Peep) and a beautiful blond boy called Marilyn in a skirt.

From Bowie such people had learned the art of style and attention-seeking; but it was punk that had taught them they too could form bands and be pop stars. And in the eighties many of them – Boy George, Spandau Ballet, Sade – would do just that.

For the moment they were locked out of the celebrity world. The old celebrity establishment – Mick, Bianca, Andy and Rod – still ruled. According to socialite and party-giver Nicky Haslam, seventies London kept the celebrity riff-raff out of the better parties and clubs. 'There were no VIP rooms (a good thing), no clipboard Nazis, no guest lists or plus ones. You were either invited or you weren't. And to make the front page the next day you had to be truly famous, like Elizabeth Taylor.'

But this type of exclusive society was already becoming a thing of the past. Commentators at the time were convinced that fame was being democratized, and complained of the invasion of the B-list people.

A new magazine called *Ritz*, a prototype of the celebrity mags of the eighties, appeared in November 1976. Based on Andy Warhol's *Interview* magazine, *Ritz* was a mix of high glamour and gossip. Tina Brown said it was full of 'overexcited hairdressers in fancy dress' and Peter York declared, 'Absolutely anyone could be in *Ritz*.'

What Brown and York meant by 'anyone' didn't mean the average person in the street, but the average person at a nightclub opening: restaurateur Peter Langan, journalist Molly Parkin, hairdresser Ricci Burns, writer Shirley Conran, *Playboy* manager Victor Lownes and Joan Collins. Such people formed what was called cafe society, which had its own It Girls like Viviane Ventura and Myna Bird.

For the most part ordinary people were not considered interesting – either to read about or watch on television, unless they appeared in the soaps. Their function was to be the appreciative audience, the contestants in quiz shows and vox-pop interviews in programmes like Esther Rantzen's *That's Life!*

Then in 1974 ordinary people got their first real break. Paul Watson's fly-on-the-wall documentary called *The Family* proved to be the big ratings hit of the year. It was just the story of an ordinary family in Reading. In retrospect, it marked the birth of reality TV and a new chapter in the history of fame.

10

Baby, Put Out A Line

In 1984, at a book launch, I saw a young woman sitting on a sofa who was all legs, pale skin, flaming-red lips, and was wrapped tight in a black bandage of a dress. She looked like a film noir beauty and had the strange, nervy manner of a shy alien. It was the journalist Julie Burchill.

To readers of the *NME* during the punk years, Julie Burchill and her husband, Tony Parsons, were legends: the 'hip young gunslingers' of punk. She was currently writing a brilliant column for *The Face*, which I never missed. You looked forward to a new Burchill column like the album release of your favourite band.

I had to speak to her, but the prospect of going over and introducing myself was terrifying. I imagined that I personified everything she hated: Americans, liberals, hippies, and the middle class. I thought of Jay and how he would handle it. He'd have gone straight towards her like a heat-seeking missile, never for a second imagining that she wouldn't want to meet him.

I took a deep breath and launched myself in her direction. 'Hello,' I said, 'I'm Cosmo Landesman . . .'

'I *know* who you are,' she squeaked.

It was a glorious movie moment.

Her words echoed in my head: *I know who you are . . .*
I know who you are . . . I know who . . .

Unbelievable! She Who Must Be Read, the hippest
girl in London, knew *my* name, knew *my* work. I had
arrived. I WAS A SOMEBODY!

And then she said, 'You're the son of that couple
with the open marriage. I read about them in *Cosmopoli-*
tan magazine when I was a little girl.'

I kept smiling and gave a little forced chuckle that
said: *Why, isn't that the funniest, most adorable thing in the*
world! But inside . . .

I wasn't surprised that Julie didn't say: *Yes, I know*
who you are. You're Cosmo Landesman the journalist. I
didn't exactly have a hot career in the media. I was in
my late twenties and I hadn't even got a toe in what
was then called Fleet Street. But in those days people
didn't have 'hot careers in the media', you were simply
a journalist or a broadcaster. (We didn't have hot
people, hot films, hot records, either – all that came
later in the decade.) I may have been a failure in the
seventies but nobody really noticed it, and even if they
had they wouldn't have said anything; such talk was
taboo. And anyway, the belief that Britain was in irre-
versible decline meant that in some sense we were all
failures together. Some of us were just more conspicuous
at failing than others.

I had drifted into the eighties, carrying on in much
the same aimless way as I had in the late seventies. I
was moving from one small rented room to the next.
For work I was managing Miles's latest band, Miles

Over Matter, with very little success, and doing a bit of editorial work for Jay Landesman Ltd.

I still had dreams of being a journalist and writing a novel. I made the occasional pitch to magazines, but no bites followed. Most of my time was spent being unhappy. For me, the early eighties were an emotional monsoon of tears. I wept for an entire year. I wept on my way to parties, I wept coming home from parties. I wept at breakfast. I'd often have a pre-lunch weep and a post-nap weep. And then at night there were tears before bedtime.

I wept because I felt I was a failure. This was odd, because I had been brought up to reject the straight world's idea of success and failure. If anyone should have been able to treat those two impostors, as Kipling had called them, with indifference, it should have been me.

I felt like a failure for one simple reason: I *was* a failure. I didn't have a girlfriend, I had very few friends and I was lonely. I didn't have a real job or any prospect of one. I had never thought about making plans, supporting myself and all that other 'square stuff'. I had been brought up to 'go with the flow' and focus on the 'here and now'. So when that big wave of weirdness receded and the glorious revolution of '68 fizzled out, I found myself drifting. Now at the start of the eighties I felt like I was drowning.

Things got better as the decade began to take shape. I started writing book reviews for a trade journal called *Publishing News*, and then for a literary journal called *Books and Bookmen*. In 1984 I got my first column in the

Literary Review. It was called 'Journal of a Literary Contender' and was a satirical account of a failed young writer trying to make it into the literary big time.

I rented a small room in a big house on the Kings Road that belonged to a friend, and lived off a little bit of money that Fran's father had left me. And thanks to my job at the *Literary Review* I had access to three or four book launches and parties every night. I was meeting people and making friends. And most important of all, I was suddenly popular with women. I stopped weeping and became happy with my lot. I honestly thought I was lucky that I had made something of my life.

Then the real eighties came along and whispered in my ear: *loser*.

By the end of the seventies people had grown tired of failure and were disgusted at the nation's economic and social decline, and so in 1979 we got Mrs Thatcher in to clean up the mess. At the heart of the Thatcher project was a rejection of the politics and culture of loserdom. Until she came along it was widely believed that the task of British politics was the 'orderly management of decline', by which was meant that it was acceptable to allow Britain to go down the toilet provided it was done in a civilized way.

But for Mrs Thatcher failure was not an option. She found the very idea repugnant. 'I can't bear Britain in decline,' she once said, as though it was personally wounding. For Mrs Thatcher and her people there was nothing funny or heroic about failure. Her solution to the threat of decline was to create an 'enterprise culture' that would revitalize the nation. Britain had plenty of enterprise, it was the culture bit that was missing. She and her supporters believed that Britain had been ruled by an upper-middle-class elite who were hostile to wealth and its creation. The Thatcher gang were going to roll up their sleeves and sweep away that whole 'decadent' affection for underdogs, heroic failures and lovable losers.

What Thatcher and her supporters wanted to do was to 'liberate the individual' from the state, collectivism, high rates of taxation and the cultural tastes of the elite. But they also wanted to liberate the individual from a state of mind, one that was embarrassed about success and guilty about making money. Once liberated, the dynamic individualism that would follow would enable Britain to be great again.

That was the theory – and for guys like me it was a bit scary. London society decided that being cute and funny wasn't enough; you had to be a winner. The charming men about town realized that the party was over and scrambled to relaunch themselves with proper jobs in publishing, journalism and the arts. You had to have a glittering career (or at least a dozen impressive-sounding projects on the go) for it was the decade of Project Man, or as the satirist Craig Brown called them, the Projectiles – young men about town who hustled, did lunch and talked earnestly about their latest projects – none of which ever seemed to reach the light of day.

We all hustled and hyped ourselves for one simple reason: to be a success. Success in the eighties could be measured and quantified in terms of your income, your house and your style of living. The key thing that success brought was money. The great English silence that surrounded the subject of wealth was finally broken. Money had always talked, but in the eighties you no longer had to pretend you couldn't hear what it was saying. The City, to use the jargon of the time, was sexy. The business of making money was now neither dull nor vulgar; it was exciting and fashionable.

Perhaps the most important thing that money changed in the eighties was the way we looked and talked about art and culture. What excited people was no longer the work itself – the film, the novel, the album – but the magical numbers behind the work. Statistics got sexy: the size of the advance for a book, the first week of business at the box office for the latest blockbuster, the advance orders for a record album – these were the things that mattered. Artists became businessmen, businessmen were hailed as the new artists and advertising was the new art.

☆

For me the eighties really began when I met two people who were to personify that decade for me. One of them was Julie Burchill, the other was Toby Young.

In 1984 Michael Young and his family had moved into the house two doors down from my parents' home in Duncan Terrace. Michael Young, then a Labour peer, was one of the co-authors of the 1945 Labour Party manifesto, and the man who invented the term 'meritocracy'. He was the very embodiment of the enlightened liberal social entrepreneur, a man who had dedicated his life to the public good. His wife, Sasha, was a novelist and painter. Together they embodied the liberal establishment that Thatcher and her kind so loathed.

The Youngs had a nineteen-year-old son called Toby, who looked like a young Kevin Bacon. On summer afternoons I'd see him hanging out of the front window of the family home, and he'd yell 'Hey, hippy!' or sing that old Nazi favourite, 'Tomorrow Belongs To Me', as I walked past. But his taunts were always delivered with a smile.

Naturally we began to hang out. I was partly horrified and partly amused by this crazy kid. Toby had a style I had never encountered before: the Right-Wing Brat style. It took an impish delight in puncturing liberal pieties and mocking hippies, feminists and do-gooders. In other words, all that his parents and their progressive-minded friends held dear.

In the eighties liberal-baiting became one of the great national sports. It had first become fashionable during the years of punk. The punks had spat in the face of the consensus, classless style of the liberal intelligentsia. But unlike the educated Young they did not take aim with quotations from Adam Smith and Leo Straus.

Irreverent and impish, Toby spoke openly of his longing for those dark forbidden things that children of progressive parents were not meant to want: money, success and fame. I realize that this must make him sound awful, but back then there was something refreshing and daring about his candour. He was the first member of what Keynes had called 'the educated bourgeoisie' I had ever met who was totally open about his fascination with celebrities.

In those days it was the mark of an intelligent person that they looked down on Hollywood stars and celebrities. But not Toby. He embraced mass culture and its garish icons as a form of rebellion from the good taste of his class. I first saw the full extent of his celebrity obsession when at a party at my parents' house he was talking about his hero Arnold Schwarzenegger and how he was the person he'd most like to meet in the world. An ex-hippy woman at the table thought he must have been joking. 'No,' said Toby, 'I'd even have sex with him!'

Everyone at the table was shocked.

It was as if he were daring you to drop all the high-minded posturing and give in to the secret lust your liberal self was repulsed by. Yes, at times he verged on the obnoxious but he managed to pull back at the last moment and make you laugh instead of groan.

The thing about Toby I spotted straight away was that he shared the Landesman hunger for attention and affirmation. At any social event he always worked the room in an attempt to be the centre of attention, and was constantly reporting on his social success or failure. For an ambitious and brash child of the eighties he had that Landesman obsession with failure and had built a whole routine and persona around it. 'I was born with negative charisma,' he'd say. 'People just don't like me. They hate me on sight. If only they'd bother to get to know the real me – then they'd really have someone to loathe!'

☆

Not long after meeting Toby Young, I found myself having an affair with Julie Burchill. After our first afternoon of cold vodka and hot sex a voice inside my head said: don't fall for this woman; she will only break your heart. After our second afternoon of cold vodka and hot sex the voice inside my head said: don't fall for this woman, she's crazy, immoral and treacherous. She's mad, bad and dangerous to sleep with. After our third afternoon of cold vodka and hot sex the voice inside my head said: don't fall for this woman. For God's sake wake up Cosmo, this broad is a sociopath, a Stalinist with Nietzschean tendencies who drinks like a fish, fucks like a rabbit and eats nice middle-class Jewish boys like you for breakfast. You have been warned: STAY THE FUCK AWAY!'

Reader, I married that woman.

☆

OK, I admit that at first I was thrilled the new woman in my life was *the* Julie Burchill. But that buzz of her celebrity didn't last long. Instead, I fell in love and by 1985 we were married.

Friends and family were happy for me. But they were even happier for themselves, for now they had a celebrity in their midst. Toby's reaction on hearing of our affair was: 'How the fuck did you pull someone as cool and famous as Julie?' What he was really saying was: how the fuck did someone like you who is neither *cool* nor *famous* pull someone who is both? To him it was a mystery, something unnatural, or to use a popular word at the time, *unsound*.

Toby was delighted by the relationship, for it worked to his advantage. He soon became the New Best Friend of Miss Burchill, and with this newfound status came an entrée into hip London society. What did she see in him? He made her laugh. And she liked his whole media-brat style, the way he got up the noses of all the hip people on the scene.

He wasn't the only one to be curious (or to benefit) from our relationship. Everyone – my friends, my friends' parents, my parents and the friends of my parents – was eager to meet Julie. Even Toby's dad Michael, a man who had met Franklin D. Roosevelt, was curious to meet the great Julie Burchill and called by for an audience.

But the enthusiasm of my friends was nothing compared to the reaction of my parents. They too had been fans of her work. Although from a working-class background, and having parents of modest means, Julie came into the Landesman family with the greatest dowry of all: her celebrity.

My mother was delighted and took to quoting her famous daughter-in-law every chance she got: at dinner parties, in interviews and at live gigs. Miles was excited by Julie's *NME* pedigree, and viewed her as an endless source of endorsements and plugs for a succession of bands. He wasted no time in asking for quotes and free tickets to concerts, a habit he continues to this day.

But it was Jay who was the most star-struck of them all. It was as if he had won the pools. He couldn't wait to tell everyone the good news. In the early days of our marriage he underwent a personality transformation, and from being my father became this other creature: Julie Burchill's Father-in-Law.

Julie and I first got a hint of what was happening to Jay when she got a letter from Tony Parsons during the early days of our elopement. Among other things, he mentioned that a friend of his had been in a pub and heard Jay 'boasting' about his connection to Julie. The friend had offered to 'sort him out' as a favour to Tony. Tony, however, was far too cool for that course of action. In the months to come I would curse Tony for not giving his mate the nod.

Once we were married, things intensified. Jay organized a small dinner party. He claimed that he was worried about the quality of our social life, but he was really doing it so that he could show off his famous daughter-in-law. To be fair, it wasn't just her celebrity status that appealed to him. He admired her originality of mind, her wit and her ability to drink like an old-fashioned writer.

Also, she produced exactly the kind of controversial copy he'd championed back in the days of *Neurotica*. She was his new Gershon Legman – the brilliant writer from Jay's *Neurotica* days – and he wanted to hang out with us and be one of Julie's gang. I assumed that Jay would soon calm down once the novelty wore off, but his Julie mania only grew worse. The first time it really angered me was when I attended a Labour Party rally with Julie, who was then political correspondent of the *Mail on Sunday*. We arrived at the venue and were met by a PR who told us of a strange encounter with an American man claiming to be Julie Burchill's father-in-law and demanding to be let in. Julie and I looked at each other in disbelief.

But this was just the start. Soon Jay began dropping

her name all over town – at parties, pubs and when confronted by doormen and head waiters for whom the name Jay Landesman failed to ring any bells.

Julie and I weren't the only ones to suffer; it wasn't long before his friends began to tire of his obsession. The journalist John Diamond told me that he wished Jay wouldn't go on about Julie all the time. Others complained that he was turning into a 'Julie bore'. Julie, on the other hand, was totally cool about it. 'I think it's funny,' she said.

I wanted to be cool about it too. I tried to see the funny side and regard Jay's Julie thing as a quirky, lovable, eccentric trait. But I couldn't. Here I was, grown up, married and living in my own flat with a child of my own (we had a son in 1986), so I assumed I'd finally escaped the embarrassment of my parents. Now this. It occurred to me that I would never stop being embarrassed by my parents.

I grew tired of people turning to me to discuss their problems with Jay. I was sick of being the child who had failed to curb the antisocial behaviour of his adolescent parent. What was I supposed to do? Go and say to Jay, 'OK, Dad, you're grounded. Now hand over the car keys and your membership to the Groucho Club?'

Eventually, however, I faced up to it and decided we needed to talk. I turned up at his place and found Jay on the phone harassing some poor book editor to review Fran's latest slim volume.

Jay: What's up, kid?

Me: I'll get straight to the point. It's embarrassing the

way you go on about Julie and try and use her name. You've got to cool it.

Jay: What are you talking about?

Me: It's not just me. Even your friends say that you're out of control.

Jay: Oh, that's crazy!

Me: No, it's a fact.

Jay: I would never try and use Julie's name. I'll have you know that the name Jay Landesman is still good enough in this town. Take my advice: don't take yourself so seriously.

He always pulled that line on me. He gave that little laugh of his and I left fuming. I also felt kind of sad for him. He was somebody in his own right who was a funny and interesting man. Jay didn't need Julie's name to impress people, did he?

I spoke to Fran about my Jay problem and she said, 'Ah well, he's getting old and wants a little attention and to be fussed over. I've got my career, you've got Julie and what has he got? So what does it hurt if he talks about his famous daughter-in-law a little?'

'I guess you're right,' I replied.

As I left she gave me a hug and handed me a piece of paper. 'Here, this will make you feel better. It's a poem I wrote about Julie.' I could tell by the look in her eye that she too was besotted with her daughter-in-law.

In retrospect I wonder if Jay regarded Julie as the son he never had: the brilliant, famous son who was a glittering success and thus added lustre to the Landesman name. If Jay was conflicted about his own success – or lack of it – he was equally ambiguous about that of his children.

During the early eighties, I ran into a young journalist whom both Jay and I knew. He reported to me that during a conversation, Jay had said something like this: *Can you help my son? Poor schmo he can't get a girl, he doesn't have a job. Can't you take him out for a drink and give him a few tips on how to have some fun in life?*

When I confronted Jay with this he said it wasn't true, but the way the guy reported what Jay had said had the ring of authenticity. 'You made me seem like such a loser!' I complained.

Of course, I knew I was a loser, but you don't expect your dad to go around and do a whole 'My Son, the Loser' routine.

He looked totally baffled by my accusation. 'But I'm so proud of you . . .' he said and began to weep. And that got me going too. We sat there, father and son, both feeling like losers, blubbing like something out of the film *Terms of Endearment*.

I think he was proud of his children because they were so much like him: creative but never commercial. He later wrote in his memoir *Jaywalking*: 'Their luck wasn't any better than mine as they drifted through their various pursuits. (I felt a certain gratification that they hadn't strayed from the Landesman credo of putting the fun back into failure) . . . Cosmo's only accomplishment in life up till then had been making an art form out of mixing the perfect Martini . . .'

☆

By the early eighties Miles had regained the confidence he'd lost after the collapse of Renoir. He was working in BOY, a punk clothes shop on the Kings Road, and living with a beautiful girl called Sarah Stockbridge in a funky one-room basement flat nearby. (She would subsequently leave him and become a star model for Vivienne Westwood.)

But Miles was optimistic about his new band, Miles Over Matter. They were part of what was being called the 'new psychedelic movement' and one of their songs had made it onto a compilation album called *A Bigger Splash*. Demos were recorded, and as a favour to Miles I helped write press releases about how we were on the brink of a 'new summer of '67' and the band would never rest until they had 'turned on the whole world'. I wrote, 'Psychedelia was the new punk.' The band supported Hawkwind at the Rainbow and played the usual collection of small rock venues, but eventually it all fizzled out and they split in 1982.

One door closed and another opened. This one was a trapdoor. Miles Over Matter gave way to Jozo and the Fiends. Once again there were endless rehearsals and Miles would be full of excitement over whichever track had been finished that day. The only problem was the band itself: a third-rate art-rock outfit fronted by Jozo, a girl with an aggressive lack of talent. I told Miles he should call the band 'Bozo and the Fiends'. They were too awful for words, and this time when Miles tried to press-gang me into writing press releases I refused.

Miles, on the other hand, insisted that they were brilliant, and he called me regularly to let me know about their forthcoming gigs. 'You gotta come man, I swear it will be brilliant. Please.' I would promise to go, but never did. Jozo and the Fiends soon fell apart. But was Miles downhearted? No way, he just got another band together. Jack of Hearts was a leather-and-mascara nouveau glam band whose repertoire included covers of old T.Rex and Alice Cooper hits. Miles reckoned they were amazing. I got roped in again to work on the press releases. 'Glam was the new psychedelia,' I declared.

Jack of Hearts folded before the year was over. Things went downhill for Miles. He went from playing in bands to hanging out with bands, to being a roadie for bands like Curiosity Killed the Cat. Yet he was always full of enthusiasm for his latest role – even when this meant being an extra in a Madness video. 'Brilliant,' he declared. I felt sorry for him at times, but he never seemed to be sorry for himself. He was always just one demo away from his dream.

For a time things weren't going well for Fran either. The publisher Hutchinson had rejected her new book of verse – more witty and wry observations on the failure of love. Plus she was suffering from writer's block and felt that she couldn't compete with a new generation of emerging poets. She told Jay, 'The only thing that cheers me up these days is the thought of knocking myself off.'

At the start of our affair Julie and I had taken refuge at my parents' house, much to the delight and terror of my folks. But when, after some months, we moved out they found themselves alone together at the dinner table, having to deal with the nightmare of dead air. All the attention they got from other people made them feel lonely when they were together. Instead of sharing affection, they shared their anxieties.

Jay: Am I interesting to you any more?

Fran: Do I bore you?

Jay: Are you tired of my old stories?

Fran: Are you tired of mine?

They chewed their rice, struggled not to talk about themselves, fell into silence and went to their separate beds.

☆

In 1983 my father's mistress, Pamela, appeared in a BBC documentary called *The Mistress* where she talked about her affair with Jay, though he was never named. Two years later it was Fran's turn to talk about her husband's philandering and her own affairs in another BBC documentary, *The Infernal Triangle*.

At first Fran had reservations about appearing, but Pamela was encouraging: 'You'll look beautiful on the box, in your bangles and beads, lying on your bed and telling your side of the story . . . it's fun. I enjoyed all the attention.'

When I heard the news of the documentary idea I went to see Fran and said, 'No, please . . . please! I beg you on humanitarian grounds, don't go on television and talk about your open marriage!' She said she'd think about it, but I suspected that she really thought that it was just me being my same old uptight self. Maybe it was, but I also had a dislike of people outside my family who went around exposing their private lives in public.

According to Jay, he told Fran that she shouldn't do

it on the grounds that they didn't need the publicity. If that's true, then it must have been the only time in his entire life that the line 'we don't need the publicity' had ever passed his lips. He maintains to this day that the only reason Fran did it was because she had a new agent who insisted that the publicity exposure would be invaluable.

On the day that Fran was being filmed by the BBC crew, sitting on her bed talking about her marriage, Jay arrived home with his new mistress – a twenty-two-year-old publicist for the Girl Guides who went by the name of Gigi. On seeing the cameras she immediately fled. Jay stayed. The cameras were rolling and it was too good an opportunity to miss. Although it was Fran's moment, Jay was ready for his close-up. 'I stuck around hoping to soak up some attention that might be left over from Fran's performance,' he explained.

The programme was widely reviewed. Mary Kenny in the *Daily Mail* said Fran was a 'kookie, likable American' who 'seems devil-may-care about extramarital affairs that she and her husband – raffish Soho publisher Jay Landesman – have enjoyed during their 30 years together.'

Byron Rogers in the *Sunday Times* called Fran 'a game old trout, revelling in the attention of the camera crew and producer'. Rogers went on to confess his amazement at the personal revelations of the film's participants. 'There are people out there, people with families who can be identified, who are quite prepared to appear on television and reveal their most intimate secrets. And there seems to be an inexhaustible supply of them. As the Sundance Kid said of the pursuing posse, "For Chrissake, who are these people?" '

Rogers's sense of amazement belongs to a time when people could still be shocked by the desire to flaunt your private life in public. It's a sign of how much things have changed that no one today would ask the question 'Who are these people?'

Of course I didn't watch the programme. I did my best to avoid any television previews of it and made sure I didn't read newspaper reviews. Julie was forbidden to mention it and I assumed Toby would be too involved in his own media career to notice it. So I felt safe and detached from the whole thing. If my parents wanted to go on television and make fools of themselves that was their business, it had nothing to do with me. I was safe in the sanctuary of my own family life.

No sooner had the programme finished than the phone started ringing. Toby was in there first.

Toby [*disguising his voice*]: Hello, is this the son of the famous open marriage? Yes, I'm doing a piece on parental slags and would like to interview you for *Old Hippy Slags Monthly*.

Me: Ha-bloody-ha.

Toby: How was *that* for embarrassing? Christ, you must want to die!

Me: I didn't watch it. Was it that bad?

Toby: Cos, honestly it was *worse* than bad. I actually felt pity for you, buddy. The good news is, I've made you a videotape!

Me: How thoughtful.

Toby: Hey, what are friends for?

Click.

The following days I discovered that all my good friends and dozens of casual acquaintances had seen the programme and they all wanted to share their reactions and feelings with me, and were eager for me to share my reactions and feelings with them. I suddenly found myself thrust into group therapy. I even met one of my mother's ex-lovers, who had seen the programme and insisted on telling me about the time they went to a hotel room in Piccadilly 'to write our names on the sheets'.

'Thank you for sharing that with me,' I said. 'Got any more hilarious anecdotes about fucking my mother?'

'Yes, I have actually,' he said. 'There was this time when . . .'

I made my excuses and left.

☆

You would have thought that the public's fascination for the rich and famous in the 1980s would have meant that my parents were to suffer from a lack of media attention. On the contrary, you couldn't keep them out of the spotlight. Every time Fran had a new book of verse published by Jay she would be profiled in women's magazines (like *Cosmopolitan* and *She*) as the witty, irrepressible Fran Landesman . . . with the open marriage.

Fran took another stab at stardom when she did a one-woman show entitled *Confessions of a Middle-Aged Juvenile Delinquent*. To my amazement her show got rave notices, and once again the old dream returned. 'We are hoping that this West End run will lead us back to Broadway,' Jay told the *Stage* magazine.

Instead of Broadway, Fran was back on the London poetry circuit. Only this time she had a new accompanist on acoustic guitar: Miles. While she wailed, he went wild, banging his head in time to the music. They got their first review together in *New Society*. The reviewer quoted one member of the public who saw Miles perform a song on his own and said, 'Come back Bob Dylan all is forgiven . . . this bloke is appalling.'

For a man like Jay with a motto like *Let's take the sting out of success and put the fun back into failure*, things were much harder. Heroic failures and lovable losers had gone out of fashion. When the journalist Stephen Pile published his *Book of Heroic Failures* in 1979 it became a best-seller. Midway during the 1980s he published the follow-up, *More Heroic Failures*, and it sold poorly. 'That sort of humour changed with the arrival of Mrs Thatcher,' Pile told me. 'The moment you say this is a meritocracy and you have to compete and win . . . English self-deprecation can't survive that.'

Jay had a kind of publishing genius. He could do everything – find original authors, generate publicity and throw fantastic parties – except publish books that would sell. He belonged to that dying breed of small independent publishers who somehow managed to always stay afloat, until the eighties came along. By 1982 we were in our death throes, although you would never have guessed it listening to Jay. He would sit at his desk in our office on Wardour Street, like a WWII commander in his bunker; only he now commanded an army of just one. He would often break into morale-boosting speeches. Sipping coffee, a cigarette dangling from his mouth, he would say, 'I got a feeling that this year we're gonna make it! I really do! We got some great titles! Come on, Cos, what do you say, let's give it our all!'

I couldn't share his optimism. We had gone from publishing Jeffrey Bernard and Elizabeth Smart (author of the minor classic *By Grand Central Station I Sat Down and Wept*) to a book on gourmet dishes for pet dogs.

Then one morning, not long after his last pep talk, Jay announced, 'It's time to call it a day.' His accountant had advised him to shut down operations at once. Although concerned about how he would react, I needn't have worried. Late one afternoon the phone rang.

Jay: Got a minute?

Me: Minutes are all I got at the moment . . .

Jay: Funny. Good news. We're back in business!

Me: But we just closed the business down yesterday

Jay: I know. The business is dead, long live the new business!

Me: Who's been hitting the Martinis?

Jay: We're going to be packagers . . .

He then proceeded to explain what that meant.

The idea was that we would come up with concepts for books that would have an international appeal, find writers to write them, and then sell the whole package to publishers. To cut down on our overheads we would close the office down and move operations to the basement at Duncan Terrace. We would make our debut as packagers at the London Book Fair.

Jay got busy like he was opening a show on Broadway. We had all sorts of original ideas for books: *The Final Note*, a collection of suicide notes; *Teach Yourself Duelling*; a defence of smoking called *Smoke Gets In Your Eyes*, and *Boo Hoo, The Complete Cryer's Manual*.

We won a lot of praise for having what the *Bookseller* dubbed the most original stall at the fair (it was designed like a sultan's harem) but unfortunately we didn't sell a single package.

The next day Jay phoned. 'It's time to call it a day,' he said. Later he wrote a farewell to publishing in the *Bookseller* that ended with the line: 'I truly loved publishing. Unfortunately, publishing didn't love me.'

After Jay had closed down his publishing business he found himself at a loose end. Things got so bad he took up gardening. Then one afternoon I went to visit him. We sat in his basement lair having tea and he started to talk about being a failure and not knowing what to do with his life.

The act had stopped, the mask had slipped and for a moment I caught a glimpse of the real Jay. It was strange to see him speaking in a normal way, rather than in B-movie dialogue uttered through the side of his mouth like he was inviting you to join him in a dangerous conspiracy.

He started to cry. He sat there, a quivering mass of hurt. The saddest tears for any boy to see are the tears of his dad. I tried a little emergency first aid on his ego, telling him that his life had not been a failure. On the contrary, I said, you've lived a really interesting life. I went through all the highlights, all the innovations and daring projects, and concluded, 'When they come to write the history books, you'll be there!'

'You think so?' he asked hopefully.

'I know so!' I said, trying to make it sound convincing.

Then Fran came in and asked, 'Has anyone seen my lead sheets?'

She ignored Jay and went to the Xerox machine at the other end of the room. I was shocked.

'Look at him!' I said. 'For God's sake aren't you going to say anything to your husband?'

She walked over to Jay, took one look at him and said, 'Have *you* seen my lead sheets?'

That evening I told Julie how worried I was about Jay. How could he live without a project?

The next day I got the call.

Jay: Thanks for the pep talk, kid. It was just what I needed.

Me: That's OK.

Jay: I'm working on the mems.

Me: The what?

Jay: The mems, my memoir. I'd started it ages ago but I think the time is right for my story. I've done a terrific opening about how at the age of eleven I had a nervous breakdown to get my mother's attention. It's very funny. Got a minute?

Me: Actually . . .

Jay: I'll just read you the opening chapter . . .

It was his mistress Pam who first raised doubts about Jay's new project. She asked him, 'Who wants to read a memoir of a nobody?' In fact, the Nobody Memoir was just beginning to take off. Following the success in the seventies of James Herriot's books about being a rural vet, Britain in the eighties saw a groundswell of people who thought their lives would make fascinating reading. The trend was started by Peter Mayle's *A Year In Provence* (1989), another book that played to the affluent middle-class dream of dropping out for a slower, more fulfilling way of life. It became an international bestseller.

Jay had finally found a topic that was endlessly fascinating: himself. He was fulfilled and happy. As he later wrote in *Jaywalking*: 'Writing about myself for eight hours a day, seven days a week and then talking about it for a couple of hours with friends and family was not a bad way to spend time.'

For him it may have not been a bad way to spend time, but for the rest of the family it was hell. The mems were all-consuming: the literary equivalent of being macrobiotic.

From my diary, March 1983: 'In the evening a birthday party for Miles. Jay spent the evening talking about himself. He was out of control. Is this a professional hazard of those who write their memoirs or has his egoism gone into overdrive?'

☆

When I was first involved with Julie she was only locally famous: that is, famous among people who read the rock press and *The Face*. Everything changed when she became a columnist with the *Mail On Sunday* and then the *Sunday Times*. She became the star and I became the husband in tow.

People would come up to Julie at the supermarket and tell her how much they loved her column. We'd go to parties and people would come up and tell her how much they loved her column. She got letters from strangers saying how much they loved her column. She got calls from my parents saying how much they loved her column.

The difference in our status was obvious to everyone, especially me. But I wasn't jealous of her success. On the contrary, I was very proud of her. I wasn't one of those envious, petty husbands who think that because they are the man of the house, they should be the success.

When Fran's career began to take off, Jay was always determined that he wasn't going to wind up as Mr Fran Landesman. The way I handled the obvious discrepancy in our levels of success was by trying to be upfront and funny about it. I once jokingly suggested to Peter York that I was planning to start the Mr Barbra Streisand Society for men who found themselves, like Streisand's husband Elliott Gould, married to women far more successful than themselves. He said he thought it was an 'awful' idea, by which he was showing his disapproval of my putting myself down.

I could handle Julie's fame and success, but Julie and Toby's success was another matter. Success sealed their newly established best-friendship; it became their own private members' club. Toby's success happened so fast that even he was surprised. In 1985 he wrote an article for *New Society* called 'The Shock of the Old'. It was a classic style-watching/state-of-young-people-today piece. It was his first article for a national magazine and he hit the jackpot. Two weeks later he'd been wooed by *Harpers & Queen*, the *Observer*, the *Mail On Sunday* and two agents. Four months later he had a contract with the *Observer* and we broke out a bottle of champagne to celebrate.

So Julie was the big name, Toby was the rising star and I was the fat girl who tagged along to the Saturday night disco with the two beautiful mates that everyone wanted to dance with.

Julie and Toby handled my lack of success with a discreet silence. They never once talked about it in front of me. My failure was like a terrible physical disfigurement that was too embarrassing to mention. But I remember Toby once saying to Julie something that did shock me: 'There isn't any natural relationship between successful and unsuccessful people.' In other words, the successful and the unsuccessful had nothing in common; nothing upon which a friendship could be maintained. This is something you don't want to hear from your successful friends.

Toby and Julie talked about 'winners' and 'losers' in a way that seemed to epitomize the callousness of the Eighties. Both would claim that they were being ironic. In her essay on the Eighties – 'McLaren's Children' – Julie wrote: '. . . most of the people playing the game were only half serious. The whole hustle was played out with a theatrical and self-conscious obsessiveness that verged on parody; we were playing Manhattan in the Fifties with much talk of *losers*, being *finished in this town*, being *wiped off the board*, the *A Party* and *Mr Nobody* with a one-way ticket to *Nowheresville*.'

It was the lingo of that New York my father had warned me about all those years ago, but transferred to London. There were plenty of people, especially those who worked in the City, who took that sort of talk seriously, but in media circles it was still taboo.

Today Toby takes pretty much the same line of defence. He told me, 'There was a great deal of play-acting, especially the use of that hard-boiled American argot. Part of the appeal of this sort of talk was a desire to shock the older generation. We wanted to ham it up as to how ambitious and materialistic we were. It was a way of flicking fleas at the previous generation who thought it impolite and vulgar to be interested in money and success. It was a way of advertising your indifference to their good opinion. It was fuelled by desire to provoke the liberal intelligentsia.'

But were Julie and Toby really so indifferent to the opinion of the older generation?

I think Julie was. She loathed people like John Mortimer, Salman Rushdie and Harold Pinter. It was partly a form of inverted snobbery, but she hated the way they demonized ordinary people who wanted to do well for themselves and their families as 'greedy' and 'selfish'.

Julie was a strange mix of bourgeois triumphalism and bohemian hedonism. She talked a lot about making it, and was very proud to be a working-class girl from Bristol who had done just that. She constantly asked people how much money they earned – and was only too happy to let them know that she earned more. But she didn't really care about success and wealth in other people. What she really liked were smart, funny people who were fun to hang out with. I was lucky to find a girl like that. In the eighties I didn't have a column. I didn't have exciting phone calls from commissioning editors dying to take me to lunch and discuss projects.

I had phone calls from my mother to invite me to her gigs.

I had phone calls from my dad to discuss his latest project.

I had requests from my brother to come to his gigs.

And I had my novel.

Yes, I'd succumbed to a literary virus that struck many bright young men at the time: the desire to write the Great London-in-the-Eighties Novel.

What made this outburst of novel-writing unexpected was that not too long before this, hip, modern people had given up on the novel, thanks to Tom Wolfe. His introduction to his anthology, *The New Journalism*, had liberated a generation of journalists from the need to prove your worth as a man of letters by writing a novel. Wolfe had argued that the new journalism (one that borrowed the techniques of fiction) was 'dethroning the novel as the Number One literary genre', and in the early eighties we believed him. We thought that novelists were old squares who didn't understand pop culture and the ways of the modern world. We preferred journalists like Tom Wolfe and Peter York to the gods of literary fiction like Rushdie and Amis.

And then around 1984/5 (with the success of Jay McInerney's *Bright Lights, Big City*) we began to hear about the Brat Pack: a new group of young, hip novelists like McInerney, Bret Easton Ellis and Tama Janowitz, with their urban tales of excess and alienation. Suddenly the novel was back and every journalist I knew was working on one.

My novel was about a group of young people on the make in the eighties. It was essentially a *roman-à-clef* featuring Julie, Toby and everyone I knew. After some months of working on it Julie asked me what I was going to call my novel.

'*The Tough and the Tender*,' I replied. I'd taken this from William James's description of two different responses to modernity, and I thought it sounded suitably F. Scott Fitzgerald-like, but Julie was not impressed. 'You fucking *ponce*!' she laughed.

I started looking for another title.

After a year of working on my Great London-in-the-Eighties Novel I had three completed chapters, six aborted chapters and hundreds of pages of notes. What stopped me from finishing was my constant rewriting. This had nothing to do with the code of the literary perfectionist, who feels that if he isn't up there with the Great Ones – Joyce, Dostoevsky, Proust – he might as well forget it. My problem was that I felt I wasn't even up there with the Adequate Ones, never mind the masters; I suffered from a crippling lack of confidence.

The contrast between Julie and me couldn't have been greater. In 1987 she sat down and bashed out a novel called *Ambition*, which went on to become a bestseller. Watching her write was an unorthodox master class in How to Write While Smashed out of Your Skull.

She would write only in the evening after she had put our son Jack to bed. Her work routine began with a bit of a tidy-up and a dusting of the flat. Julie wrote in the living room, usually with the television on, like a school kid doing homework. I knew she was getting ready to work when she would ask me to go and open a bottle – usually wine or champagne. Drink was her creative lubricant. She'd put paper in her machine (these were the days of the typewriter), alcohol in her blood and cocaine up her nose. Then it would start: she'd sip and tap ... sip and tap ... sip and tap ... tap and tap-tap-tap-tap till she had lift-off.

And then after a furious rush of tapping she'd say, 'Baby, put out a line for me.' More tapping and sipping would follow and then she'd say, 'Baby, put out a line for me. Oh, and get me another bottle, please.'

Then there would be an outburst of furious tapping. I would look over and see her hunched over the keyboard typing with one finger – just one crazy, demonic finger hopping up and down, speeding right and left across the keyboard with a frenzied life all of its own.

Then it was break time. Out would come her mirror, she'd check her lipstick, pout and put away the mirror. By now she would be thoroughly drunk and would look over at me, wink, smile and say, 'OK baby? Put out just one more line for me. Cheers!' The refreshed demon finger would go into a final frenzy and I'd hear the triumphant cry of 'Finnn-iish-ed!'

You'd think, given how drunk she was, that whatever she wrote would be incomprehensible rubbish. But it was perfectly formed copy.

I could never work at night the way she did. I was an early morning riser. Instead of a demon finger, I could type with both hands. For all the good it did me, though, I might as well have had two stumps. I sat in my small room endlessly rewriting or waiting for the spark of inspiration. I would drink coffee and have a line of coke (imitating her) and wait for my fingers to fly the way hers did. But they could only crawl across the keyboard.

Sometimes Julie would come into my study to check on my progress.

Julie: Oi, Marcel Proust! How's it going?

Me: Fine.

Julie: How many words have you done today?

Me: Loads!

Julie: How many?

Me: Umm . . . about 250 . . .

She'd give a little snort of disgust and go off to dust.

☆

By 1986 I was writing features for the *Guardian*. Whenever I had to turn in a piece I'd become a nervous wreck. At night I would have terrible sweats; in the day I went around sighing. I would go over and over every paragraph, convinced that what I was writing was rubbish. Julie was very supportive and encouraging, although there were times when she'd become exasperated with my neurotic relationship with writing and scream, 'What's the matter with you? You can't write out a fucking shopping list without doing seventeen rewrites! For fuck's sake, just *bash the fucker out*!'

The only time I could write with confidence was

when I wrote film reviews or features for Julie under her name. She had been given the job of film critic for the *Sunday Times*. After attending a few screenings she decided that she'd had enough of sitting in a dark room with 'smelly old men'. From now on I would be dispatched to go and sit with the smelly men, watch the film, and take notes which she would polish up.

It was as if in using her voice I could find the confidence I needed. I wrote some good stuff, which appeared under her name. I felt good about doing it because I was making a financial contribution to the household, and because I could earn so much more money writing under her name than my own. There were times when I wished I could have had my name on the piece but I kept quiet, afraid that if anyone found out we'd get into trouble. Julie didn't care about being found out. On the contrary, when people complimented her on one of my pieces, she had no qualms about telling them, 'Oh, Cosmo wrote that one!'

☆

Meanwhile there were times when Fran and Jay thought they were finished. He was winding down the publishing business. The 'mems' were doing the rounds of publishers and getting plenty of rejection. Publishers didn't know how to handle them. Then Fran's new agent went bankrupt before he could even get her a gig. Jay described their career situation thus: 'Two old farts who have been up to bat so many times without coming up a winner. The old lady can't get a gig and I can't get my book published.'

Desperate measures and fantastical conceits were employed to help get Fran's career off the ground. At one point Jay wrote to Barbra Streisand asking her to appear in Fran's new show, but there was one condition: 'No singing!'

He thought that was hilarious. She didn't reply.

For my parents there would be long periods when the phone never rang and the letters they longed for never came. 'We're finished,' they'd say. And then something would turn up – a little nibble at one of their projects. A producer/publisher/composer wanted to meet and talk. Hope would return, and with it speculation about how this could be the lucky break.

In 1985 a producer in America, Hope Wurdack, wrote saying she wanted to do a production of their old Broadway flop, *The Nervous Set*, in St Louis. Hope arrived in London and her enthusiasm for the project set my parents' heads spinning – especially when she suggested they both do three nights of cabaret before the show opened. Fran would do her poetry and Jay would read from his memoirs, and both would be paid $1,000 a night. 'It would be great publicity and help raise money for the show,' she insisted. What the aptly named Hope didn't realize was that my parents would have paid *her* for the privilege.

The last time Jay had been back to St Louis was twenty-five years ago, when he went to his mother's funeral; it never occurred to him that he could now be going to his own. Hope's offer had once again filled my parents' heads with dreams of the big time. 'You will be able to dance your way back into people's hearts,' she told them, and they were only too happy to believe her.

Jay immediately hit on the idea of not only bringing his book to St Louis, but his mistress as well. He thought it would stir things up if the Landesmans returned as a *ménage à trois* and showed the squares of St Louis that they were 'high-flying nonconformists'.

Fran went along with the idea, but when Jay changed his mind she was relieved. She confessed to him, 'It would have been humiliating for me to try to explain what your mistress was doing on the journey.'

The trip to St Louis was everything they had ever wanted. In the small pond they were still big fish. As soon as they landed at the airport they were treated like returning heroes. A television crew awaited them at the airport. Everywhere they went, they were recognized and showered with attention.

On the opening night Jay took to the stage first. He began reading from his memoirs about the old days of St Louis to an audience who were old enough to share his trip down memory lane. The round of applause that followed was their way of saying, 'We've missed you, Jay.' Fran's act went down even better, and the evening finished with the two of them in the spotlight dancing to a medley of songs from *The Nervous Set*.

Then they broke into one of Fran's songs.

She sang:

> *I sulked in the spotlight Wearing a frown*
> *When I should have been dancing*
> *I was putting you down.*

He sang:

> *We could have been sensational*
> *A couple of luminous stars*
> *Could have been inspirational*
> *When all those tomorrows were ours.*

Then they stopped dancing, put their arms around each other and looked into the audience:

> *When I should have been making sense of my life*
> *I was busy messing up yours.*

They kissed in the spotlight and got a standing ovation.

That old feeling came back: the *this-is-it* moment. After the show they got a full-on blast of adulation. People came up to them to shake their hands and tell them how terrific they were.

Fran had been here before, but it was a new experience for Jay and the small taste of success went to his head. He began to act and talk just like the St Louis big shot he'd been thirty-odd years ago, and Fran couldn't stand it. That night of their opening they had the worst and most intense row of their marriage. Jay had always said that if either one of them ever made it, it would put their marriage in jeopardy. Now they were in trouble.

At last *this* was the big one; he had made his comeback. His head filled with dreams of success – a tour across America, readings from the mems and his collection of unpublished novels. He was ready, America was ready, or so he imagined. For the first time in their marriage he was actually thinking of leaving Fran and starting a new life with his mistress in the States.

Jay consulted old friends, family members and even former St Louis lovers, and they all told him the same thing: *don't do it, Jay!* By the end of the week, that first rush of success began to fade and with it his fantasy of life without Fran. He sobered up and they returned to London to discover that they were going to be grand-parents.

The birth of our son Jack in 1986 saw Fran the fame-hungry poet become Granny Franny. She claimed that she was no longer interested in showbiz and stardom; nothing could compete with the sheer joy that she got from the new baby. Jay's feelings about becoming a grand-father were more ambiguous. At the age of sixty-five he felt he wasn't ready to grow up and be a grandad. So off he went on a two-week holiday with his mistress.

11

When Will I Be Famous?

The 1980s began with a bang that went around the world. On 8 December 1980, ex-Beatle John Lennon was shot dead by Mark Chapman in New York City. Fame had possessed a dark side since the early days of Hollywood: now it was both dark and deadly.

The rock star life had always had its own dangers. With fame came mob love: great hordes of hysterical girls who threatened the physical well-being of their idols. Think of the Beatles in *A Hard Day's Night*, constantly running from fans as if they were about to be lynched by love. But these fans simply wanted a souvenir – a lock of hair, a shred of clothing or the magic of a fleeting touch. Their aim was to connect, not to kill. And looking back, it's amazing that no rock star ever died at the hands of the crazed mob.

There was only one thing more dangerous to rock stars than their frenzied fans, and that was the star's own frenzied self. It was rock stars who were killing themselves with drugs, drink and a life of excess. The year 1980 alone saw the deaths of AC/DC vocalist Bon Scott (who choked on his own vomit); Led Zeppelin drummer John Bonham (asphyxiated on his own vomit after forty

shots of vodka); folk singer Tim Hardin (heroin overdose) and the suicide of Joy Division's Ian Curtis (an
overdose of guilt and depression). Now rock stars – and
everyone who was famous – had a new threat to deal
with: the lone stranger, or the 'stalker' as he was to be
called. The stalker was a far more dangerous figure, for
unlike the noisy mob he was silent and deadly.

In the 1980s fame lost its innocence. It was no longer
the sweet daydreams of pretty girls who worked in
drugstores waiting to be discovered by Hollywood
agents, or earnest young men who took acting classes in
the hope of being the new Brando. It was the sweaty
stuff that seethed in the minds of lonely, invisible men
in seedy hotels who planned to make their mark on the
world by murder. And fandom lost its innocence, too.
No longer were the fans just weepy, wailing lovesick
teens; they were simply sick. The fan had become the
fanatic. In the press and popular culture fans were
always portrayed and diagnosed as 'obsessives', 'stalkers', and weirdos.

The idea of fame as a kind of sickness (both as a
personal aspiration and an obsession about the famous)
first emerged in America. At the start of the 1990s the
Daily Mail covered a new report for the US Justice
Department by Professor Park Dietz, which claimed that
in America 'there is at large a hidden underclass of
the obsessed and the insane.' According to the *Mail*
Professor Dietz 'believes there are a quarter of a million
mentally disordered and potentially dangerous people
at large in America threatening the privacy, if not the
safety, of celebrities local and national.'

The impression given by the British press was that the phenomenon of the celebrity stalker was a peculiarly American problem, a symptom of the Americans' 'obsession' with fame. The British, readers could assume, were too sane for that sort of insanity. Although the *Mail* did point out that pop singer Kim Wilde, television presenter Gloria Hunniford and Princess Anne had all become victims of stalkers. But the great British stalker seemed harmless compared to his American counterpart. We had the determined nuisance; they had the lethal nutter.

The crazed fan and the crazed fame-hunter became hot topics in the eighties. They even got their own film in 1982 with Martin Scorsese's *The King of Comedy*, in which would-be comic Rupert Pupkin (Robert De Niro) kidnaps talk-show host Jerry Langford (Jerry Lewis) so that he can grab his fifteen minutes of fame by appearing on Langford's show. Pupkin, who is aided in his task by a Langford fanatic (Sandra Bernhard) describes his motivation thus: 'Better King for a night than a schmuck all your life.' It was a motto that many Americans could relate to and, increasingly, so could the British.

The curious feature of fame in the 1980s was that it was pathologized at the very time it was popularized. People saw its darkness and didn't care. In the seventies popular culture had warned the young about the dangers of fame; in the eighties it told them to go for it.

In the same year that Lennon was shot, Alan Parker's movie *Fame* was released, and a franchise that would spawn a hit television series, a long-running stage musical and of course the hit single, 'Fame' by Irene Carr, was born.

The television series *Fame* ran in the UK from 1982–1987, and like the film was set in New York's High School for the Performing Arts. The show followed a group of students from various ethnic and socio-economic backgrounds as they danced, sang, made music and pursued their dreams of stardom. The show was memorable for two things – the title song and the line from one of the teachers in the opening credits: 'You've got big dreams? You want fame? Well fame costs. And right here is where you start paying. With sweat!'

In *Fame* the democratic promise of postmodernism – anyone can do it – meets the punishing demands of the Protestant work ethic. Fame was being packaged and sold as the new American dream. Seen today, *Fame* looks like a lost golden era when young people had to work hard, nurture their talents and sweat a lot to become famous – not just flounce around some reality-TV show. Talent was what got you through the doors of the *Fame* school, but if you wanted real fame what really mattered was attitude, ambition and dedication. This gave hope to those who had the fame dream, but not much in the way of talent.

Fame was the perfect show for the Reagan and Thatcher years. It was fame subjected to the laws and promises of free enterprise: take risks, work hard and provide the market with something it wanted, and you got your just reward. Surprisingly, the television series was more popular in the UK than in America, and influenced a whole generation of future British stars – Geri Halliwell, Robbie Williams and Victoria Beckham. It was *Fame* that led Beckham to take her first showbiz steps. It inspired her to get her parents to enrol her into the Jason Theatre School. Looking back to those *Fame*-struck years, she would boast: 'I even had a velour *Fame* tracksuit with gold stitching.'

Victoria Beckham was typical of many young Brits who wanted to be famous but weren't weird and didn't want to be all freaky like Bowie and Bolan, thank you very much. The wholesome-looking cast of *Fame* suggested that it was OK to be a boring kid from the suburbs who didn't take drugs, as long as you wanted to work hard, do well and follow your dream. But the most important message of the programme was that you didn't have to be a genius or even particularly good to find the *Fame* kind of fame: just determined.

If you wanted to see the truth of that you had to look no further than the great diva of determination herself, Madonna. Here was a perfect example of what a girl with a little talent and a whole lot of ambition, attitude and determination could achieve.

What Jane Fonda had been to the workout movement, so Madonna was to the wannabe movement. They both sold the idea of women taking control of their lives through their bodies and the virtue of hard work. By the time she was a global star, one look at Madonna told you she was a performer who spent more time in the gym than the recording studio.

She offered young girls records they could dance to, but the music was just the soundtrack to the real product, which was Madonna. Singing was her part-time career; her real job was as a role model who showed girls how to dress (lace tops, skirts over capri pants, fishnet stockings and crucifix), how to have attitude, tease boys, be independent, swagger and find fame. Growing up a Catholic, Madonna had already found God, and now she wanted to find his kind of fame as well. 'I won't be happy until I'm as famous as God,' she's alleged to have told a British tabloid newspaper.

Given that the Madonna of today is a caring, sharing, ecologically concerned mommy who regularly attacks the vacuity and horrors of fame, it's worth remembering that she represented something very different in the eighties. Madonna helped to foster a cultural climate that said it was cool to be materialistic (or, as she put it, a 'material girl'), an exhibitionist, to want fame and focus on nothing but your career.

Madonna turned fame into something that wasn't just desirable but essential for the modern girl. She dressed up fame in clothes that concealed its selfish, needy and greedy side and presented it to a generation of admiring schoolgirls, clubbers, and intellectual feminists as female empowerment, something that was 'putting women in control', and they loved her for it. It was narcissistic individualism made to look like progressive feminism. For the Madonna generation fame, not diamonds, was a girl's best friend.

The kind of fame Madonna enjoyed was important for another reason: it was the start of a new kind of ubiquitous and unavoidable fame. Before she appeared on the scene, people who had no interest in Eighties pop music or pop culture could, with a little effort, manage to avoid such things.

But Madonna's fame changed the relationship

between performer and public. We the public weren't just intruding into the private life of a star; here was a star who intruded into the private life of the public. In the 1980s you couldn't avoid having a conversation about Madonna: what did she signify? Was she a feminist? How would she reinvent herself? An opinion on Madonna was something you were expected to have, like a view on modern art or the European Union.

In the wake of Madonna's success a new social type emerged: the wannabe. At first the term referred to any young teenage girl who wanted to be like Madonna. Later, it came to mean anyone who wanted to be famous. This reflected an important change in the fame game: people stopped talking about being a 'pop star' or a 'movie star', and began talking about 'being famous'. Fame was no longer a by-product of some other activity; it had become an end in itself. This new state of affairs was summed up by the Bros hit of 1988, which posed the question on many young minds: 'When Will I Be Famous?'

Thanks to the tabloid press we got wave upon wave of wannabes. In 1983 there were the pin-up wannabes, those Page Three stars like Samantha Fox and Linda Lusardi and 'Wild Child' figures like Amanda de Cadenet and Emma Ridley, who were photographed in nightclubs getting drunk.

Pretty girls with no discernible talent were launched as models, singers and actresses, because fame still had rules of entry. One of them was that you had to have some sort of profession or ambition – you couldn't just say to the world: *excuse me, I want to be madly famous.*

(That came later.) Also, there really was nowhere else for such people to go. With the exception of quiz shows like *Celebrity Squares* and *Blankety Blank*, there were no television formats that provided a home for celebrities who couldn't do anything but be celebrities.

For a time the most famous wannabe of the eighties was thirteen-year-old Mandy Smith, whose affair with forty-two-year-old Rolling Stone Bill Wyman landed her on the front pages of the tabloid press. She gained enough publicity from the affair to get a record contract in 1987 with hit producers Stock, Aitken and Waterman. Her face was everywhere, but her singles in the UK went nowhere.

Patsy Kensit was an aspiring British starlet who sang, acted, modelled and married rock stars: Dan Donovan, Jim Kerr and Liam Gallagher. You can see the Madonna influence in Kensit's mission statement: 'All I want is to be more famous than anything or anyone.' Her band Eighth Wonder had a couple of hit singles but her big movie *Absolute Beginners* (1986), was the flop of the decade.

Paula Yates was another famous blonde of the eighties. Brought up in a showbiz family, she couldn't sing (although she recorded a version of Nancy Sinatra's 'These Boots Are Made For Walking') or act, but she wanted to be famous. She posed for *Penthouse*, crashed her way into Fleet Street as rock journalist and friend of the stars, and then married rock star Bob Geldof.

Yates was famous not for such books as her *Rock Stars in Their Underpants* (1980), but for being Paula Yates. She successfully managed to brand herself as a rock chick. It was her lifestyle, her flirtiness that was so appealing to young women – and men, of course. She was the Jackie Collins of the rock set – a glitzy figure who provided outsiders with a peek into a 'glamorous' world they were excluded from.

Yates was shrewd enough to know how to play the fame game, but not smart enough to see through it. She thought it could solve her problems – provide her with the affection and validation she so needed. But eventually fame became the problem as the market for crazy famous blondes became overpopulated and the Paula brand depreciated. At the end of the eighties she tried a spot of Madonna-inspired reinvention, and came back as Yummy Mummy in 1990 with a book called *A Practical Guide to the Bliss of Babies*. But this didn't work and after much personal sadness, Paula the rock chick died from a drug overdose.

☆

It's ironic that the most famous woman of the decade, Princess Diana, had never wanted to be famous. Madonna was the blonde bad girl who married the king of cool (Sean Penn); Diana Spencer was the good-girl blonde who married a prince and became a princess. What in 1981 began with a 'fairy-tale' wedding ended in a media morality tale about the princess and the paparazzi.

Of course I can't be sure that Diana never dreamed of being famous, but Sloaney girls like her (at least in the days before Tara Palmer-Tomkinson) didn't do fame. The posh were brought up to look down on the pursuit of publicity and self-promotion. Attention-seeking had only one purpose: the attraction of husband material. But fame found Diana, and it wasn't long before she found that fame handy in her charity causes and battle against the Windsors.

Diana shared several of the features of the modern celebrity: an ubiquitous presence in the media, a willingness to discuss her personal life and problems (his adultery, her bulimia) as a means of connecting with the public. She had no particular talent other than the ability to relate to people, but that was enough. Her public performances – conspicuous displays of caring for the poor, the sick, the marginalized – won hearts around the world.

Diana enjoyed a kind of fame that went beyond mere celebrity. She belonged to that Eighties fame elite who were known across the world: Madonna, Michael (Jackson) and Arnie (Schwarzenegger). Her fame was rooted in her looks. Charles Leadbetter summed her up perfectly when he wrote: 'Diana was a largely silent star in a cacophonous age. Her life was meant to be seen and not heard.' When she opened her mouth and spoke, notes Leadbetter, it ruined the illusion that she was one of the people.

☆

What, you may wonder, did we all talk about before we all talked about celebrities? The answer is style. It was one of the great buzz words and topics of the Eighties. Style wasn't just clothes, it was bars and restaurants, consumer goods, corporate identities and politics. By the mid-Eighties Britain was in the grip of a style boom. It was on the high street (Next) and in Fleet Street (every magazine and newspaper carried their style section). The notion of style as a means of expressing your individuality, your separateness and even superiority from others became the Big Idea behind the whole consumer and lifestyle boom of the Eighties.

Style culture helped to kill off the idea of pop culture as an alternative to the mainstream, a place that provided sanctuary and support for the nation's rebels, misfits, thinkers, radicals and creatives. Pop decided to screw art and idealism and just take the money, the fame and run.

It's hard to think of singers more obsessed with success, self-promotion, selling records – the whole business side of the music industry – than the pop singers of the Eighties. For them the only success worth having was in the mainstream: being on *Top of the Pops* and selling millions of records; the only fame worth having wasn't rooted in the rock press but appearing on the front of the tabloid press. Bands like Culture Club and Duran Duran had no shame when it came to pursuing fame. As Dave Rimmer notes, 'The New Pop stars would do anything to get on television. They even agreed to being locked up in a cage and pelted with custard pies – which was what invariably happened on the now defunct Saturday morning kids' show, *Tiswas* – if that was what it took to get their new video shown.'

Even the bohemians of the post-punk era living in squats and keeping the idea of a counter-culture alive – bands like This Heat, the Raincoats, Scritti Politti – couldn't resist the lure of commercial forces. 'Post-punk bohemia started crumbling in the 80s when the Thatcher effect kicked in. It was time to "get real". Clamber on some kind of career(ist) track,' wrote Simon Reynolds. Scritti Politti, the Thompson Twins, Boy George, Marilyn and Hayze Fantazee all made a mad dash for the charts with innocuous reggae-flavoured pop.

Those who refused to water down their music and stay true to the cause became increasingly marginalized and broke. Cult performer Sue Gogan was part of this alternative scene. For a brief time she worked as a road sweeper for Camden Council. One morning in 1984 she was sweeping a street when a flash car pulled up beside her. Out steps a driver and opens the back door of the car. Out steps Green from Scritti Politti, every inch the pop star. 'I guess he'd "made it",' says Gogan.

The tragedy is that in celebrating the idea of stardom as the ideal life, style culture and music started to lose its originality and creativity and got sucked into that big, bland thing that eventually became known as celebrity culture. The two were never the same. Of course Boy George and that crowd worshipped Bowie and Bolan, and craved fame. They were star-struck, but not indiscriminately. You couldn't get into Blitz just because you were a big name, as Mick Jagger discovered when he was turned away at the door by Steve Strange one evening. Style culture was essentially elitist and had no interest in playing to the masses.

This prehensile longing for fame among eighties youth might seem mysterious or reprehensible, but a lot of it has to do with class. When you're young and from the working class, you don't have Oxbridge or family connections as a route to a better life. Fame is the next best thing; it's a ticket out of a humdrum existence.

Think about all those talented working-class kids, many stuck in the provinces dreaming of London and going to glamorous parties and nightclubs. There's Julie Burchill in Bristol, waiting for her life to begin. Fame, she believed, could help her find what she wanted most in life: love and money. Fame, she writes, helps you to be who you are. 'You don't really exist until you see your name in print. That you are simply not yourself till you're famous.'

There's the eighteen-year-old Morrissey in Manchester who wrote: 'I want fame now, not when I'm dead!' Later he talked about his need for fame: 'I've always had a religious obsession with fame. I always thought that being famous was the only thing worth doing in human and everything else was just perfunctory.'

Fame is the revenge of the outsider, the ultimate trump card in the everyday battle of class and status. The only alternative for people like this is to stay put and be buried alive.

Middle-class commentators who bemoan the whole wannabe celebrity culture fail to appreciate how stifling and mind-numbingly boring ordinary life can be for a certain type of sensitive and creative working-class kid. So of course when these kids dream of fame it's part of that working-class tradition of dreaming of winning the pools, or a premium-bond scoop.

☆

Diary entry, 12 January 1984: *Ran into JH on the street.*
She proceeded to tell me about what a big star she was
becoming. How she had been in the newspapers and on TV
singing some song. God what an egomaniac! The world is full
of these monsters.

Rereading my diaries from this period, I'm struck
by the number of entries complaining about the self-
absorption of not only my family, but my friends and
people I meet. I'd thought this self-preoccupation was a
twenty-first-century phenomenon that came with the
rise of reality TV in 2000. But clearly it was alive and
flourishing in the eighties. Is this self-preoccupation an
inevitable by-product of becoming the kind of meritocratic society that we'd all assumed was so good? Have
we simply democratized the right to be an egomaniac?

In a society stratified by class, your social status is
primarily rooted in birth and family. The general trend
of post-war British society has been a movement away
from the hierarchies of class and culture to a world
where the individual created a sense of identity from
work and consumption. It's often said that one of the
awful things about the 1980s was that it reinvigorated
the British class system. Much was written about the
rise of 'smart society': the Sloane Rangers, the cult of
Brideshead Revisited and the success of the *Tatler* under
new editor Tina Brown were all signs of the new class-
consciousness. For this Mrs Thatcher got the blame.

But unfairly, I think. She may have been the great
champion of the virtues of the middle class, but she was
the great enemy of the class system. Thatcherism celebrated not the privileges of class but the prerogatives

of hard work and enterprise. She was a true meritocrat who believed that the free market was a fairer means of status distribution than the accident of birth. Besides, she had no fondness for the upper classes or their way of life. She saw them as the backbone of the British Establishment, whose anti-enterprise bias had been responsible for Britain's post-war decline.

So in the kind of meritocratic society Mrs Thatcher was trying to create, people had to hustle, push and promote themselves. A preoccupation with the self is bound to increase in a society organized around the individual. You can't have a 'dynamic', 'go-getting' individualism that is modest and self-deprecating.

Instead of self-deprecation the style of the Eighties became self-promotion, which at one time was regarded as terribly *American*. Self-display – at least among the middle class – was dismissed as vulgar. When the actress Celia Johnson was asked why she didn't like being interviewed she replied, 'One doesn't talk about oneself, does one.'

One did now. There was a sense by the end of the eighties that the future belonged to the self-promoters and hustlers, and all those gentlemanly virtues that had at one time defined the English character – modesty, self-deprecation, reticence – were a thing of the past. A new kind of Americanized Englishman was emerging, one that embraced the modern world of image, advertising, lifestyle, consumerism and self-promotion. The great era of Me had begun.

12

Fathers & Sons

For some people there's nothing like the intoxicating optimism of a new decade; they get high on hope. In the first few weeks of that first month of a fresh decade, people start to dream; insane projects and grandiose plans flourish. All is possible.

I got the call one morning.

Jay: Got a minute?

Me: What's up?

Jay: Are you ready for . . . *Gatsby, The Musical*?

Me: What?

Jay: I'm co-producing a musical version of F. Scott Fitzgerald's *The Great Gatsby*. Fran is writing lyrics for it and they're sen-sation-naaal!

Me: [*silence*]

Jay: Hello, are you there?

I should point out that two weeks earlier Miles had phoned me, asking for help with his latest project.

Miles: Cos, I've written a rock musical!

Me: What?

Miles: It's called *Skytwister* and it's about this rock band from Earth that goes to this planet to play an intergalactic rock festival and these aliens who want to be rock stars so they kidnap the band and try and take their place.

Me: And what, you want me to play the lead alien?

Miles: No, I just want you to read through the script – check it out, man . . . you're the critic in the family . . . just tidy it up a bit. I need an ending. Maybe you could knock out a press release while you're at it. You're good at that sort of thing. Cheers!

Me: But . . .

Click.

So when Jay phoned I was prepared. There was a time when I would have delivered the brutal truth and a rationale of why it wouldn't work: the whole Roaring Twenties style was so dated. We'd just been through the excesses of the Eighties, and nobody was in the mood to live it again in the Nineties.

Besides, this was the era of the 'mega-musical': *Les Misérables*, *The Lion King*, *Rent*, *Whistle Down the Wind* as well as *Mamma Mia*. Broadway was full of revived sure-fire hits: *Chicago*, *Cabaret* and *The Sound of Music*; *Gatsby*'s chances would have been slim.

But this time I decided to be less negative, for one simple reason: I had discovered that my father was actually getting old. I'd always joked to Julie that God was going to punish me for being such a bad son and let my parents live for ever, but then Jay started having dizzy spells and trouble with his heart. An ambulance came and took him to the hospital.

There he was put in the hands of a cardiac specialist who wanted to be a poet. As soon as he found out about

Jay being a writer/publisher, he had his 300-page manuscript by Jay's bedside. Visiting my father there, I saw him in his thin hospital gown and caught a glimpse of his mortality.

That image came to mind as we talked on the phone and I was determined to be kinder and more encouraging of Jay's projects – even if the strain killed me.

Me: Interesting . . . *very* interesting.

Jay: Yes, isn't it?

Me: Of course the *Gatsby* movie with Robert Redford stank, but a musical? Interesting. It has great . . . possibilities.

Jay: I'm very excited about producing it. I really think that this is the one that's going to do it for us. I'll fax Fran's lyrics over to you, take a look and tell me what you think.

Me: Can't wait.

Click.

I wonder if Jay was drawn to Gatsby as a way of promoting himself, or at least the kind of man he had longed to be. After all, Gatsby had inspired him to change his name. Gatsby was the great tragic hero of modern American literature: a poor boy from the Midwest (Dakota) who reinvented himself as the rich elegant Jay Gatsby, a mysterious legend and famous party-giver. 'If personality is an unbroken series of successful gestures, then there was something gorgeous about him,' said the novel's narrator about Gatsby, and that just about sums up Jay.

It was Jay's nephew, Rocco Landesman, who first tried

to bring him down to reality with some good advice. 'To produce a full-scale musical today on Broadway would cost about twelve million dollars. It would be difficult to raise that kind of money after looking at the record of two flop films on Gatsby. Best leave it as a novel.'

But Jay wasn't going to allow a little thing like $12 million to get in the way of what might be his last chance to crack Broadway. He was of a generation that regarded having your name in lights on Broadway as the pinnacle in the pantheon of fame. The theatre was the king of the performing arts.

Hell has no hustler like Jay with a new project. He picked up that phone and started smiling and dialling like a demon. He made contact with all the big boys in the British theatre: Cameron Mackintosh, Trevor Nunn, Bill Kenwright and Andrew Lloyd Webber, striking out with every one of them. He heard that J. Paul Getty – then one of the richest men in the world – was a big fan of the book, so he got in touch with him. No luck. He then tried Lord Sainsbury, another *Gatsby* fan, and drew another blank.

The *Gatsby* musical was on the critical list when Jay suddenly got some interest, first from the actor Simon Callow, and then composer Richard Rodney Bennett. They both thought it was a terrific idea and wanted to be part of it.

With these two on board it looked like Jay was back in business, and he loved every minute of it. He was on the phone, having lunches, writing letters and listening to new songs. Things had reached a point where they were ready to take the idea and pitch it to producers in

New York. So Jay organized a platform performance of the show in New York, and afterwards everyone drank champagne.

'I gotta feeling this is the one!' Jay said, giving Fran a big hug.

Friends were enthusiastic, the performers were excited. The old Landesman dream of being back on Broadway was back from the dead. But the potential producers – who make a show happen or not – all left without saying a word. *Gatsby, The Musical* was assigned to the graveyard of Landesman projects.

☆

In 1990 Miles got married and the first thing he did was make his bride Caitlin the lead singer of his new band, Neurotica. She had never sung before (or even entertained the notion) but that didn't worry Miles. He was now supporting his mum on guitar and had his wife on lead vocals. The marriage ended quickly and so did the band. I think he was more upset about *Neurotica* busting up than the marriage. He quit forming bands for a while and became a club entrepreneur, organizing various cabaret nights. Guess who was the star performer: Fran Landesman.

☆

Jay took the *Gatsby* flop in his stride. He was disappointed, but not down in the way he had been when *Dearest Dracula* had failed in 1964. Besides, he had another project that needed his attention.

In 1992 *Jaywalking*, the second volume of his memoirs, was published by Weidenfeld & Nicolson. Jay had high hopes for this one. Not only had he found a respectable publisher but they had given him a £10,000 advance, which was a considerable amount for an author who wasn't exactly famous.

The book covered Jay's life from Swinging London in the Sixties to the start of the Eighties, via the sexual revolution, a dozen artistic movements and a thousand and one parties. Jay knew that if he wanted to attract publicity and make his book a success there was one sure way of doing it: play up the celebrity angle. He even boasted in an article for the *Bookseller* that one of the unique features of his book was that it 'set a new record in name-dropping'.

I should point out for the benefit of younger readers that there was a time when name-dropping – the habit of trying to impress others by mentioning the names of famous people as if they were friends – was considered socially gauche. These days nobody uses 'name-dropper' as a term of censure, because *everyone* does it.

Famous people are the worst name-droppers of all. Even a sophisticated guy like Martin Amis does it. In his book *Experience* Amis suddenly drops a whole pile of them apropos of nothing: Jessica Lange, Sharon Stone, Tom Hanks, Quentin Tarantino and John Travolta. He also drops the fact that he has had dinner twice with Travolta at John's rented home in Beverly Hills.

Amis is a classic case of a name-dropper in denial. He says he only does it because he is the son of the famous Kingsley Amis, and to write about his father he must indulge in certain 'bad habits', name-dropping being one of them.

Another name-dropper in denial has been me, at least until now. I'm the worst kind of name-dropper, the kind that in theory is against it but does it all the same. I hear myself casually slipping a famous name into an anecdote that suggests intimacy/a shared history of good times with a famous person, and I feel ashamed because of the phoney way I do it. I imply that the famous name – e.g. Nick Hornby or Will Self, whom I only know slightly – is not really essential to the anecdote, but a mere bit player, that this story really could be about anyone, but it just happens to be about a famous person. Of course that's a lie. My anecdote is only a way of saying: I know famous people.

My mother is also a great name-dropper. She is the only person in the world who can somehow go from a story about her shoe size to the time she met Marlon Brando, Bob Dylan, Jack Kerouac, Lenny Bruce, John Lennon, Peter Cook and Bette Davis, without missing a beat.

Jay immediately got to work on a campaign for the promotion of *Jaywalking*. This included every radio station – however small – and newspaper (local and national) that would have him. He had hoped to appear as a guest at some glittering literary event like the Foyle's Literary Lunch or a Groucho Club dinner. What he got was a support spot at a literary dinner in Birmingham, with Claire Rayner as the star. He gave a speech full of self-deprecating one-liners and failed to get one laugh.

Even for a connoisseur of failure like Jay, it was to be an unforgettable night. After the speeches he found himself in the sales hall, where the audience lined up to buy books. Nearby, a queue for Claire Rayner's table stretched to the back of the hall, while Jay sat at his table with a large stack of books, pen in hand and hope in his heart. No one was interested.

Eventually, one person approached. He took one look at Jay's book and then apologized for being in the wrong queue. After an hour of sitting there in total silence, Jay finally cracked. The humiliation was too much even for him. He asked a security guard to keep an eye on his table while he popped out for a second, fleeing into the Birmingham night never to return.

I never read the book when it came out, and as usual I went into media quarantine – avoiding the newspapers that might carry an interview or review. An extract from the book appeared in the *Independent*, dealing with Jay's relationship with Julie. Thanks to Toby Young I got to hear all about it.

Somehow Jay's book always managed to slip through my Jaydar. No matter how hard I tried to ignore it, the book refused to go away and kept popping up into my life, leaping unexpectedly out of nowhere and shouting: *Yoo-hoo, here I am!*

I'd take Jack out for a stroll on a sunny day and see it there in a bookstore window. One morning I was shaving while listening to Alistair Cooke's *Letter from America*, and Cooke began to talk about 'the old beatnik reprobate Jay Landesman' and his new memoirs.

I could put off reading Jay's book, but I couldn't put off Jay. I knew he was anxiously waiting for my verdict. It was my turn to make the call.

Me: Got a minute?

Jay: What's up, kid?

Me: Just phoned to say I've finished reading *Jaywalking* and it's a terrific book – funny and a fresh account of London in the sixties.

Jay: Really?

Me: Honest. It's one of the best things you've ever written.

Jay: Thanks a lot. I can't tell you how much it means to me.

I could tell he was deeply touched by my encouraging words and I felt like a shit. I justified my lie on the grounds that the old boy needed some encouragement, a little praise to lift his spirits. Wasn't it Fran who was always saying, 'Be nice to your dad. He's old. You don't know how much longer he will be around.'

I tried to make nice . . . and lied.

So why hadn't I read his book? Because . . . I don't know . . . because I was a) an awful, unsupportive shit-of-a-son b) I knew I would be embarrassed by what I would read, because there was stuff about Julie and me in it, and c) I'm an uptight, ridiculously oversensitive idiot who should have grown up and got over this whole parental-embarrassment thing years ago.

Take your pick.

I was a grown-up with a wife, a child and a career of my own, and yet somehow I was still stuck in that adolescent mindset that feared being judged negatively because of my parents. Would it always be this way?

☆

In 1991 I got involved in a new project as well. This was the year that Toby Young told Julie and me about his idea for launching a magazine that would be an intelligent guide to popular culture. He immediately co-opted us to join him. He would use Julie's name to give it credibility and also to help us attract writers. 'Let's call it the *Modern Review*,' she said. Julie liked the idea of having her own magazine; for her it was like some exotic fashion accessory.

The decision to start our own magazine had the spontaneity and innocence of one of those 'Hey Gang, Let's Put on a Musical!' films starring Mickey Rooney and Judy Garland. The whole operation was set up and run from Toby's sitting room in his small flat in Shepherd's Bush.

For such a small periodical we managed to get a lot of media attention. Most of the arts sections covered its launch; there were profiles of Julie and her magazine in *Vanity Fair* and she went on Radio 4's *Start the Week*, calling John Mortimer a 'middle-class nerd'.

Though the *Modern Review* was always written about as 'Burchill and Young's magazine', Toby was always careful to point out in interviews that I was one of the founders as well. In truth it was their baby – I just helped change a few nappies from time to time. That was fine by me.

Jay, on the other hand, was less happy. Although he was full of praise for the magazine I think he felt hurt that he'd been left out of the project. Not even a word of consultation from the old magazine publisher himself had been sought. When I wrote a diary piece for the

Guardian about the experience of doing the *Modern Review*, Jay said, 'Neurotica must have slipped your mind. Oh well, these things happen.'

Then in a letter to his brother Gene, Jay said of me, 'I sometimes think he's recycling my literary life.'

I think that's what he wanted me to do. For what greater vindication can a man have than that his son would want to follow in his footsteps? I suspect that Jay saw the whole *Modern Review* saga as a rerun of the *Neurotica* story. In his mind I was Jay – the charming crusader – and Julie was the brilliant iconoclast Gershon Legman. Together we were taking on the literary establishment, just as he and Legman had done. And just as Jay had Henry Luce – the founder of *Time* magazine and the most powerful publisher in America – as his enemy, so we had Robert Maxwell, who wanted to close us down after we'd used his office equipment to produce our first issue.

But it was all a fantasy. If anyone was playing the Jay role it was Toby. He was the one with a flair for generating publicity and putting people's noses out of joint. I was the John Clellon Holmes figure – the sweet guy in the background.

I sometimes worried that I had, inadvertently, played a part in the rise of celebrity culture. Of course I'm not so foolish as to think our little magazine had much impact on anything, but I wonder if celebrity culture wasn't a natural outgrowth of the kind of pop-culture crusade we at the *Modern Review* had taken up.

In our defence let me say that when we started the magazine it was because we believed that popular culture

233

deserved an intelligent scrutiny. It was never about a celebration of celebrity culture – for celebrity culture is actually the enemy of popular culture. It's the parasite that uses the forms of pop culture – pop music, art, cinema, media, etc. – as nothing more than a vehicle for self-promotion.

It strips popular culture of everything that makes it great – its art, intelligence, eccentricity and potential for subversion – and creates an homogenized culture of glossy gossip, fashion disasters, body issues and emotional meltdowns. Celebrity culture is all about human entertainment; popular culture – at its best – is all about being human.

☆

There were periods when Fran would complain that she didn't feel appreciated by the world; her career was always taking off and then stalling. An actor called Howard Samuels put together a mini-musical of her various songs, *Invade My Privacy*. He called it a 'celebration of the works of Fran Landesman'. It opened at the Riverside Studios in 1993 and was given a try-out performance at the Criterion theatre. That night Fran and Jay arrived at the show to find a sign outside proclaiming the two favourite words of anyone in show business: Sold Out.

That old, this-is-going-to-be-it feeling returned when the drama critic of the *New Yorker*, John Lahr, told Jay's nephew Rocco that the show was ready for New York. Rocco came to London and loved what he saw.

It seemed that at last the Landesmans were heading back for Broadway.

But it didn't happen; Rocco wanted changes made that Fran, Jay and Howard couldn't accept and so the show just withered away and died. When Fran was down Jay would try to boost her morale by telling her how well she had done as a mother, a wife and a poet.

But all she would say was, 'It's not chic to be complimented by your husband.'

He saw in her that longing for success that had made so many people unhappy. They'd stroll through the park, he in his raffish panama hat, she hunched over, wearing an Iron Maiden T-shirt, debating the merits of success.

Jay: Success destroys your soul.

Fran: I wouldn't know. I've never had any.

He could see that sad, faraway look she had had that day he took her away from her beloved New York.

☆

Jay invited me over for tea one afternoon. I found the man who once claimed to have taken the 'sting out of success and put the fun back into failure' in a melancholic funk because he felt like a failure. He sat at his office desk, surrounded by piles of his wife's books, his son's demo tapes and a Twin Tower-size collection of remaindered copies of his two volumes of memoirs.

He told me he felt bad that he hadn't done more to help Fran's career. 'I promised to make her a star and for some reason . . . I don't know . . . I failed.'

I could have said, 'Remember all those years ago

when Fran first started out and I told you she was never going to be a big star? And you said I was just being negative. You all said it. Remember? Well, Mr Starmaker, Mr Bernard Fucking Delfont . . . Mr Brian Epstein . . . who was right and who was wrong about Fran? Say it, loser, get down on your knees and say it loud and say it proud: *You were right, Cosmo, I was wrong!*'

But I didn't. Instead, I pointed out that Fran's act had only a limited appeal. 'You did good, Jay, you took the act as far as it could possibly go. Honestly, there was nothing more you could have done.'

He then talked about her 'terrific talent', her 'wonderful songs', and how 'she can move an audience to tears' and he made me think of Erich von Stroheim as Max von Mayerling in *Sunset Boulevard*. Max was once the husband of the great starlet of the silent screen Norma Desmond (Gloria Swanson), and has become reduced to the role of chauffeur and servant to his ex-wife's ego. He displays an absolute loyalty and devotion to his Norma, doing all that he can to keep reality at bay.

Jay's loyalty to his wife, his belief in her talent, is one of the most endearing things about him . . . even though at times it verged on lunacy. Don't get me wrong. Fran was a very gifted lyricist and writer of light verse. I wish I could have written a song as good as 'The Ballad Of The Sad Young Men' or 'Spring Can Really Hang You Up The Most. But as a performer, she was always going to be a cult act. And there's nothing wrong with being a cult, but that's not the way Jay saw it. He believed you were a star or a nobody – and no matter how much you mocked the idea of stardom or dismissed it as something shallow, once it had got into your soul it was there for ever.

☆

So Jay realized that Fran was never going to be a star, and I realized I was never going to finish that damn novel of mine. Martin Amis once said he felt sorry for people who had never written a novel; God knows what he must have felt for people like me. I belonged to that group of men who started novels, who talked about their novels, who dreamt of novel prizes and novel fame: but we are the men who never finish their novels.

I could measure my life out by my unfinished novels. I had them all: my coming-of-age novel set in the sixties; the collection of short stories about the seventies; half a London-in-the-eighties novel, five chapters of a London-in-the-nineties novel.

You'd think there would come a point in a man's life when he knows he's never going to write that novel. After all, sooner or later most of us accept that we're not going to be pop stars, so we sell that guitar. But the novel dream lingers on long after the desire to sit-down-and-do has died.

In your mid-twenties you tell yourself that you've got 'real' and given up. Then you turn thirty and you try once more. Friends laugh when you tell them, 'No, this time it's different. It's a now or never situation.' And you rewrite, rethink, restructure – and the more you do, the further you are from finishing.

Forty comes and with it another fresh start. This time around there's even more urgency because you have a vision of your future: 102 years old, telling friends, 'No, this time it's different . . . I really am going to finish my novel!'

I suspect that this is just a guy thing. It's different for women. They just write prose; we've got something to prove. That's why there are no female equivalents of Hemingway and Mailer. In writing a novel, a man can find out the answer to the big, scary question: how much talent have I got? Any smart man with a creative spark wants to write a novel, and a man who hasn't done it by his mid-thirties is a literary virgin with a teeny-weeny dick and bubble gum for balls – or at least that's how I felt.

You want to know what hurts the most? It's the fact that so many people with far fewer brains than me are managing to do what I can't: write their novel. Politicians, agony aunts and chat-show hosts, schoolgirls, dentists, accountants, marketing men and semi-literate no-hopers of every kind are getting published. I can remember reading about a ten-year-old English boy called Jacob Connors having his novel published – and he can't even read or write! What about that French guy Jean-Dominique Bauby, who suffered a stroke and was left speechless and paralysed; he managed to dictate a memoir by blinking out letters with his left eye. This guy blinked a whole book and I couldn't even write one!

I would try and comfort myself by saying, 'So what, their novels are crap.' The point is, while I was faffing around (as Julie would say), dreaming and talking about my novel, they sat down and wrote theirs.

Worse still are the friends who actually finish their novels and get them published. You tell yourself you're cool about it and meet up to celebrate. When offering congratulations to your friend you make a joke about him being a traitor to the cause of literary procrastination. He laughs. It's your round. And then he tells you he's already working on his next novel. You decide to get an early night and leave.

The publication of his novel will haunt your friendship for ever. His good reviews say something bad about you. You start wishing he would stop asking about your novel. And then, out of respect for the dead, he will stop asking about your novel and then you will complain that all he ever talks about is *his* novel.

Take a tip from me: when your friend sells his novel to Hollywood take it like a man, hold back the tears and kiss that friendship goodbye.

By the end of the nineties I was boasting to my friends that I had finally dumped My Great Novel dream. But there were times when I imagined I could hear the ghosts of my dead novels rattling in the cemetery I call my filing cabinet. I could hear them whisper to me, 'Hey, Cos, take me out ... this time it will be different. It's a now or never situation ... come on ... you know you want to.'

I would laugh and say, 'What kind of sad, stupid geek do you think I am to fall for that one? Sorry boys, but I have given up on the novel dream.'

And I would give up ... until the next time.

☆

There were times when my parents would suddenly appear right in the heart of mainstream popular culture and I would wonder: what the hell are they doing there?

It was if they had wandered outside their natural habitat – poetry and literary journals and women's magazines, etc. – to a place where they had no business to be. I remember watching *The Antiques Roadshow*, a popular BBC1 programme where the public would bring possibly valuable objects for appraisal by experts, and up popped Jay.

He's there with a painting by the Japanese painter Foujiata, and one of the show's experts tells him it's worth £50,000. The audience gasps. 'Jesus!' cries Jay, and then he turns to the woman next to him and says, 'Now will you marry me?'

After that, Jay became a local celebrity. A policeman on a horse asked him for an autograph. Cab drivers waved. An article about him appeared in the tabloid press. 'It was ironic,' he wrote in his memoirs, that 'I should have found the kind of attention I had always longed for through one small painting of three nude ladies with large necks by a Japanese Impressionist.'

Then in 1996 Fran turns up on Radio 4's *Desert Island Discs*, and when Sue Lawley asks her what luxury she would like to take on her island, Fran says 'cannabis seeds' so she can grow dope. The edition receives a huge number of complaints.

Fran and Jay even turned up in the *Sunday Times*. In the late nineties I was commissioned by that paper's News Review editor, Sarah Baxter, to write an article about my parents' open marriage. (The tie-in was an article that had appeared in the *Guardian* about open marriages, and my parents had been cited as an example.) I thought it would be just another small, light feature that would get lost among the big stories of the week. Come Sunday, I was shocked to discover that my parents' sex life was the big story of the week. The *Sunday Times* splashed it on the skyline of the front page, with a picture of me! I had inadvertently awoken the beast. My parents were inundated with requests from various newspapers to do interviews about their marriage. Jay appeared on some sort of local religious television programme to defend his marital life before a hostile audience.

The article also boosted my career. Literary agents began to call, asking if I wanted to do a book on the subject. I found myself on *Richard and Judy* talking about my parents' sex life. I was glowing with success until I realized that, just like them, I was using their private lives to gain attention. I wasn't as bad as them, of course: I was worse. At least they were desperate for some attention. What was my excuse? Could it be that I was desperate too?

☆

I remember my father once saying, 'It's hard to get laid when you're in your eighties.' But that wasn't going to stop him from trying. As well as his musicals and memoirs, Jay's other major project in life was getting laid. I always said to him if he had put as much time and effort into writing as he did into getting women into bed, he would have been the most famous and successful writer of his generation.

He replied, 'Yeah, but I wouldn't have been so happy.'

My parents were famous for their open marriage, but my dad was infamous for making a pass at any woman with a pulse. I know this because women often told me about the night they faced his sexual advances.

Girl X would tell me how he propositioned her with the line that she was beautiful and that he could help her get into movies. I'm not sure what was more shocking about this – his lechery or his corny chat-up line. Girl Y would tell me about his friendly hug turning into a 'disgusting grope'. At a small dinner party a female journalist told me, and the rest of the table, the story of how Jay Landesman had 'tried it on' with her. The curious thing about these women was that they all seemed to think that I would be utterly fascinated to hear their story.

I wanted to say: *Why in the fuck are you telling me this? Am I my father's keeper? What exactly am I supposed to do – call him up and have him apologize?* But I would just sit there with a big smile on my face as if to say: *Why, the old rascal is still at it! Bless!*

No woman was safe: the young and old, the sensible and the insane, the married, the divorced and the desperate. He was often drawn to young fat women with bad skin and complicated relationships with their fathers.

In his panama hat, co-respondent's shoes and seersucker suit, he would cruise the hunting grounds of the Groucho, the French House and Gerry's club. His chat-up lines were nearly as old as he was. He went in for mock hard-boiled B-movie talk, adopting the manner of a Bogart. 'Don't fall in love with me, baby, I'm no damn good!' he'd say from the corner of his mouth. Now here's the really weird and inexplicable thing: it often worked!

Eventually things got so bad I had to discuss it with him. One afternoon he called to tell me about his latest project: his new record label.

Jay: Have you got a minute?

Me: I'm glad you called. I need to talk to you about something.

Jay: I'm thinking of going into the record business.

Me: Really? How will you find the time to do that – and take care of your sex life?

Jay: What?

Me: I keep getting these young women complaining about you and your sexual advances. I want to warn you, you're starting to get a reputation as a dirty old man. I . . .

Jay: That's total bullshit. Who are these women?

I gave him a list of names and described various incidents.

Jay: All lies! I never did such a thing. These are young girls crying out for attention.

Me: So these are all figments of their imagination?

Jay: Absolutely. Never mind that shit. The good news is that I'm in the record business now and I'm going to release a CD of Fran singing her own songs.

Me: I'd rather listen to women complain of your sexual molestations than Fran sing.

Jay: Funny.

Click.

But I knew it was true because I had seen the old man in action. One night in the Groucho Club he was sitting at the bar, chatting to two girls. I was at a nearby table, watching nervously. He sat there on his stool with that little swaying motion of a man under the influence. Here comes trouble, I thought. He finished another Martini and then trouble arrived.

I can only remember it now as a movie moment, one that took place in slow motion. I see the old, salacious, Martini-soaked lips of Jay, puckered up and moving through space. They were approaching, sideways, the face of one of the girls. I shake my head in horror. NOOOOOOOOOO, a slow-mo voice in my head cries. And just as the heat-seeking lips are about to hit their intended target, the girl swivels to the side. Instead of the lips aborting their mission they continue to dive forward, taking the rest of Jay with them and pulling him off his stool. I see the body of my father falling through space and crash-landing on the floor of the club. He lies there motionless and then says, 'I'm all right,' as people come to his rescue. I'm not sure if the girl even knew what was about to hit her.

Everyone in the immediate vicinity looked up to see the old guy who'd taken a tumble and watch him helped to his feet. The guys at my table averted their eyes and continued talking as if nothing had happened. They were embarrassed on my behalf. I too remained silent about the incident. What could I say? But I remember seeing Jay on the ground and thinking: that's my dad!

How do I explain his behaviour? Jay had always been a womanizer, but in the latter part of the 1990s his libido went gaga. He was one of those men who use sex and seduction to bolster their sense of self-esteem. They believe it is more important to be a winner in the bedroom than the boardroom. In fact they look down on men who are only successful in the workplace.

Usually such men grow old and lose their lust for life and women. But not Jay. The fact that he was in his eighties and still chasing women didn't bother him at all. And that's because he did not see himself as the world did; he saw himself as that young, handsome and funny man he had been all those years ago.

He had to believe he had something special to offer the world. He didn't want to be some old geezer with a glorious past. He wanted to stay in the game and feel like a somebody, and sexual conquest can do that for a man. But the downside was that it made it impossible for me to go out in public, because there was always this worry that some horribly embarrassing incident would occur.

Many years later, when he was recovering from a life-threatening sickness, he asked me, 'How come you never wanted to go out and have a drink with me?'

That night at the Groucho, seeing him old and help-less and drunk on the floor, came to mind, and I said, 'Because I was always worried you'd do something to embarrass me. You made it hard for us to hang out together.'

Jay looked puzzled and said, 'Embarrassed? I've never embarrassed you in all your life!'

☆

In 1995, after a fight between Julie and Toby, the *Modern Review* came to an end. Toby got a call from Graydon Carter to go to New York and work on *Vanity Fair*. Tom Shone, our film critic, got a call to go and work for Tina Brown at *Talk Magazine*. I got a call from Julie to tell me our marriage was over.

The end of a marriage between two journalists would not normally raise much press attention, but the context – high-profile feud between magazine owners, and the fact that Julie had taken off for another woman – meant it was newsworthy.

I found myself in a media whirlwind, with journalists calling every day on the phone and ringing at the front door, asking if I wanted to 'tell your side of the story'. In the past it had always been my parents' life that had embarrassed me; now it was my own.

I avoided the papers, but learned that I was referred to as 'Julie Burchill's estranged husband'. I hated the thought of being the 'estranged' one, for the word has such awful connotations – it seemed to me to suggest that you are somehow *strange* and that's why you were dumped.

For me, one of the things that went to making a successful life was a good marriage, and to achieve that you had to be a good husband. OK, I had failed on that score. But what about the Good Dad factor? Fatherhood had become fashionable in the nineties. Where once hunky male models were pictured swathed in babes, they now had babies wrapped in their protective arms.

Now that Julie had moved out, and we'd agreed it would be best for Jack to stay where he was, here was my chance to put into practice what I preached.

Once Jack and I were living alone I found that I was suffering from an acute form of Dad Anxiety. This is the worry that you're not really up to the task of being a good dad. And I don't mean dealing with the practical side of parenthood. For, contrary to the Hollywood image of men as innocent incompetents, dealing with nappies, bottles and crying babies is the easy bit.

Dad Anxiety is about not knowing what it means to be a good father, not knowing how to be patient, how to nurture and provide the moral marrow that will enable your son to grow to be a good human being. Most men start to worry about being a good dad around the time their children are in the lower reaches of adolescence. But my wife wasn't even pregnant before I was having dad-anxiety attacks. It got worse after Jack was born in 1986.

I tried to talk it over with Julie. 'Shouldn't I be teaching him the moral codes that will make him into a good man?'

'Jack is only six weeks old, you moron!' an exasperated Julie cried.

As soon as I learned that Julie was pregnant I began developing this fantasy of the kind of dad I would be: the normal dad I had wanted when I was a teenager. I longed to be one of those strong and silent dads with a shed in the garden. Jack would be my devoted assistant, carrying 'Dad's toolbox' around the house as I performed miraculous feats of DIY. We'd go to football on Saturday, fishing on Sunday, and I'd show him how to fix that puncture on his bike.

But Jack never wanted to do all those father–son things. People talk a lot about the changing nature of parenthood, but the really big change has been in the nature of childhood itself. Kids such as Jack no longer automatically learn how to play football, or get on their bikes and seek out adventure.

When I was young the streets were where the action was. Now with computers, videos and hi-tech games, being in your bedroom is no longer second best to being out on your bike. So instead of bonding with his dad, by the time he was seven Jack was bonding with his mum. She had something I couldn't compete with – a Nintendo video console and a capacity to play video games for hours on end.

I hated playing them and was determined to win Jack back. I remember one sunny day going into the living room with my latest plan for male bonding: a basketball.

'Hey, Jack, what do you say we go to the park and throw a few hoops?' I said, bouncing my brand-new bribe.

He and Julie were sitting in front of the television, utterly wrapped up in a video game of Super Mario Brothers. Neither looked round. Together they just let rip with a cry of 'NOT NOW, WE'RE BUSY.'

I felt jealous of Julie, and a bit of an outsider in my own home. She was brilliant with Jack. No matter how much she drank the night before, she would be up to make sure he had breakfast and was ready for me to take him to school. It wasn't easy being a dad with a mum like that around. She could earn more money than I could, but she couldn't wash a dish or cook a meal to save our lives. And while she had many wonderful qualities, Julie believed there were only two ways of doing things: her way and no way. Consequently I had to fight for my right to wear the apron in our home.

With the end of our marriage I had the chance to be the Superdad of my dreams. From now on Jack and I would do everything together. I'd teach him how to cook; he'd teach me to zap space monsters like Mum used to. And we would sit down and have proper meals, with the television off, thank you. I'd fill the place with the smells of home-baked pies and pastry instead of takeaway curries and M&S dishes.

But first I had to explain to Jack that his mother wouldn't be living with us any more. Instead he would visit her on weekends and see her on alternative nights. 'Think of this as a new, fun way of life. You'll have two homes and you and me will have a chance to get close and spend time together. It will be great,' I said.

Here was my first challenge: helping Jack to adjust. In the first weeks of her departure I did everything I could to make up for his mum's absence. I fed him, entertained him and made sure he had clean clothes for school; I read to him at night and told him 3,000 times a day how much I loved him. But most important of all, I was careful never to let him see my sadness. Like the Superdads of old, I would be strong, and endure.

I would protect and provide. I could and would do anything for him, but I couldn't stop that terrible noise that came into our lives and made living in our flat so unbearable: the silence of her absence.

It usually struck around dinnertime. I'd come in with a specially cooked supper and a specially prepared smile, and soon we'd be sitting in silence. Within two weeks of Julie's departure, Jack's brave little face began to show signs of strain. He acquired a series of nervous tics and twitches. His eyes would blink rapidly while he'd flick his head back and forth, and from side to side, like someone with brain damage. He would gnaw on his lips and sigh.

One day I said to him, 'Jack, I think we need to talk. Is everything all right?'

'Yeah, Dad, everything is fine,' he said, looking down at his food.

But I could tell he was going through hell. Eventually he said to me, 'Dad . . . I don't like this new life of ours.'

When I heard that, I knew that if I didn't get a grip on myself I would break down and weep. I had to be the strong single dad whose shoulder Jack could cry on – and not the other way round.

'I know you miss your mum and things around here aren't perfect. But hey, let's give it a chance. Things will get better, wait and see.'

Here I pushed my lips into the shape of a smile and gave him a confident thumbs-up sign. I looked at him and saw a little boy with a mop of blond hair, his eyes blinking madly, his head jerking left and right. Jack put on a sad imitation of a smile and said, 'OK, Dad, let's give our new life a go. It will be great.'

And then he raised his little thumb at me.

That was it. 'Excuse me, Jack,' I said, 'I've got an apple pie in the oven I need to check on.' I bolted from the room, but before I made it to the safety of the kitchen I broke down and wept. He found me, Superdad, in the hallway on the floor, a heaving and wailing wreck of tears and trembling limbs. At first he was embarrassed and looked away. This was the first time he'd seen me weep, and for a second his face stopped twitching. That was when his tears started. He came and stood by me, not knowing what to do.

I wanted to apologize for being so weak and pathetic. Through the tears I started to babble on about what a failure I was as a father. Suddenly I went silent and Jack said, 'Dad, I've got some bad news.'

Oh no, I thought; he wants to go and live with his mother. I've lost him!

'What is it, Jack?' I asked.

'Your pie is burning – I can smell it.'

That night we ate burnt apple pie with ice cream and watched *The Simpsons* on television. It made us laugh. For the first time since Julie had gone, Jack and I were having a laugh together. It was then I realized that I had not only lost my wife, but my dream of being one of those Superdads, too. But I had, at last, gained a son.

13

In From The Cold

Towards the end of the eighties I had said to Julie, 'God, I'm so bored with the nineties!'

I was experiencing premature decade fatigue, a condition created by advertisers, pundits, market-research experts, professional trend-spotters and think-tank boffins who had all written so much about what the nineties were going to be like that you felt you'd already lived them.

By 1987 we'd all seen the future; and it was going to be less materialistic, less competitive and more sharing and caring. Turbo-capitalism was going all touchy feely. Leading advertising agencies were claiming that the way to sell your product was to associate it with compassion instead of status consumption.

Everyone was eager to get with the new caring zeitgeist just around the corner, even Mrs Thatcher. The *Sunday Times* reported that she had pledged to make the 1990s 'a caring decade' and to build 'a Britain . . . [where] help will always be at hand for those who cannot help themselves'.

Mrs Thatcher had certainly changed her tune, but it was too late. In November 1990 she was dumped by her own party for being an electoral liability. It was fitting that the woman who wanted to create a society for winners should have fallen from power because her party perceived her as a loser.

The fact that John Major won the 1992 general election, and not the Labour Party as the opinion polls predicted (and did it with more votes than any party in British political history), suggested that the nation wasn't ready to be *that* caring and sharing.

The change from Thatcher to Major was more one of style than substance. She had been confrontational and strident; he was cosy and reassuring. She had wanted to create a go-getting enterprise society; he wanted a society 'at ease with itself'. Major managed to tell us what many wanted to hear: the eighties were over.

The obvious symbols of that decade – Filofaxes, red braces, Porsches, buzz words like privatization and talk of winners and losers – fell out of fashion. Money still talked, but in the nineties it had to lower its voice. Now that the wicked witch at Number Ten was gone it was safe for all the nice people, the charmers, the fun-to-be-with failures and the freaks to come out of their hiding places.

We saw the first distinct forms of post-eighties life emerging from America in 1991, and they were called Generation X. The term – in its most recent incarnation – came from the novel *Generation X: Tales from an Accelerated Culture* by Douglas Coupland, a young Canadian writer. His book chronicled the lives of members of a disaffected, post-yuppie generation. A year after Coupland's book we got *Slacker*, a film by Richard Linklater that that featured Generation Xers walking and talking and not much else.

The media portrayed Generation X as apathetic and alienated. They were the overeducated and under-employed kids in America who had 'McJobs' and were hostile to the pop-culture icons of the baby boomers, and antipathetic to the go-getting values of the Yuppies. Educated middle-class youth who had been on a steady course of downward social mobility during the 1980s must have breathed a sigh of relief. Once they were called 'failures' and dismissed as 'losers'. Now they went by the cool-sounding title of Generation X.

With America's Generation Xers enjoying such a high profile, it was inevitable that the English media would want to find out what was going on with post-Thatcher youth. In a 1993 feature for *Harpers & Queen*, journalist Daisy Waugh set out to define them. The heading of her article dubbed them 'Major's Children', which didn't quite have the hip ring of Generation X.

Never mind. Waugh wrote of Major's Children: 'We have reacted against the greedy Eighties. We don't want money and fast cars and . . . and we don't like looking after number one.' What's more, they didn't speak the same go-getting lingo of Thatcher's Children: 'the words ambition, materialism, hedonism and – above all – suc-cess' have been 'banished from our vocabulary'. What she saw was a 'more thoughtful, philosophical gener-ation from whose minds the threat of Aids, the rate of interest, the depletion of the rain forests is never far.'

This made them sound a rather earnest lot who had no time or capacity for fun, but fun they had. As Waugh pointed out, the essential character of Major's Children was shown in their love of rave culture. Unlike the fragmented and tribal nature of rock culture, rave had a communal we're-all-in-this-together openness. Here was the first youth culture not founded on the idea of tribal affiliations or narcissistic individualism. There were no 'we' and 'them', 'squares' and 'straights' to rave culture; everyone was welcome to join the party. 'It's all about pretty clothes, bright colours, face paint. It's classless. It's all about free love without sex. It doesn't matter what kind of job you do. Nobody cares,' said Imogen Edwards-Jones, then the twenty-five-year-old rave correspondent for the *Independent*.

The British media, eager to appear aware of the latest trends of youth, sought to find some home-grown slackers. Typical of the new breed was Cambridge-educated Mark Marignac de Cote, who told the *Sunday Times*, 'I don't believe there's such a thing as a job I'd enjoy. I just can't see the point of having a job.' The same article featured twenty-five-year-old Al Clayton, who decided to give up his 'yuppie' job as a human resources consultant and become a clown.

There even appeared a new wave of youth magazines – *Phat*, *The Zine* and the *Idler* – aimed at Major's Children. They all shared an anti-style, anti-success ethos celebrated in aspirational Eighties youth journals like *The Face* and *Sky*. *Phat* ran articles on career guides for losers, and the *Idler* was a lifestyle manual for a new breed of the urban aristocratic loafers, dedicated to the quality of life through leisure.

The great heroes of Eighties enterprise – yuppies,

City whizz-kids, and entrepreneurs like Richard Branson and Alan Sugar – all fell out of favour. Now it was the turn of outsiders and oddballs to be celebrated. Typical of the new breed was Tracey Emin, who described this change: 'During Thatcherism . . . if you didn't fit in with the crowd, you were on the outside, and if you were on the outside then you were a Nobody. And that was the general feeling for everything, no matter what your place was in the hierarchy: you had to fucking fit in, and if you didn't – forget it. But get rid of Thatcherism and everything was turned around. Then it became the cult of the individual, the loser, the outsider – because those were the types who had been ignored for fifteen years.'

Of course popular culture's fascination with winners didn't suddenly come to an end just because *Dallas* was off our screens. The popularity of those psychologically damaged divas like Courtney Love, PJ Harvey and Björk didn't mean that Madonna, that very embodiment of Eighties aspiration, was finished, either. But mainstream popular culture and media gave a space to people and voices who would have been ignored or marginalized in the 1980s.

There were the violent and druggy Scottish lowlifes of Irvine Welsh's novel *Trainspotting* (1993), which was the iconic novel (and later film) of the decade. When Bruce Robinson's cult classic *Withnail & I* – a tale of two debauched actors played by Richard E. Grant and Paul McGann) was first released in 1987, it bombed at the box office. Re-released in 1996 the film became a cult classic, finding a whole new audience among the young. Two of the most famous and popular losers of the decade were MTV's *Beavis and Butt-head* – animated teenage figures that *Time* magazine called 'totems of decline and non-achievement'.

Then there was the group of young and dynamic creatives who became associated with Cool Britannia, like those bad boys from Oasis, the Gallagher brothers who swore like troopers and swaggered like rock stars. There was the 'daring' fashion designer Alexander McQueen, the raffish Jarvis Cocker, the boho Kate Moss and a whole group of 'controversial' Young British Artists like Damien Hirst, who were hitting the head-lines around 1995. They were all young, gifted and out of their heads – or at least that was their image. Tales of wild drug-fuelled nights at exclusive London clubs began to circulate in the media. The house magazine of this lot was *Loaded*, and it celebrated working-class hedonism for a new breed of middle-class kids – e.g. David Baddiel – who longed to be mad, bad and lad.

Any idea that here were a group of young rebels, forging a new creative spirit and cultural style that offered an alternative to the mainstream, was an illu-sion; they all made a mad dash to the mainstream and scooped up the money and fame. The drugs, the drunken behaviour, the controversial art meant that the kiddies of Cool Britannia could clamber up the ladder of success while still looking like outsiders and rebels. The road of excess – sex, drugs and rock 'n' roll – did not lead to the palace of wisdom, as Blake suggested, but to drinks with Tony Blair at Number Ten. It led to contracts with big fashion houses like Givenchy and Dior (see John Galliano and Alexander McQueen); and for artists, large exhibitions at the Royal Academy ('Sensation', featuring the YBAs) and celebrity. Being an outsider was the quickest way of becoming an insider.

☆

The Nineties was the decade in which the Big Bang of celebrity happened. It became a growth industry, spawning new media, creating new forms of celebrity life, driving consumerism and driving broadsheet commentators to furious tirades against our 'obsession' with celebrity culture. Philip Howard wrote in *The Times* in October 1990, 'Fame is the spurt of scum on top of society. We are obsessed with celebrity.' He was the first columnist in Britain to make this claim, referring to an infestation of minor celebs (like Julia Carling, wife of rugby star Will Carling) and It girls (Tamara and Tara) who had ubiquitous media presence. And then along came the first real queen of Nineties celebrity culture: Elizabeth Hurley.

In 1994 she was just another unknown pretty actress looking for a break. Hurley had tried to launch her acting career in Hollywood and failed. Then one evening in May 1994 she went to the London film premiere of *Four Weddings and a Funeral* – with her then boyfriend Hugh Grant – in a black Versace dress. And, like Byron, Elizabeth Hurley woke up to find herself famous.

At first there was incredulity – at least from some sections of the press – that Hurley should acquire so much fame for having done so little. It was the Sabrina syndrome all over again. 'Her list of non-achievements is impressive indeed,' wrote Ross Benson in the *Daily Express*. Why was this woman so famous, they asked.

After all, Hurley *doesn't* appear in the film; she *doesn't* give a dazzling performance. Hell, she doesn't sleep with the director or even take her clothes off. She merely turns up at the premiere of someone else's film and becomes a star!

Hurley earned the dubious distinction of being the pre-eminent symbol of the emptiness of modern fame and the way our society had become obsessed with celebrity. But essentially the same thing happened almost a hundred years earlier to Lillie Langtry, the nineteenth-century London society beauty.

Langtry became an instant celebrity in April 1877 when she attended a fashionable society party in London. Such was her striking beauty, she found herself surrounded by famous artists, writers and society figures. Overnight she became the talk of the town. Artists like Whistler asked to paint her portrait. Her image on postcards sold in tobacconists all over Britain, and whenever she stepped outside the house she was mobbed. Like Hurley, she earned a fortune from her face.

Lillie and Liz had much in common. They'd both wanted to be actresses and only succeeded in becoming models. Lillie had Oscar Wilde as her best friend; Liz has Elton John. Both owe their international fame to a sex scandal. Liz Hurley was an unknown in America until Hugh Grant was caught with the prostitute Devine Brown in 1995. Lillie Langtry only became known outside England when her affair with the Prince of Wales became public knowledge in 1870.

There is one important difference between the two. The morning that Hurley awoke and found herself famous, we woke up to find that we now had someone in our lives called Elizabeth Hurley. In the years to come she would always be there – in our daily newspapers, Sunday supplements and on the covers of glossy magazines. At dinner parties people would talk about the Hurley 'phenomenon', and discuss Liz as 'an icon of our times'. By contrast, Langtry never played that large a role in public life.

The Nineties are important for one reason: they mark the time when ordinary people were invited to join that once exclusive club called celebrity. While commentators raged against the cult of celebrity, what was less discussed was the cult of the ordinary. As far as television was concerned, real people – that is, ordinary people – became all the rage. In 1992 MTV's *Real World* featured a group of young people living together in a loft in Manhattan. A year later the BBC came up with a similar format called *The Living Soap*, featuring the everyday lives of six students sharing a house in Manchester.

From these human soaps there developed the docusoaps like *Hotel*, *Airport* and *Pleasure Beach*, featuring ordinary people at work. These were documentaries that had the narrative drive of the soap opera. *Driving School* (1997) was about a group of learner drivers and the various disasters that beset them as they prepared to take their driving test. Welsh cleaner Maureen Rees became a celebrity after audiences of up to 12 million watched her fail her test six times. She went on to record a cover version of the Madness hit 'Driving In My Car', which reached number 50 in the UK singles chart.

Another popular series, *The Cruise*, made a celebrity of crooner Jane McDonald. In 1997 British television even got its first real-person sex symbol in Charlie Dimmock, the bra-less gardener from the BBC series *Ground Force*.

The cult of the ordinary even seeped into the coverage of the arts. A taxi driver was given a column in the *Literary Review*, while a nun (Sister Wendy) got her own history of art series. The BBC's premier arts programme, *The Late Show*, had a panel of 'real people' reviewing fiction, while Channel 4's film programme *Movie Watch* used ordinary people as critics. BBC2 came up with an arts programme, *Off the Wall*, featuring real people buying art.

A popular form of viewing was watching ordinary people pretend to be famous. One of the most popular shows of the decade was *Stars in Their Eyes*, which first aired on 21 July 1990. Ordinary members of the public would dress up and perform as their favourite star, and the audience – both at home and in the studio – would vote on the best imitation. Winners would go on to lucrative careers as star-imitators.

The Nineties saw the rise of tribute bands like Abba imitators Björn Again, and the growth of celebrity look-alikes. At times it was hard to tell who were the real pop stars and who were the imitators. Watching Molly Dineen's fly-on-the-wall documentary on Geri Halliwell (*Geri*), you got the feeling that the singer was imitating a pop star as much as any contestant on *Stars in Their Eyes*.

In the early part of the 1990s a man named Alan Conway – a gay, ex-alcoholic travel agent from Harlow – went around pretending to be film director Stanley Kubrick. Conway would go to a theatre, turn up backstage and tell such stars as Julie Walters and Patricia Hayes that he was considering them for a film he was doing. He would use Stanley's name to gain entrance to the Groucho Club in London.

What was interesting about Conway's con was that it was not some meticulously planned, *Stars in Their Eyes* transformation, where Alan Conway from Harlow steps out into the world looking, sounding and acting *just* like the legendary American film director Stanley Kubrick. On the contrary, Alan remained Alan. The clean-shaven Conway made no attempt to look like the bearded Kubrick, and his fake American accent was said to be 'appalling'. Conway acted in a way that made his gayness obvious, while Kubrick was a heterosexual.

Another curious thing about Conway was his lack of interest in Kubrick. He was not your typical fan/fanatic who knows everything about their hero's life and work. Conway had only seen a few of Kubrick's films. What made Conway's deceit possible was that Kubrick (who was then shooting *Eyes Wide Shut*) was said by the press to be something of a 'recluse', a man who had exiled himself to his guarded home in Hertfordshire. By recluse, people meant someone who did not wish to cash in on their fame; someone who was not seen at film premieres, gave no press interviews nor courted public attention.

What was Conway's motivation? Attention. 'That's all he wanted,' said Brian Cook, director of a film based on Conway called *Colour Me Kubrick*. 'He didn't do it for the money, he just needed to be a somebody.'

☆

There was a sub-section of ordinary people who wanted to be entertaining, but had no talent for entertainment. That was OK, because in the nineties you could always make an exhibition of yourself. In 1991 a Channel 4 youth programme called *The Word* first appeared and featured an item called *I'll Do Anything to get on TV*, which involved people doing disgusting things – drinking snot, eating insects, etc. – just for a moment of television fame.

It's an interesting reflection of attitudes to fame in the early nineties that such people were regarded as 'saddos' and 'losers' for debasing themselves. Given the revolting antics of participants in *I'm a Celebrity Get Me Out of Here!* nearly a decade later, *The Word* wannabes were simply ahead of their time.

If, on the other hand, you were an artist like Tracey Emin, it was permissible to go on television and make an exhibition of yourself. Emin had been a cult artist until 1997, when she appeared on television drunk and began to swear, abused fellow panellists and charged off the set. It was her Bill Grundy/Sex Pistols moment, and she gained instant fame. But no one thought she was a 'saddo' or a 'fame-hungry exhibitionist'. On the contrary, her supporters said she was saying something significant about self-confessional culture, though nobody was quite sure what.

Emin had grasped better than most that art shouldn't be about difficult abstract ideas, but a way of telling stories about yourself. She became the high priestess of confession, who had nothing to declare but her genius for pain and self-revelation. Tracey's pain could be seen in the titles of her shows, like 'Every Part of Me's Bleeding' (Lehmann Maupin, New York). This woman could bleed for Britain; indeed she did that when in 2007 she represented Britain at the Venice Biennale. Emin was demolishing the line between art and autobiography, exhibitions and exhibitionism. She gave the world her abortions, naked body, used condoms, the names of everyone she had ever slept with, and soiled sheets.

In 1996 Emin pushed the envelope of exhibitionism when she accepted an invitation to do a show at the Galleri Andreas Brandstrom in Stockholm. She would spend two weeks in a special room where she would eat, sleep and make art – while naked. Sixteen fish-eye lenses set into the wall enabled the public to watch her live and work.

In the same year that Tracey Emin was allowing the public to spy on her in Stockholm, a young American student called Jennifer Kaye Ringley invited users of the Internet to watch her eating, sleeping, working, showering and occasionally being naked and having sex with her boyfriend. It wasn't long before Ringley's site was getting between three and four million hits a day.

Was this art or mere exhibitionism? Neither. Ringley believed she was a crusader, fighting for the rights of ordinary people to be as worthy of attention as celebrities. 'I make people feel better about their ordinary, unglamorous lives ... I'm trying to prove the point that no matter what you look like, you're still as interesting as the people on the TV or in the magazines.' Three years after she began her crusade, a programme appeared in Holland called *Big Brother* that would do just that.

If Tracey Emin was the queen of the new confessional culture, then its princess had to be Diana. In the 1980s she embodied the Live Aid ethos: celebrity glamour harnessed for good causes such as Aids victims, victims of landmines and the homeless. She managed to strike a chord with the forgotten people of the 1980s – the lonely, the neglected, the loveless – and yet also the rich and powerful. Diana was a one-nation celebrity.

But in the nineties she found a new way of connecting with the public: confession. Her problems – divorce, an unfaithful husband, eating disorders – moved centre stage with the publication of Andrew Morton's biography, *Diana: Her True Story*, and then in 1995 a notorious interview on *Panorama* where she discussed her husband's affairs and her own. The more she presented herself as suffering Diana – first at the hands of her husband Prince Charles, and then later tormented by a heartless media – the more the public loved her. Here was the most famous and glamorous figure in the world, and she was just as miserable as everyone else. In 1993 she announced her retirement from public life, but the public – and their servants the press – had no intention of letting her go.

☆

The Nineties were the time when serious commentators started to deal with the phenomenon of fame. In 1993 Clive James made a BBC television series (*Fame in the 20th Century*) that helped him to become more famous, and broadsheets began running think pieces on modern fame. The general consensus was that it was a kind of modern pathology. Writers went to bizarre lengths to connect celebrity with sickness or evil. In his novel *Alma Cogan*, Gordon Burn linked the fame of Fifties singer Alma Cogan and the child-killer Myra Hindley. In her essay 'The Cult of Celebrity', the writer Jacqueline Rose made a similar connection between the fame of Princess Diana and the young child-killer Mary Bell. Others complained that we were 'dumbing down' and sinking in a sea of cultural trivia. Hardly a day passed without some new survey appearing, showing that the names of soap stars were better known to the British public than the names of members of the Cabinet.

Still, no one had the smoking gun that could prove what celebrity culture had done to Britain, at least until the death of Princess Diana in 1997. To the critics of this culture, nothing exposed the pathology of modern celebrity more dramatically than the bizarre outburst of national grief that followed her death.

That event evoked the first real anti-celebrity backlash among the general public, who blamed the French paparazzi for her car crash. Couldn't they have just left her alone, her grieving admirers asked. Pundits pointed out the obvious contradiction of a public who had an insatiable hunger for photos of their darling princess, but who now blamed the media for providing them. Others went further and claimed that 'we were all guilty' of her death. For Princess Diana, like John Lennon, was killed by a crazy fan . . . and that fan was us.

But it wasn't long before the doubts and denunciations about celebrity culture and the 'hounding' of Diana faded away, and it was back to business as usual.

14

Love, Loathing and Landesmania

In 2003 I met a girl called Maxine and we fell in love. She was innately chic, effortlessly beautiful and had a big, trusting heart. There was something glamorous about her goodness.

She came into my life when I was facing fifty and feeling that mandatory sense of failure that all men of my age feel. But Maxine changed everything. We had a baby boy we called Dexter, and then we got married. I felt like I had won love's lottery – my first prize being a second chance to become the good husband and the good father I had longed to be.

Our true romance soon faced two challenges: my famous ex-wife and my infamous parents.

Max knew all about Julie, but had no idea that her ghost would be such a presence in her marriage. If you're married to someone who was married to a celebrity – even a minor media one like Julie – there's no escape. You can divorce a celebrity, but you can never be free of their fame.

Actually, my media friends showed a quite surprising sensitivity and rarely mentioned Julie in front of Max. It was *Max*'s media friends who went on about her. At dinner parties with Julie's pals, Max would have to sit there and try and smile as I dodged questions about my marriage to bloody Rebecca de Winter. Whenever Julie wrote something in the papers or was written about, it was her friends who were on the phone straight away to discuss it.

Dealing with the ghost of my ex was one thing; dealing with the reality of my parents was another. When we first started dating I had tried to warn Max that my parents were a little on the eccentric side. And I had tried to warn my parents that Max was not some showbiz media tart who was fascinated by the Landesman family.

With the prospect of the first meet-Max dinner on the horizon, I briefed them on how to make a good impression. 'Look, for heaven's sake don't spend the whole evening talking about yourselves . . . try to take an interest in her . . . ask her questions about what she does . . . and for God's sake don't go on about Julie . . . And Jay, no jokes about her being Chinese.'

It was as if I were a teenager again, pleading with my parents to try and act normal. I should have known by now they didn't do normal.

We arrived for dinner, and we hadn't even taken off our coats before I realized that my briefing had failed. They wasted no time in finding out what Max thought . . . about them.

Jay: Big news, Max – I've got two publishers in America fighting over my novel *The Nervous Set*. Have you read it yet?

Fran: Never mind that. Max, Cosmo says you're an art director at the *Sunday Times*. Will you look at this flyer for an album of my new songs and tell me what you think? I did the design myself.

Jay: Fran, I was talking. It's rude to interrupt.

Fran: Jaybird, you've been interrupting me for forty years!

Jay: Max, what about the cover of my book? I see a picture of me as a dashing young man in the fifties, Martini in one hand, surrounded by a bevy of beauties. Has Cosmo given you *any* of my books?

Max: Well, I . . .

Fran: Max, take some of these flyers and give them to your friends. It has a list of gigs I'm doing this month. I would love it if you would come and hear me.

Jay: Max, here's the cover of my last volume of autobiography. For the new one I need something fresh and eye-catching.

Just then Miles enters the room.

Miles: It's here. The final mix of my greatest demo hits. Here, Max, have one of these.

Me: Miles, how can you have a greatest hits made out of demos that were never hits?

Miles: Man, you've got to relax a bit. This is a collection of demos that *would* have been hits, had they been released. OK?

I look at Maxine. On her lap sits a little pile of Landesman projects, past and present. They will give her a bag for all her Landesman goodies.

That was the night she asked me, 'Do your parents ever talk about anything but themselves?'

☆

Unfortunately for Max, she came into my life when my parents went from being lovable eccentrics to exasperating egomaniacs.

They have friends and lovers who will tell you that this change never happened, because Fran and Jay have always been that way. I once asked Pam, one of my dad's former girlfriends, if it was true that my parents had always been so self-obsessed. 'Always!' she said without a moment's hesitation. 'Fran hasn't asked me a question about myself in thirty years.'

But I disagree with this diagnosis. Maybe they'd always been prone to self-preoccupation, but they knew it and made jokes about it. The truly self-obsessed can't step outside their self-obsession and see themselves as others do. Consequently, they're never funny about their condition. My father would invite Julie and me to dinner and say, 'I promise we won't talk about ourselves – even if the strain kills us.' Those days were gone.

Once they had been supportive of other people's talents and concerned for the lives of their friends. My parents had belonged to that special breed of the self-preoccupied who can still look up from their own lives and respond to the needs of others. They had the gift of generosity and were always gracious hosts.

But all that slowly changed. They lost their interest in other people. They no longer had dinner parties, and old friends faded from their lives. In their place came admirers, good listeners and people who could help them get their projects off the ground.

My dad lost his curiosity about other people; he used to long to know your story and probe around your personality in the hope of finding those buried treasures of the self we call our secrets. He loved talking about you, in those days, *almost* as much as he loved talking about himself. Now he saw every new face as just someone who would listen to his old stories.

There was a new note of self-obsession in the kind of projects he was taking up: they were the ideas of the desperate and the delusional. Typical was the one I heard about on the phone one afternoon.

Jay: Got a minute?

Me: What's up?

Jay: Who's this guy Izzy Ackboryn?

Me: You mean Ozzy Osbourne?

Jay: Yeah, that's the one. I caught his show last night, the reality thing with his family – what an awful act he's got! I can't understand a word he's saying. And the wife, *oy*!

Me: Sharon Osbourne.

Jay: Yeah . . . what an awful, foul-mouthed yenta she is!

Me: Well, the Osbournes are very popular.

Jay: Really? Well, I was thinking about this reality TV thing and . . .

Me: Please, don't tell me . . .

Jay: Why the hell not? The Landesmans are far more interesting than those squares.

Me: Jay . . . don't you even think about it!

Jay: OK, don't get so upset. It was just an idea.

Click.

The next day I got the synopsis in the post.

It was entitled *Life as a Work of Art – an Idea for a Documentary*.

The Characters. Jay Landesman, Fran Landesman his wife, Cosmo Landesman their elder son, Miles Landesman their younger son.

I read a section to Maxine.

'Movers and shakers of the alternative Establishment, the Osbournes of the cult circuit, the Landesmans live in a creative paradise. Each member of the family has made their mark on the literary and musical Establishment. It is a dynamic dynasty which should be captured on film.'

'Oh and get this,' I said to Max. 'Jay ran the best bar in the States, Fran wrote the best songs and lyrics, Miles is a record producer and Cosmo married Julie Burchill.'

'I think I need to lie down,' I said.

'Your poor deluded parents,' said Max, shaking her head. 'This isn't a project; it's a cry for help.'

☆

Jay's next big idea even took Fran and Miles by surprise: the Jay Landesman Museum. I've already explained the basic concept at the start of this book – it was a chance for the public to tour the house at Duncan Terrace and see what an interesting life Jay had led.

Actually, I do think Jay has had an interesting life. But having an interesting life and writing about it is one thing; inviting the public into your home, to traipse around your bedroom and have a look at your 'interesting life' is another. Also, there's the assumption that there is a sufficiently large audience to justify such an undertaking. Only a crazy man could believe such a thing.

As well as being curator of his own museum, Jay had found a new occupation: movie producer. He had found a 'terrific story' for the screen: his own. So he hired a friend, Terrence Doyle, to rewrite his screenplay *Neurotica*, which was about Jay's days in New York as the publisher of *Neurotica*. Armed with a screenplay, Jay and Terry went to Cannes with hopes of making a deal. They managed to have fun and generate a lot of publicity, but no one wanted to make their movie.

Over the next two years Jay was always finding and losing producers. He changed his screenplay more times than his underwear. Every time I saw him he insisted on reading me the latest draft – I didn't have the heart to tell him it was the same as the last one. His project brought back his old excitement. He was already casting before the film had been sold. And because I was a film critic, I was the first call for approval.

Jay: Got a minute?

Me: Yes.

Jay: Drew Barrymore is going to play Fran!

Me: Does Drew Barrymore know this?

Jay: No, it's a surprise. I've got a new producer who says he can get the script to Drew.

Over the following month the list of people he intended to play him included: Adrian Brody, Jim Carrey and Johnny Depp – who actually got a copy of the script, but for some reason turned it down. For Fran

Jay had Michelle Pfeiffer, Jennifer Jason Leigh and Susan Sarandon, as the older Fran.

I began to worry when Jay was actually considering investing £100,000 of his own money into getting the film made. It was then that I knew he was suffering from Insane Project Syndrome. But I managed to talk him out of it. It wasn't easy. I felt like I was talking to a man who is on the edge of a rooftop and threatening to jump. Slowly I eased him back to reality, and he put the screenplay and his movie dreams in the bottom of his crowded project drawer.

Other men would have given up at that point, but not Jay. He bounced back with a new project: a book called *Landesmania!: A Biography*. The book, commissioned and paid for by Jay, was a rewrite of his past two biographies by his drinking buddy Philip Trevena.

Landesmania! would have been the perfect catalogue for the Jay Landesman Museum, because it was a celebratory tour through Jay's life. It's no wonder that he loved *Landesmania!*: it was one hundred and fifty-five pages of what a wonderful, original, stylish and interesting guy Jay was. And he was anxious that the rest of the world should know this as well.

I once asked Jay if he didn't think it was odd to be paying someone to write a book about him.

Jay: No, why? Should I?'

Me: But isn't it the worst kind of vanity publishing?

Jay: Not at all. It's the best kind of vanity publishing. Philip has brought a unique perspective to my story. He really gets what I've been all about. And besides, I like to encourage young writers.

Me: Yeah, young writers who write about how wonderful you are!

Jay: I can't think of a better and more important topic!

He mounted one of his media blitzkriegs to whip up publicity for *Landesmania!*, but this time there was little media interest. Jay sent the book with a personal letter to dozens of literary editors, suggesting they might like to review it. You have to admire his cheek. His letter to Alexandra Shulman – editor of British *Vogue* – begins by reminding her of the time he tried it on with her at Biba back in the 1970s! The poor woman has probably been trying to forget that nightmare encounter ever since.

All Jay's friends and family were roped in to help promote the book. He insisted that Maxine send it to her friend who was then the books editor of the *Sunday Times*. The woman never replied or spoke to Maxine again.

Despite Jay's best efforts, *Landesmania!* only got one review, and guess who wrote it? Julie Burchill in the *Spectator*. The entire review was based on her memories of the Landesman family. Jay was thankful that he had at last got a review, but later said, 'It would have been nice if she had mentioned the book!'

Christmas Eve 2005. Max and I are talking about my parents' increasing self-absorption. We wonder how far it can go. I said to Max, 'Oh well, things could be worse. At least they're not banging on about their open marriage any more.'

'Thank God for that,' said Max.

Christmas Morning 2005. I turn on Radio 4, and Fran and Jay are talking about their open marriage. They were part of Francine Stock's *Pick of the Year*, a look back at the high points of Radio 4's output throughout 2004. They had been included in a series about people who had been married for over thirty years.

I was just about to turn it off when I told myself, grow up! You can't always duck and dive from your parents. So I decided to be brave and listen. At one point the interviewer asked Jay about the possible damage their affairs had caused to other people, and Jay said he didn't believe he had caused any damage. 'On the contrary, I was giving people a reason to live!' It was said partly as a joke, but it came across as the deluded vanity of an old crazy man.

I cringed and let out a long cry of anguish.

Max came into the bathroom, and seeing me curled up in a foetal position on the floor, said, 'Someone around here needs psychiatric help – but I'm not sure if it's you, your parents – or *me*.'

☆

What was the reason for Jay's crazy projects and his growing self-obsession? I asked Philip Trevena why Jay wanted him to write *Landesmania!*, and he told me, 'I think he felt forgotten. And he felt his footnote in history wasn't large enough and he wanted to embellish it with an outsider view of him. He wanted it to be a bit of a promo job for the old Landesman legend.'

My dad was now in his eighties. He once said to me he didn't fear dying, he feared dying anonymously. I think he felt this was his last chance to make his mark on the world, to try and get from it the affirmation that his mother never gave him.

At this point in his life all his projects had stalled on him. He'd written a third volume of memoirs – a completely rambling account of his daily doings – and everyone had told him it was 'crap'. The movie project had collapsed and even his sex life was in trouble.

In her book *Bohemians: The Glamorous Outcasts*, Elizabeth Wilson writes, 'Many bohemians . . . poured their creativity into that most ephemeral of arts, the "art of living", dedicating their lives to the evanescent arts of adornment, outrage, wit and conversation.' And that's what Jay did. He removed the creative means of display – the plays, the novels and the memoirs – for the display itself: his life. He even went one step further and saw himself as a kind of lifestyle guru. He'd already tried to sell *Landesmania!* as a book 'for all those bored citizens in the West who would like to change their lives, but do not know how to do it.' The museum had also been an attempt to show people a more 'interesting' way to live.

It wasn't long before we clashed over his new calling. He'd phoned to discuss the party for *Landesmania!*, but somehow the topic of conversation went in a completely different direction. I asked him if he ever worried that he would be remembered as the man with the open marriage and not as the writer, producer, etc. In other words, would the publicity he attracted to his life eclipse his work?

Jay: No. I want to show people how to live a more fulfilling life.

Me: What are you, some sort of makeover life coach?

Jay: You could say that. There are a lot of people whose lives could use a good makeover.

By this he meant me. And so I retaliated.

Me: You always say that you've been more interested in making your life work than making it. But that's not true. You're in denial!

Jay: Screw the success game! Look at all those so-called successful novelists, like Mailer and Bellow; they're all phonies because they didn't live their lives right.

Me: Who the fuck are you to say they lived their lives right or wrong?

Jay: Living is something I know all about. Look at you. The reason that you've been such a failure is that you're so square and bourgeois.

Me: Hold on! Where did that come from?

Jay: Straight from the heart.

Me: OK, if you want to strut around as Mr Lifestyle Guru, go ahead – but you're gonna have a following of one: yourself.

Jay: Ha! We'll see about that.

Click . . .

☆

'*I walk down the street thinking I'm the legendary Fran Landesman . . . Me . . . The legendary Fran Landesman.*'

Fran in conversation with me, 2004.

I didn't know what to do about Fran's descent into self-obsession. I wanted to be supportive and feel proud of her, and pleased that she had something in her life that she loved and gave people pleasure. But . . . I felt that if I had to hear her say *they loved me . . . they loved me . . . they loved me . . .* once more. I would strangle her.

Of course I felt bad about my reaction. I tried to tell myself not to be so irritated. After all, it was just the love-hungry little fat girl starved for parental approval who was talking. The little fat girl wanted their approval, my approval, and the world's approval . . .

'Well,' said the voice inside my head, 'it's time somebody told Fatso to shut the fuck up!'

Things came to a head between Fran and me one afternoon in my parents' garden. It was a lovely summer's day, and we were having tea. Fran started in with her they-loved-me routine and I let out a groan. She immediately shut up and I could see she was miffed.

A few minutes later out popped, 'Maxine could at least come to one of my gigs. Even Julie did that.'

I couldn't believe what I was hearing. It had never occurred to Fran that maybe Maxine was too exhausted by the baby to go to anything in the evenings. But I was determined not to spoil the afternoon, so I kept quiet.

Then Jay started talking about his new book. He was planning to do a greatest hits of his memoirs: selections from his first two books and a few chapters from his unpublished memoirs. 'I'm calling it *Cultural Slumming*,' he said. 'Great title, don't you think?'

I thought it was one of the worst titles I had ever heard. I didn't say that, though. I tried to explain that 'cultural slumming' was used as a term of criticism. Jay insisted that I had it wrong. I insisted that I had it right.

And Fran insisted that unless we started talking about something else she was leaving.

'What?' I asked in disbelief.

'You heard me,' Fran said. 'We've done this topic, Mr Cosmo. It's becoming boring and repetitive.'

'But I'm trying to make a point about Jay's book,' I replied. I turned to Jay and said, 'Look, Jay, the thing is that your title . . .'

Fran threatened me with, 'I'm counting to three and then leaving.'

And so the battle began.

Me: Why don't you just fuck off now?

Fran: You're boring and repetitive.

Me: What? Boring and repetitive? I've had to listen to you go on and on about oh they love me, and listen for thirty-five years to your fucking stories about the Crystal Palace and what a drunken Jack Kerouac said to you, the same fucking story, and you call me repetitive.

Fran: I'm leaving.

Me: No, I'm leaving . . . you self-absorbed cunt. You can't stand to have any conversation that isn't about you!

I left vowing never to return, just like I had a million times before.

The next day I got a letter from Fran saying she was sorry. 'Won't you forgive your crazy old mum?' The PS read: 'Here's a flyer for a gig I'm doing. If you could get it mentioned in the *Sunday Times* I'd appreciate it.'

It wasn't just my parents who were so self-obsessed, but everyone I knew. There were times when it seemed that all my friends were turning into my parents. They wanted me to read their books, their screenplays, their latest articles, and hear their demos. They wanted me to be an adoring audience. I was constantly being invited to gigs, asked to contact so-and-so in the media on their behalf, which I was happy to do because that's what friends are for, aren't they?

We never talked about our lives – only our forthcoming projects. Once we shared secrets, now we shared reviews of our work.

I had friends who only got in touch with me via an email to everyone they knew, announcing that they would be appearing on such and such a programme. The curious thing is, no one ever wondered if their acts of self-promotion might be considered in bad taste. There was no hint of embarrassment, none of the nervous tics of irony that suggested self-doubt about what they were doing.

Not since the 1980s had everyone become so shamelessly involved in promoting themselves. However, this time around it wasn't for the money; it was for the celebrity.

☆

When we decided to have a baby, Maxine thought she was marrying into this warm, loving, supportive Jewish family that would embrace their new daughter-in-law and fuss over their new grandchild. But things got bad between my parents and us after the birth of Dexter in 2004. After an initial burst of excitement, they seemed to have little interest in spending time with their new grandson. They never came over to visit, or offered to mind the baby to give us a break, the way other grandparents did.

My parents' lack of interest in our son was embarrassing. Maxine couldn't understand how a project could be more exciting than a baby. Things weren't helped by Fran constantly referring to the great days when she used to spend so much time with Jack when he was a baby.

Maxine couldn't help but notice the difference between their behaviour towards Julie's son Jack and her son Dexter. Was it a case of the star's kid getting preferential treatment? No, I told myself, not even my star-struck parents could be like that . . . could they?

I tried not to make a big deal about it, and then it reached the point where I had to say something. I was talking to Fran, and suddenly out it popped.

Me: How come you spend so little time with Dexter? You never come to see him.

Fran: Because I'm fucking old! And I'm losing my sight and I can't get the fuck around like I used to!

Me: If that's true, how is it you always manage to get around when there's a chance for you to perform in front of people?

Fran: It's called Dr Footlights. Performing gives me that big rush of energy that gets me going.

Me: But seeing your grandson doesn't?

Fran: It's not the same.

Me: Obviously for you it's not the same. If you have the chance to show off you can travel halfway across

England, but you can't take a ten-minute bus ride to see your grandson.

Fran: Oh fuck you ... I'm too old. I don't want to fucking live, can't you see that?

It was at this point that Jay came and joined us, and I turned my fire on him.

Me: Tell me something. How come you can manage to go to the Groucho Club, drink Martinis and chat up women, but you never spend any time with your grandson Dexter?

Jay: I don't do that sort of thing ... it's too bourgeois.

Me: You mean you're too busy to spend time with my family because you want to go out and try and impress people that you're a big shot.

Jay: That's right!

Me: Remember how when you were sick I helped you out? How come you never help me out? We could have used some help with the baby.

Jay: You did nothing for me when I was sick.

On hearing this, something inside me finally snapped. The one time I needed my family to help me with my family they refused to do it. It was as if all the years of my anger and embarrassment came rising to the surface and I lashed out at my father – it was more of a slap across the side of his head than a punch.

I looked at Jay. He sat silently in his chair, looking at the floor. His glasses were dangling from one ear, and his old head was bobbing around like one of those dog ornaments you see in the back of cars. He looked pale and in a state of shock.

Miles ran up and stood between us, saying, 'Cos, please don't kill him!'

Before I left I managed to get in one last cruel blow. 'Oh and by the way, your last book stank!'

15

Generation Me

In retrospect it seems that celebrity culture entered our lives by stealth. It sneaked in with the post-war rise of our affluent consumer society, and was aided and abetted by the seduction of television. It began with a few famous faces, a magazine or two, and before we knew it we had a full-blown celebrity culture on our hands.

For a short time it was something safely tucked away within the confines of the tabloid press and glossy magazines. No need to worry, we said, this was ironic England, not fame-obsessed America. But then in the nineties the invincible ooze of celebrity culture began to seep and spread.

By the end of the 1990s there seemed to be more celebrity-based trivia, both in serious newspapers and in our lives. It crept into our conversations. One was expected to have an opinion on Madonna and Liz Hurley. One read think pieces on the model Caprice and watched documentaries on people like Geri Halliwell.

Some of us started to worry that we were dumbing down. New works of literary fiction were bought but never read – at least not beyond the first chapter or two. I had a growing stack of untouched copies of the *New*

York Review of Books that silently sulked in the corner of my room. Once, in the dentist's waiting room, I pulled out my new hardback copy of Francis Fukayama's *The End of History* . . . and then grabbed a copy of *Hello!* instead. I told myself: relax. You're not dumbing down. You're just keeping tabs on the zeitgeist.

Defenders of celebrity culture claimed it was bringing a fragmented nation together, providing it with the stuff of a national conversation. 'Around the office water fountain or in the family kitchen, the teenager and the fifty-something alike indulge in talk about *Big Brother* excesses and favourite soap operas,' wrote Cristina Odone in the *Observer*. She warned the liberal elite that 'if you ignore football or Liz Hurley and seal yourself off in a highbrow citadel you will fail to communicate with anyone.'

What Odone had failed to grasp was that by 2000 it was no longer possible to seal yourself off in some imagined highbrow citadel and live free from the cacophony of celebrity culture. 'Celebrities. Like flies in a summer forest, you can't move for them . . .' was how Radio 4's *Analysis* began an edition devoted to a discussion of celebrity culture. 'And now even the citadel of *Analysis* surrenders its status as celebrity-free zone. If you're appalled, you're not alone.'

Was I appalled by the rise of celebrity culture? Yes. No. Maybe. I couldn't go along with the postmodern populists who defended it as 'democratic', 'empowering' and 'fun'. And if the national conversation was going to be dominated by talk of Kylie or Jade, then I'd rather stay silent.

But there was another national conversation, one that was all about the horrors of celebrity culture. There was an England that groaned and grumbled about the latest celebrity horror show – e.g. *Big Brother* or *I'm a Celebrity . . . Get Me Out of Here!* – to be a hit. Commentators from the left and the right, celebrities and non-celebrities, they all joined in a denunciation of celebrity culture – and nothing changed.

But at the same time I didn't want to take the line of intellectuals and the liberal intelligentsia that we had entered a new era of 'dumbing down' and 'cultural decline'. For beneath such talk I sensed something nasty at work: good old-fashioned snobbery. These critics weren't bothered by the fact that the people who were becoming famous had no talent, for they knew that since the dawn of Hollywood and the rise of Pop, plenty of no-talents had found fame. No, it was the sort of people who were becoming famous that they disliked, what they saw as ghastly working-class women from docu-soaps, and all the Jades and the Jordans, the hunky nobodies and the nice, bland boys from next door. They were appalled by the vulgarity of these 'half-attractive half-persons' (Salman Rushdie); these 'non-entities who no longer realize that they are non-entities' (Clive James).

There was a time when critics like James and Rushdie would have never have attacked the likes of Jade and co., for the simple reason that such people were invisible. The etiquette of television – as well as the tastes of its predominantly middle-class controllers – kept them off our screens. But with the unexpected success of *Big Brother* in 2001, the rules of the fame game changed.

☆

It started like this. September 1997 saw the opening of the 'Sensation' exhibition at London's Royal Academy of Art. Featuring such works as a shark in formaldehyde (Damien Hirst), child mannequins with penis-like noses (the Chapman brothers) and a large portrait of child-killer Myra Hindley (Marcus Harvey), it provoked out-raged headlines in the tabloid press and protests outside the exhibition. Brit Art had taken over from Brit Pop as the arena of shock and celebrity awe.

Two weeks before the opening of 'Sensation', a cre-ative brainstorming session in Holland was under way at the house of Dutch TV producer John de Mol. He and his production team were in search of a new television format that would conquer the world. From that session emerged an idea for a new television programme that would eventually become *Big Brother* – a show that was to be the Brit Art of broadcasting: controversial, daring, taboo-busting, headline-grabbing and very popular, especially with the young.

The programme had become a big hit in Holland, Germany and Spain – but how would the British respond? Within the television industry there were doubts about its suitability for UK audiences. Even Peter Bazalgette, the man who would eventually bring *Big Brother* to Brit-ain, thought it was 'far too cruel . . . for the UK market.'

Before *Big Brother* went on air there was much anguished talk about what this show said about us as a nation. According to press reports, we were about to witness scenes of explicit sex, nudity, drunken behaviour, lurid confessions and emotional incontinence. It all seemed terribly un-English. Once again commentators asked: what has happened to the stiff upper lip?

The outpouring of national grief that followed the death of Princess Diana suggested that the stiff upper lip was no more. We were, it was said, a nation of grief bingers who were happy to let it all hang out in public spaces or on television.

By the end of the 1990s a new picture of the British started to emerge. 'The famous British reserve is crumbling fast and we are now more desperate than the Americans to secure 15 minutes of TV fame,' declared the *Daily Express*. The evidence for this was an NOP and Omnitel poll of 1,600 people that suggested that the British had become even more exhibitionistic than the Americans. One in ten Brits said they'd bare all and streak for fame; one in five Brits said they would 'kiss and tell' after a night with a celebrity, compared to fewer than one in ten Americans.

There were other signs that suggested this poll was right. The daytime television confession show *Jerry Springer* first appeared on British television in 1999. The received wisdom at the time was that it was too American – i.e. too exhibitionistic – for British tastes. But a spokesman for the show said: 'We were stunned to receive 30,000 applications to appear on the first show. We were expecting the British to be much more buttoned-up and reserved but, if anything, they're more game than their American counterparts.'

A year later *Big Brother* made its British broadcasting debut on 14 July 2000. It seemed rather tame, compared to the series in other European countries. Britain's voyeurs must have been very disappointed; there was no on-screen sex. Yes, eyebrows were raised when six of the ten contestants stripped and smeared themselves with wet clay. However, the drama that came to grip the viewing public was one rooted in that old-fashioned British sense of fair play, and not fornication.

What offended everyone wasn't the puerile displays of flesh but the Machiavellian tactics of one of the contestants, ex-public schoolboy Nick Bateman, who was caught cheating. (Bateman had tried to manipulate his fellow housemates into evicting certain contestants to enable his own victory.) For a while the housemates didn't know what was going on, but the public could see Bateman at work. The tabloid press had a field day with tales of the man they dubbed 'Nasty Nick'.

When Bateman was eventually confronted by his fellow housemates we got a trial by television. The fate of Nasty Nick became the topic of the day, and when it was announced that he was to be expelled from the house it made the front page of every British newspaper except the *Financial Times*. *Big Brother* was one of those shows that you could experience without actually having seen it.

Likewise, the second series of *Big Brother* was pretty tame stuff. This time the big drama was based on the rather sweet story of two lovers: Helen, who revealed a passion for blinking, and an ordinary guy called Paul who revealed a passion for Helen. The audience and the tabloid press may have wanted to catch the couple in flagrante bonko, but they refused to play along. Could the shamelessness of the British have been over estimated? In the Dutch series of *Big Brother*, contestants Bart and Sabine did it (under the covers) and Kerstin and Alex did it in the German version. But, in terms of sex, Britain's *Big Brother* series was still a virgin

Nor had we produced a true 'Trash Hero' like Germany's Zlatko Trpkoviski, a twenty-three-year-old car mechanic who admitted that he hadn't the faintest idea who Shakespeare was. And what's more, he didn't care. Zlatko was dumb and proud of it. He was the voice of the average bloke and it made him into a star. Ten thousand German Zlatko fans marched on the *Big Brother* house outside Cologne to see him evicted.

The best that Britain could produce was a posh cad like Nasty Nick. The rest of the *Big Brother* contestants were not the crazed wannabes and exhibitionistic weirdos we'd expected. They were all shockingly . . . *normal.* It wasn't until the third series that *Big Brother* finally got someone who lived up to people's low expectations.

Jade Goody was a large snub-nosed twenty-year-old dental nurse from Bermondsey in south-east London. She had a loud cockney voice and appeared able to give Zlatko a run for his money in the stupid stakes. Goody thought chickpeas came from a chicken and that Cambridge was in London. The fact that she was to become the first and only reality-TV millionaire suggests that she wasn't as dumb as people thought.

As we have seen, it was in the 1990s that ordinary people made their debut into the media spotlight. In

2000 we started to see a different breed of ordinary people. Instead of lovable lollipop ladies or endearing biddies learning to drive, we saw young working-class men and women who drank, swore, had sex and didn't sit around discussing the state of the English novel. Instead of cuddly Maureen Rees we got gobby Jade Goody.

There's a theory that traces our current cult of celebrity back to the age of the Romantic artist and the idea of the fascinating individual. In the eighteenth and nineteenth centuries, the artist was seen as championing the values of self-expression and personal fulfilment in a world of mass production and mass anonymity.

In the twentieth century, the oppositional values associated with the free-living artist – living for the moment, hedonism, the celebration of the body beautiful, freedom from constraints of social etiquette and deference, the cultivation of style – were co-opted by the new consumer society of the 1950s. In other words, people who were not artists were encouraged to act and think like artists and bohemians.

George Walden, in his book *Who's a Dandy?*, argues that our obsession with fashion, personal appearance and the display of provocative individuality suggests that we're all dandies now. If you want to see how the artistic/bohemian/dandy life has trickled down into the mainstream, then look at Jade Goody. It's tempting to dismiss her as a Trash Heroine, but actually she was the people's Tracey Emin. Both were working-class girls who found fame by appearing on television drunk; both were exhibitionists who used the shock tactics of sex as a means of securing attention. *My Boyfriend Fucked Me in the Arse and I Liked it* – who said that, Tracey or Jade? (Answer: Tracey. It was the name of one of her works.)

Goody did her own piece of performance art when one night in the *Big Brother* house she got drunk, stripped naked and started shouting, 'My kebab's showing!' She, allegedly, went on to perform oral sex on one of the housemates beneath a duvet. Did she blow or was it all show became the question of the day.

Emin had showed the art-loving middle classes the seamy side of real life – *nostalgie de la boue* – and now Jade was doing it too. But Jade was a touch too seedy and real for them. Emin had the authority of art, her celebrity and the media behind her; Goody was loathed by everyone. She was the real outsider, the *enfant terrible* who was too terrible both for the tabloid press and the Tate Modern crowd.

In Goody the British public found a great pantomime villain to whom everyone, no matter how vulgar or villainous, could feel superior. The tabloid press dubbed her 'Pig Brother' and 'the most hated woman in Britain'. Outside the *Big Brother* house members of the crowd carried placards that read 'Kill the Pig'. It was an echo of the humiliation that Emin had suffered as a teenager back in Margate, when boys would circle around her at the disco and chant 'slag . . . slag . . . slag.'

By 2005 reality TV was displaying the old bad behaviour of rock 'n' roll with the uninhibited look-at-naughty-me exhibitionism of the Young British Artists. For the first time ever, ordinary people came to play the role of the avant-garde.

Big Brother was denounced not only by the *Daily Mail* and the Pope, but as we have seen by such spokespersons of the liberal intelligentsia as Salman Rushdie and Germaine Greer. Not even Damien Hirst and co. had managed that combination.

One can see why Rushdie and his kind were so horrified by *Big Brother*. It wasn't the bad behaviour that bothered them; it was the banality of these reality-TV people that was so shocking. Their rise represented nothing less than a cultural revolution. For reality TV overthrew the existing system and standards that defined who was interesting and worthy of media scrutiny and fame, and who wasn't. In effect, *Big Brother* said that these ordinary people, just doing ordinary things, were as interesting as all the Rushdies and Greers in the world. Here was relativism with a vengeance.

But *Big Brother* is important for another reason: it marks a decisive turning point in the history of fame. For with its appearance the frazzled, tenuous bond between talent and fame finally snapped. Of course the talentless had found fame before *Big Brother*, but now you didn't need some justification for your fame. You didn't have to tell people you wanted to act or be a model or a singer. And you didn't have to be funny, smart, beautiful or even have big tits to deserve your fame! Reality TV tore up the fame rulebook and said: *you can be famous for just being you . . . bland, ordinary, unexceptional, ungifted you!*

Britain now had a new gang of reality-TV stars dominating the national agenda and office-water-cooler talk. Their presence upset the traditional fame hierarchy.

Commentators began to complain that B- and C-list celebrities didn't know their place any more. *Evening Standard* columnist Polly Vernon was shocked that C-list people were mixing with the A-list people and all these trashy *Big Brother* D-list types 'have become stars, revelling in the glare of A-list style paparazzi attention'.

Vernon wasn't the only one upset that the old celebrity hierarchy was crumbling. Comedienne Jennifer Saunders complained of the new equality, 'There doesn't seem to be any difference between someone who has done six movies and someone off *Big Brother*. Juliette Binoche's photo is next to Tamzin Outhwaite and you think what is going on here?'

Ever since the 1960s, commentators had claimed that celebrities had formed a new aristocracy. At the start of the twenty-first century, we got a replay of the nineteenth-century clash between New and Old Money. Now the 'stars' of reality TV were cast as the vulgar parvenus of New Fame who were challenging the supremacy of the Old Fame elite. And there were plenty of signs that New Fame was winning. Talent had always been Old Fame's trump card, but now not even that seemed to count any more. 'In this climate, actually having talent has become a distracting liability,' wrote Bryan Appleyard. 'Winona Ryder, who can act, turned up at the London premiere of *Planet of the Apes*. But the Hollywood star was ignored in favour of Helen and Paul, the couple who found love in the latest series of Big Brother.'

Leading the New Fame pack were David and Victoria Beckham. Pictures of their ostentatious marriage ceremony in 1999 showed the couple sitting on golden thrones. This, plus their purchase of a mansion they dubbed Beckingham Palace, earned them a reputation as being the vulgar faces of New Fame. Dame Barbara Cartland, she of romantic novels fame, was reported to have said on hearing that they were moving into the neighbourhood, 'They have lots of money but no class and no idea how to behave themselves.'

The Beckhams hurled back the most vicious insult New Fame could imagine: they asked, who's Barbara Cartland?

☆

There was a widespread sense that the whole fame game had just gone too far. Bryan Appleyard spoke for many when he wrote: 'This new power of fame, absolutely detached from all other values or talents, is now out of control.'

Even priests were beginning to speak out against this new celebrity-saturated world. The Rt Rev. James Jones, the Bishop of Liverpool, warned that we are 'creating a strange world in which the frivolous is being taken seriously and the serious treated flippantly'. He summed up a nightmarish vision where 'stars will become not only our rulers but also gods'.

Given the power and presence of celebrity, it was inevitable that satirists and comedians would lead the fight back. They'd last been in action during the 1980s when they took on Thatcherism; now celebrity was their number one target.

Harry Enfield, who'd made his mark with 'Loadsamoney' in the eighties, had a go in 2000 with a new television series called *Celeb*, about a burnt-out rock star. But the series was a critical and ratings failure. Ben Elton, another voice from the eighties, joined in the attack with novels like *High Society* and *Dead Famous*, satirizing the *Big Brother* celebrity culture, which seemed odd for the man who wrote the musical about Queen, *We Will Rock You*.

In 2001 the *Ab Fab* girls Patsy and Edina aimed at the celebrity target with their third series. Commentators like Libby Purves in *The Times* and Bryan Appleyard in the *Sunday Times* welcomed them with open arms, because if anyone could show the silly banality of celebrity culture it was our Patsy and Edina. But it was the series itself that wound up getting critically mauled, and not celebrity culture.

Others were more successful. Louis Theroux became the quiet assassin of celebrities – such as Jimmy Savile and Neil and Christine Hamilton – with his series *Louis Goes Into* . . . There was a new kidder on the block called Ali G (Sacha Baron Cohen), who tricked celebrities into thinking they were talking to the voice of 'yoof'. But no one managed to put the boot in so effectively as the accomplished prankster Chris Morris, whose *Brass Eye* programmes would trick celebrities into supporting imaginary public campaigns.

And then in August 2002 we got a new show that was especially designed to satisfy our longing to put celebrities in their place. *I'm a Celebrity . . . Get Me Out of Here!* promised to deliver hardcore celebrity humiliation. It was set in the Australian jungle and featured eight minor celebrities having to do various disgusting things, like eating ants or animal testicles, or lie in a coffin full of rats.

The programme led to plenty of think pieces about the rise of humiliation TV and the lowering of decency. But what do you know – the show became another celebration of celebrity, as we saw the contestants being 'good sports', showing pluck and stiff upper lips. Many of the contestants emerged from the programme more loved than when they went in. Instead of celebrity humiliation we got celebrity rehabilitation. Suddenly, people began to say that actually they admired Tara Palmer-Tomkinson, and the model Jordan went from bionic boob to feminist icon after her appearance in the third series. In 2003 *I'm a Celebrity* even won a BAFTA for best entertainment programme. Nothing, it seemed, could stop the rise of celebrity, not even terrorism.

On the morning of 11 September 2001 two planes flew into the Twin Towers of the World Trade Center. Here was a brand of reality TV the likes of which we had never seen before. Commentators immediately announced the death of celebrity culture.

'Things that were considered fringe and frivolous are going to disappear,' said *Vanity Fair* editor Graydon Carter. Given the power of his magazine's role in the promotion of celebrities, this was like a papal dictate. Likewise Peter Kaplan. the editor of the *New York Observer*, said, 'I think the days of pure celebrity voyeurism are gone. The idea of the pornography of celebrity is suddenly passé.'

There was talk about the 'new seriousness', and how

we were rediscovering the values of 'heroism'. Given the solemn mood of post-9/11 America, you might have expected such comments. But the anti-celebrity backlash happened in Britain as well. It was as if we could show our sympathy with America by sharing their sentiments towards celebrity: solidarity through seriousness.

Observer columnist Barbara Ellen wrote that 'what we seem to be dealing with here is the end of celebrity as we know it.' For *Daily Mirror* editor Piers Morgan it was a moment of revelation. 'For the first time in 30 years, people in this country are rejecting the *Big Brother*-style trivia they so adored and are realizing there are more important things in the world.'

The world was shaken, stirred and ready to face reality. No longer would we bury our heads in the froth of fame trivia, or so the enemies of celebrity culture believed. But it was just a fantasy. Less than four weeks after the terrorist attack on the Twin Towers had supposedly killed off the beast, celebrity culture bounced right back. Britain was in the grip of *Pop Idol* fever.

This was a modern variation of the old talent-show competition, with the prize being instant pop stardom. (Around 10,000 hopefuls applied for auditions.) The songs and the singers weren't as important as the dramatic subtext: stardom as a gladiatorial battle of survival. And once again we the voting public could ultimately decide the winners and losers.

For a time in February 2002 it really did seem that the whole nation was talking about the forthcoming battle between the two finalists, Gareth Gates and Will Young. You felt like a right old sourpuss if you didn't want to take part. Even the *Guardian* came out for Gareth, and panellists on the BBC's current affairs programme *Question Time* had to face the question of the moment: Will or Gareth?

Meanwhile, faced by the onslaught of celebrity-based programmes that connected with the public and generated huge amounts of publicity, real culture decided that if you can't beat 'em, imitate 'em. In November 2002 the public got a more worthy form of *Pop Idol* with the BBC series *100 Greatest Britons of All Time*. It featured celebrities like Jeremy Clarkson, actor Alan Davis and Andrew Marr making the case for their own greatest Britons, while the public made the final decision with their votes.

The BBC followed this up with *The Big Read*, which set out to find the nation's best-loved book. Once again we had celebrities advocating their favourite books and letting the public decide. Great Britons and Great Books – here was the BBC's attempt to offer an alternative to celebrity culture by using the allure of celebrities.

One would like to think that in an office somewhere in England, two people were by that mythical water cooler engaged in a hot debate about the literary merits of Jane Austen and Zadie Smith, just as they did about Will and Gareth. But I doubt it ever happened. These were just sad attempts by old folks to get on the celebrity bandwagon and ring the bell for culture.

By contrast, *Big Brother* became the seminal television experience for an entire generation, who would remember Jade's kebab moment the way kids in the seventies remembered Bowie on *Top of the Pops* singing 'Starman'.

Who was this generation? Tim Gardam, director of programmes at Channel 4, said they were 'fundamentally different from generations before. They had no sense of propriety, no sense of modesty. They were open, honest and candid with each other.'

This generation never got labelled and summed up the way previous generations were. I call them Generation Me. They were people in their late twenties and early thirties who didn't want from television – or films and books – a window onto the world; they wanted a mirror that reflected them and their life.

Gary Carter, the director of licensing for Endemol, the company that created *Big Brother*, summed up the world view of Generation Me when he said, 'In times like these, it's comforting to be able to turn on the TV, watch the Internet, read my phone and find ten really ordinary folks like me talking about really ordinary things which concern me and who sound just like me . . .'

Me-Me-Me. It's the great mantra of the new millennium, the mission statement of Generation Me.

Generation Me was not like other youth cults. They never had a style of dress or a series of bands that would define them, and that's because they are the first generation of youth to have turned their back on youth culture, preferring the infinite and instant pleasures of celebrity culture.

You can understand why. By 2000 there was nothing left to say about Britpop, and the whole movement had run out of steam. The screaming mobs that once belonged to Britpop could be heard outside the *Big*

Brother house on eviction nights. Television programmes like *Big Brother* and *Pop Idol* – not rock gigs or pop festivals – were the big communal events that provided the social glue for Generation Me.

They had grown up in a world where the consumer was king, and they had little in the way of convictions, but it was a world of infinite choice. For Generation Me, pop music wasn't an art form; it was just something you did to become famous. It was the singer and their bad-hair days and heartaches that captured their imagination, not the songs.

Generation Me were free from the bonds of class, the youth culture of the past – they were free-floating consumers who communicated through the world via mobile phones, the Internet and texts. They had networks, not communities. They had their own celebrities – Jade, Jordan, Chantelle – and their own Internet sites: Facebook and Popbitch. And they had their own magazine, *heat*.

This was the perfect magazine for Generation Me, because it took celebrities and showed that they had far from perfect bodies and less than perfect lives – just like their readers. Readers of *heat* gorged on the gritty realism of celebrity – pictures of cellulite thighs, sweaty armpits and wayward nipples – and ignored the romance of perfection that stardom offered. They didn't want gods and goddesses – they wanted to gaze upon ordinary people like them who happened to be famous.

And you couldn't get anyone more ordinary than *heat*'s most popular cover girl, Jade Goody. Her story is a modern-day media fairytale – the Ugly Sister who goes to the ball and is chosen by Prince Fame. It used to be said that a celebrity is someone famous for being famous. In the Jade age a celebrity is someone who becomes a celebrity because they are so un-celebrity-like. When pundits tried to explain the appeal of Goody, they all said the same thing: she's real, down to earth, no-bullshit. In other words, a non-celebrity celebrity.

Generation Me may seem the most celebrity-obsessed generation ever. They devour the trivial minutiae of the most banal celebrities imaginable. How could one possibly be interested in a Paris Hilton clone like *Celebrity Big Brother* contestant Chantelle, when the original herself is so uninteresting? The answer is simple: Generation Me is too self-absorbed to be obsessed by celebrities. They are nosy, curious and amused, but not obsessed. Nor does Generation Me have any illusions about their value, or why they should become a celebrity. 'There's no point to me. I've got no talent. I just want to make as much money as I can,' said wannabe model and Jordan rival Jodie Marsh.

As the new millennium progressed, Me Generation narcissism began to spread out of traditional media and onto the Internet. The television and tabloid rejects could always find a place on MySpace and YouTube. People of my generation looked at life in cyberspace and saw Generation Me in action: gross exhibitionists, fame sluts, celebrity cranks spewing forth their banal thoughts, criminally bad poetry and dumb photos. Remember that television critic who in the seventies had responded to seeing Fran and others talk about their open marriages by asking: *who are these people?* That's what we were beginning to wonder about Generation Me.

But we knew we had no grounds for complaint, for in the sixties we were the ones who had said: *let it all hang out and don't be so uptight.* In the name of freedom we rebelled against the repressive bonds of bourgeois taboos and restraints. And now we wanted the young to embrace restraint and reticence.

Generation Me, on the other hand, regards such exhibitionistic behaviour as absolutely normal. As the American writer Emily Nussbaum points out, 'from their perspective, it's the extreme caution of the earlier generation that's the narcissistic thing. Why expose yourself on the Internet? This is not a meaningful question for a 16-year-old. The benefits are obvious. The public life is fun. It's creative. It's where their friends are. It's theatre but it's also community.'

The combination of reality TV and the digital narcissism of such Internet sites as MySpace have created the sense that self-exposure is no longer odd – it is we who talk of privacy and reticence who are the odd ones out.

Generation Me have grown up in a culture that sets out to seduce them with flattery, that says we want you to vote for your favourites, share your opinions, make a comment, send a text and send us an email. The most blatant example of media flattery was the cover of *Time* magazine, January 2007. It featured a picture of a computer with a mirror-like screen, and it had a cover line that read: The Person of the Year: You.

Time pointed out that Thomas Carlyle's idea that 'the history of the world is but the biography of great men' took a beating in 2006. It saw and celebrated the way the Internet was leading to the democratization of culture. 'It's about the many wrestling power from the few and helping one another for nothing.'

The Internet and the rise of the blogging phenomenon has created something unique: a whole generation that never stops to wonder, am I really that interesting? Are my opinions and the events of my life worth recording for the public to read?

The Diary of a Nobody was an English comic novel first serialized in *Punch* magazine in 1888. It was the fictional diary of Mr Charles Pooter, a middle-class clerk who worked in the City. Part of the comedy comes from Pooter's conceit that his ordinary, humdrum life would be fascinating to the public at large. You couldn't write such a satire today, because the boring person who thought they were interesting is not a comical conceit any more.

The pop biographer Fred Vermorel once complained that in the age of the celebrity memoir 'we have little time or taste any more for that forgotten genre of modest reckoning where "nonentities" could find publishers and publics for nothing more or less than life led . . .'

Nonentities no longer have to find publishers; they just go on the Net and find a public with their blogs. The first blog – the word is an abbreviation of Web log – appeared in 1997, and by 2007 it was estimated there were around 70 million of them. There are essentially two sorts of blogs: those diaries of the self that chronicle one person's life, and blogs devoted to serious debates about ideas and the great issues of the day.

The latter make up a minority of the world's blogs, and have enriched our cultural and intellectual life. It's the blogs of Generation Me that I question. If everyone has something interesting to say, is anyone really interesting? There was a time when an ordinary person who thought they had an interesting story to tell was dismissed as a Pooter; now in the era of the blog he or she is celebrated as a latter-day Pepys, their diary considered to be a valuable form of social anthropology.

You don't have to be an old, non-blogging cynic like me to have doubts about the benefits of such sites. Even bloggers question the value of blogging. Rhodri Marsden (described by the *Guardian* as a leading blogger) is quoted as saying, 'Very few people blogging have anything to say as such. I certainly don't.' Another blogger, Gary Wright, was quoted by the *Guardian* as saying, 'I don't really read many other blogs. I'm not interested in anyone's life, just my own.'

It's too easy to dismiss cyberspace as the province of Generation Me, a place where MySpace hoodies hang around waiting to mug the world with their boring lives and lists of favourite records. The good stuff is out there somewhere; we're just going to have to work a little harder to find it.

16

My England

When Jay said that he moved to London because it was a good place to be a failure, he was only half joking. Not long ago I asked him if he thought that was still true. 'Oh no,' he said, 'everything has changed. It's more like America now.'

I suspect that most of us – at least those of a certain age – feel that with the rise of celebrity culture something has changed. We confront a public realm and a popular culture that seems more trivial, narcissistic and creatively empty. Yet at the same time we face the accusation – usually from ourselves – that such comments are the arthritic moans and groans of an ageing generation who grew up on a pop culture that has now left them out in the cold.

So have things really got as bad as people say? There's a large group of commentators, writers and sociologists – I call them the apocalyptic school – that believes with the rise of celebrity culture, everything has changed for the worse. Whereas in the past Hollywood stars and celebrities were dismissed as a trivial distraction, for the apocalyptic school they are seen as a destructive force.

What makes such a view apocalyptic is the belief that all the other values that once informed our lives – family, friendship, social solidarity and respect – have been crushed beneath celebrity culture's hegemonic heel. Consequently, the values of celebrity culture are now *the* dominant values of society as a whole.

The apocalyptic view may be summarized as follows: our culture only values money and celebrity (John Lancaster in the *London Review of Books*). We no longer value people for what they do, we only value a person's celebrity (John O'Farrell, the *Guardian*). Friends and family are fine, but what we really crave is fame (Bryan Appleyard, *Sunday Times*). Celebrity is the only measure of aspiration we have, it preoccupies us day and night and infiltrates our dreams ... nothing exists in the universe without the mark of celebrity (Ziauddin Sardar, *New Statesman*).

Furthermore, celebrity culture has killed any idea of the heroic, of excellence, of achievement and talent. It has turned politics into a branch of show business, art and culture into lifestyle consumerism. It has become our new religion, replaced the class system and made wealth and fame the defining goals in life. Oh, and did I mention it's also responsible for teenage self-harming, juvenile delinquency and rising levels of adult depression and mental illness?

It's not only adults who are put at risk by the noxious fumes of our fame-fixated society, but our children as well. If such commentators are to be believed, we're producing a whole generation of fame-hungry little media monsters, Internet exhibitionists, embryonic Becks and mini-Jades who are more interested in a place on the front page than a place at university.

One often reads personal accounts in the press by middle-class media parents who have gone to their own child's school and discovered that – Shock! Horror! – they want to be famous. And here's the thing that parents find so scary: they want to be famous *for nothing in particular*.

Along with these anecdotes there are the statistical horror stories, like the 2007 poll by the Learning and Skills Council of nearly 800 youngsters aged between sixteen to nineteen years, that found 'The lure of celebrity is so great among teenagers that almost one in ten would abandon their education if they had the chance to appear on television.'

It would be foolish to claim that celebrity culture has had no, or little, impact on English life over the past forty years. But the view of the apocalyptic school and many others is based on gross generalizations about contemporary life and the values and beliefs of the great mass of ordinary people.

The apocalyptic school is convinced that we have become 'obsessed' with celebrity. (By 'we' they don't mean the cultural elite, they mean the masses.) It seems a self-evident truth. We look at the proliferation of celebrity magazines (in 2007 the market for such publications hit £1 billion for the first time), celebrity-based television shows, and how celebrities dominate the news. We conclude from our survey that we must be 'obsessed' by celebrities and hungry for fame.

This is to assume that our celebrity-saturated media

is an accurate reflection of the state of England. The media may be a mirror of our times, but it can often be one of those funfair mirrors that grossly distorts what it reflects. Take one example. If you had followed the media in January 2002 during the transmission of *Celebrity Big Brother*, you would have thought that it was a programme that the whole nation was watching. In fact, *Celebrity Big Brother* drew only around seven and a half million viewers, and while such a figure was high for a Channel 4 programme, it was not in itself a large figure compared with the average audiences of 10–13 million that regularly tuned in to soaps like *EastEnders* and *Coronation Street*. But *Celebrity Big Brother* had a far higher media and social profile than these soaps. Even people who didn't watch it found that they had to have an opinion on it, and thus became part of the event by default.

Over the past four decades there has been a huge growth in the audience for celebrity-based entertainment – television programmes, magazines, biographies, gossip and so on – but why should that make this interest an 'obsession'? Using the term 'obsessed' is a way of making an aesthetic judgement – i.e. celebrity culture is trash – sound like a therapeutic one. Obsession suggests something pathological, a passion that's out of control. And while this may be true of certain individuals with regard to celebrity, it's difficult to say with any certainty if we as a society are obsessed or not with the subject.

Little in the way of empirical research has been done to test the thesis of celebrity obsession. In 2003 reports appeared in the British press claiming that scientists had discovered a new ailment: Celebrity Worship Syndrome (CWS). CWS was the discovery of two American psychologists – Lynn McCutcheon from DeVry University in Orlando, Florida and James Houran from Illinois University School of Medicine in Springfield – as well as John Maltby from the University of Leicester in the UK.

Even a respected journal like *New Scientist* reported that 'psychologists are starting to suspect that worshipping celebrities is the top of a slippery slope that leads to depression, anxiety and psychosis. If you can't keep your nose out of *Vanity Fair* or *Hello!* magazine you could be already headed for big trouble.'

But when I interviewed John Maltby about CWS for this book he told me that his work actually presented a very different picture of Britain to that reported in some publications. His research *challenged* the claim that we are a society 'obsessed' by celebrity. His study surveyed 1,723 people in the UK, 781 males and 942 females between the ages of fourteen and sixty-two, to find out their level of celebrity interest. Only 25 per cent of those surveyed could have been said to fall into the category of serious celebrity-worshippers. 'That means that 75 per cent of the population have no real interest in celebrity lives,' Maltby told me. 'So no, I don't think we are obsessed with celebrity.'

And neither do I. There's no doubt that people are fascinated by the lives of celebrities, but fascination is not the same as obsession. One can become a football 'fanatic', a 'telly addict' or 'hooked' on celebrity magazines and biographies, and still care more about family and friends than about the rich and famous.

The apocalyptic view ultimately rests on a perception of the masses as living such impoverished and meaningless lives in the twenty-first century that they are compelled to worship at the altar of celebrity. But the idea of celebrities as gods is not new. In the 1940s, commentators regularly complained that the British public worshipped the movie stars of the time like they were gods. The novelist J.G. Ballard writes of the difference between then and now: 'People today who never go to the cinema, or who only watch videos at home, have little idea of the godlike aura that surrounded the giant stars such as Clark Gable and Gary Cooper, Joan Crawford and Carole Lombard.'

No one would suggest that today's celebrities have a 'godlike aura'. They exist not to be worshipped but to provide us with fast, disposable entertainment. We love them for a laugh and torment them for our sport. The old gods of Hollywood never had to face such cruel and capricious followers as today's celebrities do.

The other great claim about modern celebrity is that we live in an age where everyone – small children, teenagers, adults, intellectuals, scientists, politicians and businessmen – wants to be famous. There are even radical Islamic groups that are more wannabes than Wahhabi. In 2001 writer Roger Howard visited a group of radical Muslims in Britain known as Al Muhahirn, and was surprised to see his hosts eager to display, not the Koran, but a book of their press clippings. Howard concluded that the radical Muslims he met that day were as hungry for fame as any *Big Brother* contestant.

The claim that we all want fame is a cause for much

hand-wringing about the superficiality of the age we live in. In an article for the *Sunday Times*, *Newsnight* presenter and author Jeremy Paxman complained about the ubiquity of photographs of 'someone called Abi Titmuss', and then went on to declare: 'that's the spirit of the age; nobody actually does anything any more, they just get photographed.'

The unintended irony of the piece was that Paxman was writing about his sixty-second cameo appearance in the film *Bridget Jones: The Edge of Reason*, in which he did nothing but add a bit of celebrity-presenter glamour to a scene featuring Bridget (Renée Zellweger) at work for a television station. It's tempting to say now *that's* the spirit of the age: serious presenters of current affairs want to appear in films as themselves, and then write about how vacuous the modern desire for visibility is.

But has fame really become *the* dominant aspiration of our age? We have no surveys or studies of the UK population to confirm or deny this. I think the best we can say is that more people aspire to be famous now than at any time in the recent past. That said, we should be cautious about claiming that *everyone* wants to be famous. If you were to ask people in the street, 'Would you like to be famous?' they'd probably say 'Yes.' But then if you asked them if they'd like to win the lottery they'd probably say yes to that as well. Wishing for fame in your daydreams is not the same as wanting fame to the point where it's the defining aspiration of your life.

There are good reasons for doubting the claim that everyone wants to be famous. In 2002 it was assumed that one of the quickest ways to find fame was to appear on *Big Brother*, then at the height of its popularity. In that year the programme received only 150,000 applications to appear on the show – which is not that high a figure, considering that it is a programme with a young, supposedly fame-obsessed audience of millions.

Six years later, you can find various sites on the Internet that offer the public a chance to appear in television programmes as either members of an audience or as participants. One of the most popular of these sites is www.beonscreen.com, which claims to have 70,000 subscribers. This is a rather low number considering we, allegedly, live in a country where everyone wants to be famous.

Another claim that's often made is the belief that anyone can become famous. We now have the technology – as well as the formats – to make it happen: docudramas, daytime confession shows, video diaries, reality-TV contests, YouTube, Facebook, blogs and webcams. Never in the history of mankind have so many had so many means to be visible to so many people. Frances Bonner in her study of reality TV (*Ordinary Television: Analyzing Popular TV*) estimated that British television features close to a quarter of a million 'ordinary people' on screen per year, with over 20,000 having a speaking role.

Still, it doesn't follow that fame is open to anyone. At least, fame in the traditional sense of the word: enjoying a recognition rooted in achievement, that lasts beyond one's own lifetime. Yes, it is now possible for a greater number of people than ever before to achieve a certain type of ephemeral visibility or notoriety, but that is not the same thing as being famous.

Contemporary celebrity offers a kind of game-show fame where you compete in the public arena and win a holiday in the headlines, before being dropped back into obscurity. Even celebrity is not open to everyone. You can be famous – like a politician – but to be a celebrity requires an ongoing storyline, a narrative that holds the public's attention.

We have this new kind of fame that offers all the trappings of traditional fame – wealth, glamour and social mobility – but doesn't actually offer much fame itself. Hence the phenomenon of the celebrity that almost nobody has actually heard of.

In 2003 former *Daily Mirror* editor Piers Morgan counted the name of every 'famous' person to appear in the tabloid press for a month, and concluded that there are over 500 celebrities in Britain. But how many of them – from the world of reality TV – could you actually name?

Here's my attempt: Jade, Nasty Nick, Kate what's-her-name from *Big Brother*, the weird-looking guy with Tourette's syndrome who won *Big Brother*, that chubby transsexual from *BB*, Chantelle, Jordan, Peter Andre, Paris Hilton, Kerry Katona and umm . . . that's about it.

OK, I'm not a typical celebrity fan. So I tested two young friends of mine, both readers of celebrity mags and avid *Big Brother* fans, and they could only name six or seven more names than me. Fame, contrary to what you may have heard, is still very much in the possession of a small elite of the creative and the accomplished.

☆

Even though I question the doom and gloom of the apocalyptic school, that doesn't mean I believe that nothing has changed or there's no cause for worry. The worst thing to happen over the past few decades is that the values of celebrity culture keep seeping into all other areas of our cultural life – art, literature, ideas, media – and increasingly determine what is produced and published, who is promoted and what is prized.

My fear is that the original, the innovative, the challenging, the eccentric and the learned get marginalized to make way for famous faces and recognized names. I wouldn't claim that celebrity culture has led to a general dumbing down; it's led to the dumbing down of smart people. I define such people as the gatekeepers of cultural values – critics, editors, publishers, television producers and opinion formers – who have failed to offer any kind of resistance to celebrity culture. They have become as enamoured of buzz, hype and big names as anyone else.

Why else would a respected journal like the *Spectator* have someone with little journalistic experience like David Furnish contribute to its prestigious diary column, if he wasn't the boyfriend of Elton John? Why in 2004 did the *New Statesman* choose Michael Portillo to be its theatre critic over its former critic Sheridan Morley? 'Portillo is simply too big a name to turn down,' said then deputy *NS* editor Cristina Odone, with remarkable candour.

Few in the arts and culture industry can resist the allure of a name. Celebrities like Jerry Hall and Sophie Dahl become critics (Hall was a judge for the Whitbread Prize and Dahl for the Orange Prize for Fiction) and critics become celebrities (Germaine Greer). Even a serious current affairs programme like Radio 4's *Today* can't resist the appeal of celebrity, and has invited the likes of Bono, Sarah Ferguson, Yoko Ono and Damon Albarn to be their guest editors and set the programme's agenda.

Of course quality newspapers have to include items on celebrities if they're to attract younger readers. But shouldn't there be limits? The news section of the *Guardian* (26 January 2005) carried an article featuring the doodles of five celebrities that were analysed by Erik Rees of the British Institute of Graphologists to see what they revealed about the celebrity and their doodle. Readers were invited to have a go and try and match the doodle with the celebrity.

Broadsheet newspapers have become so saturated with celebrity-culture coverage that they increasingly resemble glossy celebrity magazines. As one *Guardian* reader put it in a letter to the paper (5 March 2002): '*Pop Idol* on the front page, James Bond on page three, Starkey, Black, Lynam, Norton, Tarrant and Vorderman on page five. Did I buy the *Guardian* this morning or *heat* magazine?'

To ask for a celebrity-free media is to ask for the

impossible. Also, we don't want a press that is so worthy it's dull. It's the sheer excess of celebrity culture, the way it infiltrates into everything, that's the problem. I remember watching an episode of *MasterChef of Britain*, which is a TV cooking contest. One of the contestants was asked about her ambitions and she said, 'I would like to be a celebrity chef.' This struck me as odd. Once it would have been enough to be considered a master chef who provided wonderful food – now people want to be *seen* providing wonderful food, by millions of other people who aren't even eating your wonderful food! These days the proof isn't in your delicious pudding, it's in the appearing on television.

In this age of high-celebrity visibility, what has happened to that old English fondness for the underdog, the heroic failure and the lovable loser? It still exists out there on the margins, as the success of Toby Young's book *How to Lose Friends and Alienate People* shows. But overall I think the English no longer find him so lovable; a loser now is just a loser. The old affection we once had for him has given way to the animosity of *Schadenfreude*. We no longer laugh with losers, we laugh at them. With the success of television shows such as *The Weakest Link*, *Dragons' Den*, *The X Factor* and *The Apprentice*, the spectacle of a person failing has been turned into a popular form of entertainment.

Increasingly, it looks like we are becoming a nation of winners and losers. In the 1970s Michael Bennett, the director of the American musical *A Chorus Line*, said, 'Unfortunately in America today either you're a star or you're a nobody.' In Britain in the 1970s no one would have said that. Thirty years later it has became a common observation about English life. Ed Wilson, the director of the National Youth Theatre in London, said, 'Everybody wants to be a bloody celebrity. There is this sense that if you are not famous you are a nobody, that you have failed.'

At the start of this book I said that my dad suffered from a feeling of being a nobody simply because he wasn't a somebody. I used to think this was something peculiar to him, but it seems he's not alone. Over the past decade there has emerged a whole series of quasi-medical-sounding labels to describe the damaged mental state and decreasing sense of self-worth caused by our celebrity-saturated society. The sociologist Chris Rojek writes about 'achievement famine' which he defines as 'a psychological condition that results from frustrated desires for material and romantic achievement of the sort the rich and famous enjoy.' Rojek claims that 'The celebrity race is now so ubiquitous in all walks of life that living with failure is oppressive for those of us who do not become achieved celebrities.'

The psychologist Oliver James uses the term 'affluenza', a condition he defines as 'placing a high value on money, possessions, appearances (physical and social) and fame.' According to James, 'The great majority of the English-speaking nations . . . now define their lives through earnings, appearances and celebrity, and those things are making them miserable.'

There are many studies and surveys that suggest that such commentators are right, in the sense that we are far less happy than we were in the 1950s. For example, in May 2006 an opinion poll by GfK NOP found that the proportion of people saying they were 'very happy' had fallen from 52 per cent in 1957 to just 36 per cent today. Whether this is due to the impact of celebrity culture remains uncertain.

What has happened over the past forty years is that the public provision of socially based esteem has been in decline. By socially based esteem I mean those things that are not provided by the free market – like patriotic pride or class identity – that give individuals a sense of worth. This sense of worth goes by many other names: self-esteem, renown or respect. They are basic human wants.

'People need to feel that they matter to others ... they want to look in the mirror without self-loathing,' writes the sociologist Richard Sennett. The problem we have now is that 'Modern institutions are bad at dealing with individuals who are ordinary – at according them respect even though they are nothing special.'

In the past the 'ordinary' and those who were devoid of special talents, or the gift of beauty, could still find a sense of worth in all sorts of places, from their role in the family or in their community, for example. People got a sense of self-esteem by belonging to a certain class, a profession, a church, a trade union or a political party.

However, these collective provisions have become increasingly ineffective in providing people with a sense of self-worth. Take the example of patriotism. Once you could feel that you were somebody simply by being British. But now what it means to be British in a multi-cultural society – or for that matter English – is continually contested and debated.

Likewise, the sense of solidarity and social status that you received from belonging to a certain class has also diminished. As good meritocrats we're not even meant to recognize class any more, much less take pride in our class origins. Consequently, we've had no confident middle class since the 1970s. The old status enjoyed by such solid middle-class professionals as the teacher, the bank manager and the doctor has totally disappeared, unless you're a famous doctor or teacher.

One of the few collective ways of finding self-worth is through sport. People take a pride and feel like winners by sharing in the victories of their local and national teams. But even that offers very little, as there are rarely the great national causes for celebration like the World Cup football championship of 1966.

We now have a Britain where the new division between haves and have-nots is based not just on wealth, but also on social esteem. There's a Britain basking in the warmth of renown, applause and celebration – and a Britain on the outside in the cold. When the young talk about their longing to be famous for nothing in particular, what they are actually saying is that they want – among other things – the respect, the sense of worth and being a somebody that celebrity promises to provide. As *Guardian* journalist Madeleine Bunting put it: 'Callow 16-year-olds with nothing inside their heads but how to be famous are not selfish, but simply looking to fulfil basic human needs in the only way that our culture indicates.'

In effect we've had the privatization of the collective provision of self-esteem. Consumerism has tried to fill the public void but as numerous surveys have shown, we are no happier now that we are wealthier. We have been freed from the confines of class and now seek our status from merit. For many that is a great and liberating opportunity; for the less capable, the restrictions of class were also a kind of safety net, and now many are slipping through its holes.

One of the admirable things about England in the past was that you could fail without feeling like a failure. If you failed in life, you didn't have to feel too bad about it, because the inherent unfairness of the class system meant that the odds were stacked against you in the first place. But now you can no longer use the excuse of class for your failure. In a society where – in theory if not practice – all that matters is talent and anyone can rise to the top, it becomes harder to blame anyone for your failure except yourself. In fact, what we have is the worst of two possible worlds. We neither have the equal opportunity for all that a meritocracy promises – rates of social mobility have decreased since New Labour came to power in 1997 – nor do we have a functioning class system that you can fall back on and blame if you fail.

No longer are we able to take our sense of self-worth for granted, and consequently 'There has grown at the root of society a craving for approval,' claims the philosopher Roger Scruton. This craving for approval is what is fuelling the steady increase of reality TV and Internet-based exhibitionism. The modern self – unsustained by the old social bonds that bring meaning – is compelled to put on a show, and celebrity culture has become the main stage for the attention-hungry self in need of affirmation.

This is why celebrity culture has been so successful; it promotes itself as the panacea for all our personal problems – the perfect love potion and popularity pill that will cure that big ache at the heart of modern life which cries out for attention and appreciation. It promises every person who feels like a nobody that they too can be a somebody.

The trouble is that the esteem that celebrity culture offers is, in most cases, an illusion. There are exceptions. We may assume that media-created celebrity offers a shallow and a worthless way of life, but it would have been hard to convince someone like Jade Goody – at least before her fatal illness – that her pre-celebrity life as a dental nurse in Bermondsey was really more authentic and fulfilling than her life as a rich celebrity.

So we have to concede that the shallow celebrity life is, for some people, a vast improvement on their former life. But it is a solution open to the few. The democratic promise of celebrity culture is as fake as the claim that anyone can win the lottery. Jade Goody was the exception to the rule that most so-called stars of reality TV actually fall back to obscurity and ordinary life.

Celebrity culture may be good for a laugh for its participants, but it can't solve the need we have for recognition, self-worth and belonging to a society. No one has provided more evidence showing the failure of celebrity culture to do this than celebrities themselves, with their tales of rehab, addiction, marital failures and the mental-problems that come with fame.

What has been missing in this whole debate we've been having about celebrity culture for at least the past two decades is an awareness that there is another England that is not connected to the grid of celebrity. It consists of millions of ordinary people who are happy to get on with their lives, and have no interest in David Beckham or watching reality-TV programmes. The hard truth for many of us to accept is that celebrity culture is not going away – I only hope that this other England won't go, either.

17

My Family

Jay

People have often said to me: *You should really try and talk with your dad and sort out your relationship before he dies; if you don't you'll regret it for the rest of your life.*

I tried having a Big Talk with Jay at various times over the years, but it never worked out. The last time I gave it a go I said something like: I admit I've been oversensitive and I took things too seriously, but you on the other hand have made it hard for us to be friends. Maybe if we met halfway we could sort out our problems?

The conversation ended with Jay saying that the problems of our relationship were down to one thing: I was jealous of him.

'I've made a success of my life,' he said. 'You haven't!'

I don't think he believed what he was saying. It was a glib dismissal of my feelings and a way of avoiding his. I've always felt that if he could only drop his act for a few minutes, we could talk. Trying to get Jay to drop his act is like asking a shark to stay still. He's one of those men who are always on stage. His performing self will never allow his real self to make so much as a guest appearance; it might ruin the act.

Then in the summer of 2001 Jay had a heart attack and I decided that I had better try one more time. He was recovering in a hospital near to where I lived. Most days I would visit, put him in a wheelchair and take him off to the local park for lunch. But I found it hard to begin our Big Talk, and we always ended up with small talk, sandwiches and silence for dessert.

So as a way of getting into Big Talk mode I started to read the second volume of his autobiography *Jaywalking*, which covers his years in London. I was impressed with the quality of his writing and even more impressed with the quality of his life. I felt that my life had been dull and undistinguished compared to his.

I wanted to tell him: *You're a success! You've had a very interesting life. Your days have been your own. You've never had to do boring work and you've never been poor. You've written a great novel (*The Nervous Set*) and two funny volumes of memoirs; you've produced numerous original plays, you've lived life with real style and panache. You're still married to the same woman who after forty-five years still loves you – despite having numerous affairs with beautiful women. And you have two children who are relatively sane and love you. What more does a man want from life?*

And here's what I said: *You're an awful name-dropper who tries to impress the reader with how many famous people you have met in your life. You use the celebrity of other people to give your own life the sheen of glamour and importance.*

All your life you've strived to be a somebody, which is a shallow and unworthy pursuit.

OK, I didn't say those exact words. Honest. I said something along those lines, about how he should have written more about himself and less about his encounters with the famous. I said the sound of name-dropping in his book was deafening. I asked him: why was he so obsessed with names?

But looking at the expression on his face, I felt as if I had said those terrible things. He went all sad and silent and slumped back into his wheelchair, like he'd had the wind knocked out of him.

I felt bad. The old man was recovering from a heart attack – did I mention that he'd also had a minor brain haemorrhage? – and he was all frail and vulnerable, and here I was knocking his celebrity preoccupations and the way he lived his life. So I started applying emergency doses of praise. I told him, 'All I was trying to say was that your whole thing about being a somebody, this thing with names that you have, it's all a waste of time ... don't you see, you can't judge your life this way. You've had a great life! Forget being a somebody!'

Then Jay said something unexpected. 'You got me wrong ... I never cared about all that somebody stuff.'

I was shocked. Now it was my turn to slump back in my seat. I couldn't believe what he was saying. It was like hearing the Pope declare that he'd always been misunderstood, that he'd never cared about all that religious stuff.

How could Jay say that he'd never cared about being

a somebody? This is a man who could walk into an empty broom cupboard and still worry about being the biggest name there. This is the man who called the second volume of his autobiography *Rebel Without Applause.*

Maybe it was the comment of a man who'd just had a near-death experience and had acquired a new and bigger perspective on life. Death had whispered in his ear and opened his eyes, that kind of thing. But I knew that even before his heart attack Jay had often claimed that he wasn't really interested in all that 'somebody shit'. In his last book *Tales of a Cultural Conduit* – Jay's very own greatest hits compilation of chapters from his memoirs and various writings – he portrays himself as a man who didn't really give a damn about making it and recognition. The only thing he took seriously was his marriage and 'making one woman happy'. As for his career, he writes: 'Of all the careers I've had, doing nothing was the best one and the most profitable.'

This was a piece of grand self-mythologizing. It was the Gatsby in him talking, the posturing of the romantic poseur hoping to woo posterity. Yes, he did care. But I think he was embarrassed by this desire; he didn't want to be like everybody else. The rebel in him was repulsed by what the nice Jewish boy in him craved; and the nice Jewish boy wanted his inner rebel to go away. One wanted the glory of the outsider, the other, the status of the insider. And both wanted the love and admiration of a small, frail, Jewish mother called Cutie.

So are we to conclude that he was an old phoney and that his whole 'romance of failure' routine was just a way of dealing with the pain of failure? I used to think it was, and that Jay was just a big kid whistling in the dark with all his let's-put-the-fun-back-into-failure stuff. He couldn't admit that he wanted success because he could never really get it, or at least the kind of success and renown that he wanted. I told him that you should face failure head on, and not try and be funny and ironic about it.

However, writing this book has made me see that Jay's attitude to success is more complicated than that. He wanted to find some alternative to the orthodox view of what it means to be a success, one that had nothing to do with social status, wealth and celebrity. Coming of age in America in the 1940s and 1950s, he saw what the drive to make it did to people: the way it made egotistical monsters of men and women; how it compromised talent and originality; how it wrecked lives with drugs and drink, and ruined marriages. To paraphrase Allen Ginsberg: Jay saw the best minds in America destroyed by success.

So he didn't want to play that game. He wanted to find a way to live outside the 9–5 routine, in the company of creative and interesting people. Jay wanted to be a playboy, a dandy, a dad and devoted husband. He wanted to turn his back on straight middle-class society, but the sirens of success were always luring him away from his chosen path.

It wasn't like he never got any praise from the world at large. He got plenty, but it was never enough. But that's success's greatest secret: *there's no such thing as enough*. It's like a drug high; when the latest hit of praise has worn off, you want another line of it ... and then another ... and then ...

Jay once had a chance of conventional success. In the early 1950s he was faced with an offer that few in his position would have refused. An envoy from Mr Henry Luce (then the publisher of *Time*, *Life* and *Fortune* magazines, and one of the most powerful media moguls in America) came to see Jay to discuss the possibility of buying *Neurotica*. Luce had this idea that there was room in the market for a popular magazine on psychology. Jay was tempted, but his collaborator Gershon Legman thought Luce – and all he represented – was the enemy, and begged Jay not to sell the magazine. 'Stick with me, Landesman,' said Legman. 'I promise you a footnote in history.'

So Jay had a clear choice: sell the magazine to Luce and become a wealthy somebody, or stick with Legman, the brilliant lunatic maverick, and end up either in jail or as a footnote. Jay chose Legman. Together they ran a series of articles in *Neurotica* attacking *Time* magazine. Written by Marshall McLuhan, the series was called 'The Psychopathology of Time and Life. The talks with Luce's people ended.

I look back with pride on Jay's refusal to sell to Luce. He took the selling-out test and passed with honours. These days nobody says no to the offers of corporate culture, but Jay did. And now he wonders if he will ever get his footnote. When I was a teenager I used to sadistically tease him about his lack of footnote fame. I would show him a new book on the Beats or the

New York culture scene of the 1950s and say, 'Hey, look at this ... for some strange reason you didn't get a mention!'

'No!' he'd say in a tone of shocked disbelief. 'Let me have a look at that!'

He would grab the book from my hands and rush to the index to see if his name was there, and I would watch as his face crunched up into disdain. 'I've never even heard of this guy,' he'd say of the author. 'What does he know? He wasn't there!'

If Jay couldn't have the success he wanted, he tried to develop a playful relationship with failure. Back in the 1950s, when he had the Crystal Palace, he used to do a stand-up comedy routine called The Mystery Comic. He would go on stage and talk to the audience about the failures of his childhood and his problems with his mother – and bomb every night.

Jay claimed he was creating a new type of comedy, one that was laughter-free. The Palace waitresses claimed that he was emptying the room and thus robbing them of tips. Nobody liked the act, but Jay didn't mind.

He discovered that he had one fan. There was a man who kept coming back night after night, and always sat on his own. Eventually Jay asked the man, 'What is about my act that you like?'

The man looked embarrassed and said, 'I'm just curious to see how much rejection you can take before you crack up.'

But Jay never cracked. He's always enjoyed rejection,

because it's an inverted form of attention. Back in the eighties he would find himself occasionally mentioned in *Private Eye* as that great 'bore', Jay Landesman. He was delighted by the *Private Eye* attacks and made sure everyone knew about them.

It was in his late eighties that Jay decided that he didn't really care about fame. What he really wanted was recognition for things he'd created, like his books and plays. This feeling came when he started rereading his first volume of memoirs, *Rebel Without Applause*. When published it had got some good reviews, and Jay received some nice compliments from friends, but sales were disappointingly low. He never said anything, but I suspect he thought it would do a lot better than it did. Sixteen years later he was still thinking about that book and what he could do to bring it back from the dead.

I got the call one evening.

Jay: Got a minute?

Me: What's up?

Jay: I'm thinking of relaunching *Jaywalking*.

Me: Why?

Jay: Because it's such a damn funny book. I've been reading it again and it's really the best thing I've ever written. Have you read it lately? It's a fascinating document.

Me: Yep, it's damn good.

Jay: I was thinking maybe you could send it around to a few people?

Me: Umm, like who?

Jay: I don't know ... A.A. Gill, Bryan Appleyard, Toby Young ... you could send it to them.

Me: (Sigh) And what would that achieve?

Jay: I don't know ... maybe I would get the recognition I deserved. I'd like a *little* recognition before I die.

Me: Is that all you want, Dad?

Jay: No. I'd like a *lot* of recognition before I die!
Click.

Jay has been dealing with the problem of success and failure most of his creative life. The opening line of his first novel, *The Nervous Set*, written in 1952, is: 'You can't stay married if you want to make it in New York.'

The desire to be a different kind of success has made him a bohemian, a beatnik, a hippy; it even made him macropsychotic. He has fought success and treated it with indifference and reverence. It is the longest love affair of his life. It has picked on him like a bully and infatuated him like a lover.

The real tragedy of it all was that he'd already found the alternative to success. It was there in the way he'd lived his life: there in his cocktail-drenched afternoons, the fun parties and the living rooms of St Louis and London that he lit up with laughter.

It was there in the thousand and one projects that he did – the brilliant original ones that were ahead of their time and the crazy ones that should never have seen the light of day.

It was there in the love and admiration of his wife and children.

'The best defences against the terrors of existence are the homely comforts of love, work and family life,' wrote Christopher Lasch. Jay had all those comforts. He was the most successful man I've ever known.

Too bad he's never realized it yet.

Fran

You might think that Fran, with her whole I Want to Be a Star routine, was the last person in the world you could accuse of being in denial about success. But this isn't quite true. She's always claimed that the happiest days of her life weren't standing in the spotlight soaking up all that applause – no, it was her time as Granny Franny. She'd always tell me, 'The best time I ever had was being with Jack when he was a little boy and we would play in the park together.'

I always would say, 'Yes, those were the days!' And I always would think: you poor deluded woman! But now, I don't know. I think she did have a wonderful time with her grandson, and she was an outstanding granny. But even he was an audience of one, whose laughter and love gave her the adoration she craved.

So how can I explain my parents' descent into self-obsession? I'm not sure I can. It's tempting to point to what was happening in the culture at large and conclude that Fran and Jay were just products of their time. I could argue that they got into self-obsession before it was fashionable. But I think that as they got older they got more desperate. Time was running out. So they were forever making one last mad dash for the spotlight.

I think Fran's problem was that no matter how much success she had in her career, no matter how much love she got from her husband, and her various lovers, at a certain level she was always that little fat girl who wanted her parents' approval. In this she was not alone. The presenter Ulrika Johnson, talking about fame, once said, 'I was always seeking praise from my parents, and when you don't get praise from them you go somewhere else to look for it.'

This was true of Jay as well. He was the nice Jewish boy who wanted his mother to say: well done. And when she didn't, he went looking somewhere else for it.

Miles

Does Miles want fame? I'm not sure. He always puts on a brave face when he talks about his career in rock music. I find it hard to believe that after nearly forty years of failure he's not a mass of misery, bitterness and envy. Miles is not some deluded no-hoper without talent. On the contrary, he's written some great pop songs, and yet he's had to watch people with less talent than him become successful.

You're bound to assume that he's all twisted inside. I've had a modest amount of success in journalism and yet I'm this seething volcanic mass of envy lava and bitterness that could erupt at any minute, so how can

Miles be so contented? I think it's very simple: he just loves to make music. That for him is the buzz.

He recently did a gig with his band Daze Like These and I asked him how it went. Miles said, 'Ah, man, you should have been there. It was a really brilliant gig. We were so tight. '

'How many people were there?' I asked.

'The place was completely empty,' said Miles. 'Even the bar staff walked out on us. But it was an amazing night!'

Only Miles could play to an empty room and call it a triumph. Some people might say that is the comment of one very deluded loser. But not me. I admire him, and envy the purity of his passion. All his other friends have hung up their guitars and kissed their dreams goodbye. I don't know if Miles will do the same one day, but I hope not.

You

Are you, dear reader, in denial about fame and your fascination with the famous?

When commentators talk about celebrity culture they always refer to the kind found in the tabloid press and in magazines like *heat*. But there is another type of celebrity culture, one that provides an educated/bookish audience with gossip, scandal, soap stories and personalities from the world of arts and letters.

There is a curious double standard operating here.

When ordinary members of the public appear on a game show like *Big Brother* they are considered to be attention-seeking wannabes. But when the likes of Martin Amis, the critic Al Alvarez and the playwright Patrick Marber appear on a Channel 4 game show like *Celebrity Poker*, no one sees them in a negative light. You can understand why ordinary people would want to appear on *Big Brother*, but why would Amis et al. want to appear on *Celebrity Poker*?

Those who complain about the ubiquity of celebrity gossip are happy to read endless arts-page features and biographies about the marriage of Sylvia Plath and Ted Hughes. They have become the Posh and Becks of literary England. And for some highbrow soap, how about a film like *Iris*, which presents the great writer Iris Murdoch not as a literary figure, but as a celebrity cruelly struck down by disease?

Why is it that a busty blonde who sells her story about sex with a footballer is the object of ridicule, but when a former arts presenter like Joan Bakewell reveals in her autobiography that she had a seven-year affair with Harold Pinter, it's considered perfectly acceptable?

Consider the cultural bias against ordinary fans. The fan who hangs around stage doors and airports in hope of an autograph is seen as a bit of a saddo, who lives his/her empty life 'vicariously' through celebrities. But the literary fan who treks off to events like the Cheltenham Literary Festival or the *Guardian*'s Hay Festival, to see the big names of the literary world in the flesh and get their book signed by Nick Hornby, A.S. Byatt or Germaine Greer, is never looked down on. Why is autographing a page in a book any more culturally acceptable than autographing a piece of paper?

Maybe we should all just admit that we're as starstruck as the next person, and not look down on such people as sad geeks. We cultured bookish people are just a different breed of geek, that's all. Could it be that *we're* the sad ones, because we have the education and culture that should enable us to see through the whole charade of fame?

So here's my question: if you were to go to a dinner party and had to choose between sitting next to a Celebrated Man like David Beckham, David Eggers, Jonathan Miller or Brian Eno, and a Good Man like Mr Smith, who for the past thirty-years has delivered Meals on Wheels to the elderly for the local council, who would you choose?

Liar.

Me

Finally, there's me. Do I really believe all that stuff I said to Jay about being a somebody not mattering? In other words: am I really indifferent to the allure of fame?

We intelligent, media-wise people are meant to see fame as one of the most unworthy of all modern desires, and to regard a serious interest in the doings of the famous as suspect. Writers in particular have a high disdain for fame hunger. John Updike calls fame the 'mask that eats the face'. Zadie Smith, who tackled the subject of celebrity in her second novel *The Autograph Man*, says, 'I've noticed that a lot of young writers, people in all media, want to be famous but they don't really want to do anything . . . I can't think of anything less worth striving for than fame.'

Martin Amis even had a conversation with his eleven-year-old son Louis about fame. The boy asked his dad, 'If nothing else was changed by you not being famous, would you still want to be famous?'

And Amis tells his son, no. 'Fame is a worthless commodity. It messes with the head.'

Question – Who has conversations with eleven-year-olds about the nature of celebrity? Do we now have to impart to our children the facts of fame alongside the facts of life?

Of course, Amis's reply seems disingenuous. Fame has become a very important commodity, especially when it comes to getting your book published. Only someone like Amis, who has been famous for so long, could possibly think fame was 'worthless'. What the poor bastard fails to grasp is that his career as a writer is kept afloat more by his fame than his books.

I'm prepared to admit that being famous can be more fun than being anonymous. I know this because over the decades I've been to plenty of parties featuring the famous and the anonymous and, believe me, the famous in the room have a better time than the unfamous. Writing about the perks of fame, Amis concedes that it will 'occasionally earn you some special treatment . . . if that's what you're interested in getting.' Ha! Who is he kidding? It will earn you special treatment not occasionally, but *all the time*.

This is how the fame game works at a typical party in London in the twenty-first century. At the top of the fun pyramid are the famous. Everything you would want from a party – love, sex, work, contacts, drugs and friends – they can find. No, they don't find it. It finds them. People and pleasures are served to them like canapés on a tray, and they take their pick of conversations, of bodies and of lives.

Below the famous are people who are not themselves famous, but are well known among the famous. They usually have lots of famous friends and so they have an entrance to the magical circle and can enjoy some of the privileges of the famous. Next come the people who don't know the famous or their unfamous friends. These people are called nobodies. Why? Because nobody wants to talk to them. To illustrate this point, let's consider a Famous Me at an A-list party full of famous people, and an Unfamous Me at the same party, and compare the experience.

Famous Me. I'm talking with my new best friends Martin Amis, Salman Rushdie, and Zadie Smith. Bono joins us. So do Sam Mendes and his charming wife Kate Winslet. Sam is actually a very sweet guy who loathes showbiz. Look, here comes Cate Blanchett. We talk about what we're working on and mutual friends. She's charming.

Unfamous Me. I'm talking to Heather – one of the girls who are serving wine. She's pretty and hopes to be a veterinary surgeon. Her boyfriend is studying politics at Bristol University. Isn't that Bono over there?

Famous Me. People – publishers, journalists, agents, pretty PR girls – keep coming up to me to tell me how much they loved my book. I thank them. They try to amuse me, they try to be charming. Wherever I look there are eyes watching me; eyes that want to meet me, to be friends with my eyes. They want to invite me to their homes/parties/beds/lives. (Yes, of course I can spot the ones who are merely interested in my celebrity, and not the real me.) I glow. I feel a strange kind of love for everyone in the room.

Unfamous Me. Waiters come up and offer me little snacks and drinks. The Thai chicken is particularly tasty tonight. I stand and munch/drink, and then I move on with a drink in my hand. I look like a man who is scanning the room in search of a lost friend. What people don't know is that my lost friend is an imaginary friend. I've made him up because I don't want to look like I don't know anyone here, so I keep moving. Isn't that Martin Amis?

Celebrity Party Tip Number One – If you don't have anyone to talk to, it's important to keep moving. Stand alone with a drink for more than 3.2 seconds and alarms go off; suddenly everyone sees you're the Lonely Guy in the room. But don't worry: everyone will notice this except the celebrities. You can see them, but most of them can't see you.

It's funny. When you're young you think how great it would be to be an Invisible Man – and then you grow up and go to parties with famous people, and you realize that you *are* the Invisible Man and it's not so great after all.

Famous Me. 'There's that guy again. He keeps rushing around like he's searching for a friend. I wonder if I should go and talk to him? He seems kind of lonely . . .

Unfamous Me. I go back to the bar for another drink – and then I continue to move through the room like a man with a mission. I spot another guy with a drink, pushing his way through the crowd with an air of purpose, as if he's looking for a friend. He looks at me. I look at him. He knows that I know his secret: he's the other Lonely Guy in the room.

So we both charge around looking purposeful . . . and then I spot another drink-in-hand guy charging around. He spots me but keeps moving. There are now three of us, charging across the room, criss-crossing each other. There will come a time when the other two will connect with someone they know, and Unfamous Me will be on his own again. Pissed, melancholic and full of despair, I will decide that it is time to give up and go home.

Famous Me. I eventually leave the party with a gang of people and we go to a club and spend all night discussing the state of the novel and taking drugs with beautiful women.

So yes, I know all about the advantages of being famous. But when I told Jay that he was a success even though he wasn't famous, did I really believe that? Yes. You can be successful without being famous, and you can be famous without being successful.

Here's my problem: I want to be that guy who quietly

gets on with his work and ignores the whole celebrity circus as it passes by the window of his book-lined study. I want to be the guy who can look at friends caught up in their frenzy of self-promotion, and who can watch them collect the glittering prizes and all the praise that will never come my way, and smile with Zen-like detachment.

But I'm not that guy. I am an attention-starved award-hungry journalist. I want to be famous. I want name recognition from every person I meet. I want glittering prizes. I want to arrive at my office and find ten phone messages from very important media people, instead of one message from my mother about her forthcoming gig. I want a dozen new emails offering me jobs and praise for my latest piece, instead of dozens of emails offering me Viagra and a larger penis.

The other calls and emails I get are from my friends with exciting news about *their* books. I have six friends all with a book out as I struggle with this one. My friend Mohsin has his book (*The Reluctant Fundamentalist*) shortlisted for the Booker Prize. My friend Antonia (*Madame Depardieu and the Beautiful Strangers*) emails to tell me that David Letterman wants her on his show. Her book is brilliant. Toby is flying to New York to appear in the film of his book *How to Lose Friends and Alienate People*. My other friend Sebastian Horsley (*Dandy in the Underworld*) has just sold his book in America – and my fucking publisher has had my manuscript for forty-five minutes and still hasn't got back to me!

You know that old line of Gore Vidal's about every

time a friend succeeds something inside you dies? Well, by Vidal's law I should be dead by now.

What makes it all so much worse is that all these people have written great books, and now I am consumed with anxiety ... is my book as good as theirs? Will I get as much attention? Will it sell? Will it cause a buzz? Will I get invited to literary festivals so that I can read from my book and talk about my book? Will attractive women from arts pages come to interview me so that I can talk about me-me-me?

There are days when I catch a glimpse of the future me: a crazed, ranting, embittered old guy, his soul wracked with arthritic envy. I sit on the sofa in pee-stained pyjamas amongst swirling clouds of cigarette smoke and self-pity, mumbling to myself about all the journalistic mediocrities who have done so much better than me. Spread across the floor are my old newspaper articles, stained, yellowing and covered in toenail clippings – on the television a video of the youthful me on some BBC2 arts programme is playing

I once confessed this 'future vision' of myself to Maxine, and she said: *what do you mean, the future*? No, I don't want to be that kind of guy. I want to be a man who is happy with what he has.

And I am happy with what I have – a loving wife, two great children and a great job. There is not a day goes by when I don't consider myself a lucky man, and yet that dumb fame dream turns up and I fall head over heels for that fake floozy.

I want to believe ... no, I do believe ... that there are

higher things to which we all should aspire. OK, so I'm not famous, but I can say that I'm a good person – doesn't that count for something? This depends on who you ask: the Idealistic Me or Cynical Me.

Idealistic Me. Yes! Yes! You're right – caring does count for something! There's nothing so glamorous as goodness and kindness. For as good people, we touch the lives of others in ways that are more profound and lasting than the fast flicker of self-aggrandizing fame.

Cynical Me. Excuse me Mother Teresa, but does anyone give a fuck that you're kind or caring? Please, let's get real and look at the world as it really is, and not how it should be. Let's face the fact that what people really care about is whether you are a name or not.

Idealistic Me. But what about friends and family? They will always love me for who I am and not my status in the world.

Cynical Me. Yes, of course your family loves you! But your star-struck parents would love you even more if you were a bigger name.

Idealistic Me. That's absurd!

Cynical Me. Oh yeah? Remember how happy they were to have Julie as their daughter-in-law!

Idealistic Me. OK, but it wouldn't matter to my friends.

Cynical Me. Ha! Are you nuts? Of course your friends would prefer a more famous you. Everyone wants to have famous friends. Your friends would certainly treat you better if you were famous.

Idealistic Me. How so?

Cynical Me. Do you think if you were famous your

345

friends would take so long to return your phone calls? When George Clooney calls up someone for dinner, how long do you think they take before getting back to him? Would your friends cancel dinner or lunch dates with you as often as they do if you were their famous friend?

Idealistic Me. OK, you may have a point there, but not everyone is so star-struck, I would never be like that with my friends.

Cynical Me. You're the worst kind of fame phoney – the kind that pretends not to care if someone is a celebrity, but as soon as you're around someone famous, you're down on your knees with your tongue out like a panting dog that wants to be petted by his master.

Idealistic Me. That's not true!

Cynical Me. Oh yeah? I'll give you an example. That little story you like to tell about that girl you were with at a party in the eighties, the one who you introduced to Robert De Niro, and she said to him, 'And what do you do?' You tell that story as an illustration of the ridiculous lengths people will go to to appear cool before the famous, but actually the real point of the story is to tell people that you were at a party with Robert De Niro, and there's the implicit claim that you and he are friends.

Idealistic Me. Guilty as charged. But I think you're wrong on the fame point. Bruce Willis once said to Jay McInerney, 'Everyone wants to be famous,' and . . .

Cynical Me. You're doing it again. You could have made that point without name checking-two famous people.

Idealistic Me. Fine, what I mean is that we live in an

age where it is assumed that everyone wants to be famous, and if you deny it then people think you're lying or kidding yourself. There was a time when you didn't have to prove your innocence when it came to wanting fame. Not wanting to be famous was considered the norm.

Cynical Me. Sorry, but those days are gone. Now everyone wants to be famous and we are fascinated by the famous. And so are you; you just can't admit it. By the way, what about this book?

Idealistic Me. What about it?

Cynical Me. Have you thought how you are going to promote it and yourself?

Idealistic Me. I don't have to play that game. I can simply try and write a great book and leave the marketing and hype to others. Unless writers take a stand against it, nobody will ever do anything to stop celebrity culture from devouring everything! We will just become part of the whole damn circus!

Cynical Me. You had better stop all this whiny *I wanna quietly get on with my book and ignore the celebrity game* shit tout sweet. Cos if you don't, your book is going to disappear without a trace. You won't have to be indifferent to the celebrity carnival, it will be indifferent to you and you will be sorry and you'll be sitting around and moaning: *nobody paid any attention to my book.* Well, boo fucking hoo! Get real, grow up, get out there and hustle!

Idealistic Me. OK, maybe you have a point. But it is possible just to focus on your work. I read this interview with the writer Douglas Kennedy. The author of the piece was saying that Kennedy had 'a deep cynicism about celebrity hype and a clear perspective about what really matters in an artist's life: work'. Now, he sounds like a guy who has got it right.

Cynical Me. Oh you innocent baby! Kennedy's book is all about the phoniness of Hollywood and 'the importance of being fabulous' as he calls it. He went out to Hollywood to do the screenplay for his novel and got his sorry ass fired. He came back to London and now he gives interviews like that.

Idealistic Me. What are you saying?

Cynical Me. It's always someone who goes to America to make it – in Hollywood or at *Vanity Fair* – and when they fail, they return to London saying how they have no time for phoney values and can see through celebrity culture. Funny, their good wholesome artistic values never keep them from taking the money and going in the first place.

Idealistic Me. Well, you've certainly given me something to think about!

Cynical Me. Fuck off, loser.

Here's the other thing that worries me: was I a shitty son for not being more supportive of my parents? I thought I was supportive, but they don't agree. Jay once criticized me for being such an awful, undutiful son. 'You never gave me any appreciation . . . you never wanted to go out and drink with me . . . you never . . .'

What kind of son would they have preferred? I can imagine him. He would go to every one of his mother's gigs and bring his wife, his ex-wife, his friends, his ex-lovers, his children, his casual acquaintances and colleagues from work. He would stand transfixed by her performance and at some point he would shout from the back of the room, 'Hey, everybody, that's my mom up there!'

He would go backstage with flowers and tears in his eyes and would say to his mother, 'Remember how years ago you said, "I'm going to be a big star," and I laughed at you? Well, I'm not laughing now because you are a star . . . a magnificent star!'

He is the son who would help his dad with everything: his latest film script/volume of memoirs/press releases. The one who would deliver advance copies of his father's memoirs to literary editors and who would give copies to friends for weddings, birthdays and bar mitzvahs.

But they got me: Mr Fucking Sensitive. The King of Cringe. The son who hid on the outskirts of the audience, sweating, fretting . . . who squirmed at the back, pretending he had no idea who the crazy poet lady on the stage was. Maybe I wasn't the adoring fan they wanted, but I hope they know that I was the adoring son.

For a time I had lost sight of the other Fran and Jay. The mum who took care of me when I was a sick child and tucked me into her bed, brought me cinnamon toast and tea and read wonderful stories that made me want to be a writer. And there was Jay, simply the funniest guy in the room, whizzing the family off to a pop festival and getting us front-row seats in the press section.

For a while they were monsters of egotism, but I'm glad to say they've changed since then and become the wonderful mom and dad I always wanted them to be – and for that I'll never forgive them.

18

Have You Got A Minute?

After the big fight with Jay in 2003, I didn't visit my
parents for a long time. Their phone calls stopped and
so did Fran's letters announcing new gigs and invites to
dinner. But then one afternoon I found myself near their
house, so I decided to pay them a surprise visit.

I arrived at Duncan Terrace and I stood outside the
house and looked through the windows. When I was
young, I had always feared strangers looking into
those same windows and seeing the weird forms of life
within. I worried about what they might think, and
was always trying to get my parents to shut the blinds;
their visibility made me vulnerable. I feared that I – or
my family – would suffer reprisals for being different.
We would attract nutters, skinheads, drunks and gangs
of rampaging teenagers. I wanted all of us to be safely
hidden behind the armour of net curtains.

My parents thought I was just being uptight, and
they were right. Whenever I pleaded for curtains my
father would quote his mother: 'Let the neighbours buy
the curtains.' That's something I've said to my wife, so
maybe I've made some progress in the uptight stakes.

Nowadays people walk by those same windows, but they never stop and stare. My parents are no longer weird, they're just old. And besides, the world has caught up with them; everyone is a little weird now.

I always thought that when they got old my parents would see through the vanity of success and the futility of longing to be a somebody. After all, when you're old it's easier to see the big picture of life. You realize that what matters isn't being treated like a star. No, what matters is family, grandchildren and finding big pleasures in small things like sunny strolls through the park with your wife or husband of fifty-six years by your side.

Unfortunately, nobody had told them that. I assumed that one day it would dawn on my parents that it was time to retire. In my fantasy the scene always resembled a Noel Coward play. Over cocktails my father in his white tux would be tinkling away at the piano, and then, turning to my mother, he'd say: *Well, old girl, we gave it a terrific shot. I think it's time to call it a day, what say you?*

My mother, spread across her chaise longue puffing on a joint held in her ivory cigarette holder, would reply: *Yes, dear, of course it's time. This way we'll leave them wanting more.* (And here a small tear would fall from a stoned red eye.) *Darling, summon the children. I want them to be the first to know . . .*

So they'd bow out with a farewell performance and at last I would have them where I'd always wanted them: out of the spotlight and tucked safely away from public view. Forty-five years of embarrassment would thus come to an end. But no, they'd refused to surrender and go quietly into that good night of anonymity.

Going inside the house, I experienced the strange sense that nothing here ever changes and yet everything had changed. The living room looked old and tired. There were dark dusty corners, grubby walls and no-go areas full of the detritus of four decades of never throwing anything out. I was standing in the middle of the junk shop that time forgot. The battered furniture looked exhausted. The mattress on the floor, that once bore stoned bodies like a raft on a sea of swirling psychedelia, seemed to have sprung a leak and had sunk deep into the floorboards.

And yet the house still humming with creative activity. I could hear the sound of a drum track coming from Miles's room at the top of the house. In the middle was Fran rehearsing her act and down in the basement was an excited-sounding Jay on the phone. Father, Mother and Child – the complete set of mad people I had longed to lock up in the attic.

I started at the top with Miles. He was at his eight-track mixing desk. 'All right?' he said.

He told me that his band Fancy Dress had broken up and I mumbled commiserations. Oh dear. Another day, another dead band. Their remains would go into the graveyard of Miles's groups where all the other demo tapes, handmade flyers for gigs, Polaroid snapshots, reviews, song sheets and press releases lie resting in peace.

I wondered if he would now quit. How many dead

bands can a man endure before he calls it a day? Could he bear to go through the whole process of getting another band together: the search for singers, the rehearsing, lugging your gear from one grotty gig to another, delivering your demo tapes to people who will never play them, and then finally the heartache of another band falling apart.

But Miles was not downhearted. The band had died, but so what? There were tapes of Fancy Dress to be remixed into a sort of 'best of' compilation.

'It's going to be a collectors' item,' he told me.

I left Miles to go and look for Fran. On the floor below was my old bedroom. I looked through a crack in the door and in the semi-darkness was the hunched figure of my own son Jack, sitting on a mattress on the floor playing his bass guitar with the headphones on. His hair was long, just like mine had been in the summer of '67 when I too had sat in this room and strummed a guitar. Suddenly I had a terrible vision: my sixty-year-old son Jack still in that room with his bass guitar. My parents' home could do that to you – it was the *Twilight Zone* of talent. I snuck away.

'What a nice surprise to see you, Mr Cosmo,' said Fran when I walked into her room. 'How are you?'

But she didn't wait around for an answer. She told me she was going blind (Fran had macular degeneration), that her bones ached, her feet had turned purple and that there were days when she felt like killing herself – 'But other than that, I'm terrific. I got a gig coming up that I'm doing with Miles. You should come.' Gigs were her miracle cure. No matter how awful she felt doing a performance, getting that warm rush of love from the audience was like a shot of the most perfect painkiller. But looking at her sorry state, I could see that her days as a performer were numbered.

We chatted for a bit, she showed me a new poem and then I said goodbye.

Jay was at his desk, alone with a Martini and his cat. His basement pad had the look of a decaying opium den owned by a syphilitic aesthete who hadn't left his room in three decades. On walls hung art objects, hats and old photos of a young and dashing Jay. There were stacks of books and scripts and tapes sprouting up all over the place. On the radio was the sound of melancholic jazz.

Jay mixed me a Martini and said, 'Well ... I'm through. Finito. I'm no longer interested in playing the make-it game.'

It seemed that all his various projects had come to a halt: the New York revival of *The Nervous Set*, the attempt by the German film-maker in Stoke Newington to do Jay's movie. Even his latest volume of memoirs had been getting the thumbs down from various publishers.

'Sorry to hear that,' I said.

'Well, what can you do. I gave it my best shot. It's time to call it a day.'

I told him that we'd been here before. But he insisted that this was different. 'It's no fun any more. It's a different world out there now. I mean, what people are interested in. Even the smart, hip ones are so ... mainstream now. All that celebrity horseshit.'

I felt sorry for him. What would he do with himself? How could he fill his days without some sort of project to work on? What could he talk about? Could he be content just being an old guy with a rakish hat, a string of one-liners and an interesting past?

Yet if I'm I honest, I was kind of glad that he had retired from the limelight. He'd had a good innings. Now it wouldn't be long before the others in the family would follow, and the stage would be free for me.

As I walked home that night I thought about what Jay had said. It was the end of an era. Sixty years of big dreams and dumb dreams, great ideas and ideas born of desperation were over. There would be no more talk of 'the mems'. No more cringing when I heard them on the radio. No more requests to read this, write that, send this off to a friend or someone I barely knew.

When I got home I hugged my wife and cried, 'Free at last . . . Free at last!'

'What's happened?' she asked. I told her the news. 'Don't you see, it's over . . . the whole self-obsessed read-me-hear-me-talk-about-me Landesman thing is finished!'

'Praise the Lord!' Max said. 'This calls for a celebration.'

So we drank champagne in bed and reminisced about the various horrors we had endured at the hands of my parents. Now that it was all over, we could look back and laugh. That night I slept well and dreamt that I won the Booker Prize for the best unfinished novel.

The next day I got an early morning phone call.

It was Jay.

He wanted to know if I'd got a minute . . .